D0769086

Religion, Power and Protest in Local Communities
The Northern Shore of the Mediterranean

Religion and Society 24

GENERAL EDITORS
Leo Laeyendecker, *University of Leyden*
Jacques Waardenburg, *University of Utrecht*

MOUTON PUBLISHERS · BERLIN · NEW YORK · AMSTERDAM

Religion, Power and Protest in Local Communities

The Northern Shore of the Mediterranean

Edited by

Eric R. Wolf,
Herbert H. Lehmann College
of the City of New York

MOUTON PUBLISHERS · BERLIN · NEW YORK · AMSTERDAM

Library of Congress Cataloging in Publication Data

Main entry unter title:

Religion, power, and protest in local communities.

(Religion and society ; 24)
Contributions to a conference held at the Free University of Amsterdam, 1979.
Includes indexes.
1. Mediterranean Region--Religion--Congresses.
I. Wolf, Eric Robert, 1923- .   II. Series: Religion and society (Mouton (Firm)) ; 24.
BL21.R433 1984   306'.6'091822   84-8407
ISBN 3-11-009783-4

CIP-Kurztitelaufnahme der Deutschen Bibliothek

Religion, power and protest in local communities:
the Northern Shore of the Mediterranean / ed. by
Eric R. Wolf ; Herbert H. Lehmann. — Berlin ;
New York ; Amsterdam : Mouton, 1984.
(Religion and society ; 24)
ISBN 3-11-009777-X

NE: Wolf, Eric R. [Hrsg]; GT

Preface

Daniel Meijers (for the Free University of Amsterdam) and
Jojada Verrips (for the University of Amsterdam)

Thinking up a conference is easier than setting one up, as Dr. John
Davis discovered while serving as a Visiting Professor in the
Department of European and Mediterranean Studies, Anthropology-
Sociology Center, University of Amsterdam, in 1977-1978. In a recent
book, which essays a critical synthesis of what anthropologists have
written about the *People of the Mediterranean* (1977), Dr. Davis
observes that little systematic study has been made of religion as
Mediterranean people practice it. To help remedy this deficiency,
Dr. Davis proposed to hold a conference on the subject attended by
outstanding scholars of Mediterranean society, and drew up a list of
prospective contributors. His colleagues in Amsterdam received both
suggestions enthusiastically, but finance was another matter. Hence
it was only after Davis had left Amsterdam that funds were obtained
to underwrite the gathering he had planned. Finally, in December
1979, two years after Davis first proposed his idea, the conference
was held at the Free University of Amsterdam. For three days anthropologists and sociologists discussed each other's conference papers,
most of which (suitably revised) appear in the present volumes,
edited by Ernest Gellner and Eric R. Wolf, who chaired the proceedings. We are deeply indebted to Professors Gellner and Wolf, both
for their splendid management of the discussion, and for the labors
they undertook afterwards to prepare these books for press. They have
our heartfelt thanks.
    Their good work would have come to naught, however, but for the
financial support graciously provided by the Subfaculty of Sociology,
Cultural Anthropology, and the Sociology of Nonwestern Peoples at the
University of Amsterdam; the Subfaculty of Social and Cultural
Sciences at the Free University of Amsterdam; and the Netherlands
Ministry of Education and Science. We also wish to thank Ir. J.H.H.
Hasenack, chief administrator of the University of Amsterdam subfaculty, and Mr. W. Buitenhek, his counterpart at the Free University,
for their personal interest and help in making this conference
possible.
    After John Davis left Amsterdam, we the undersigned took charge

of organizing the conference. Hence we wish to thank our colleagues
in the Departments of European and Mediterranean Studies, University
of Amsterdam, and the Anthropology of Religion, Free University, for
their continuing trust and support -- in particular, Drs. Tom
Nieuwenhuis (University of Amsterdam) and Drs. Miep Stam-van
Ginhoven, Dr. Adrianus Koster, and Freeke Falkenhagen (Free
University), whose assistance was indispensable. At a later stage,
Ms. Gay Woolven, Department of Philosophy, Logic, and Scientific
Method, London School of Economics, Dr. Katie Platt, Ms. Hannie
Hoekstra and Ms. Nettie Westerhuis, University of Amsterdam, and
Ms. Marijke Kreuze, Free University, helped prepare the final
manuscript for our publisher, whose kind cooperation is hereby
gratefully acknowledged. Thanks, too, are due to the Administration
of the Free University for aid in translating several key contributions from French.

We owe thanks, in addition, to Drs. Bertus Hendriks, Drs. Edien
Bartels, and Professor Sydel Silverman, who rounded off the
discussion with clear summaries and sharp comments.

Lastly, we wish to thank Professors Leo Laeyendecker and Jacques
Waardenburg for their advice and support.

A conference like this can succeed only if the written contributions are of high quality and, moreover, if a certain community
of interest develops among the participants. The reader can best
judge whether the first condition has been met. As for the second,
all we can say is that despite the multinational composition of the
discussants, the division of the proceedings into two segments
concerned, respectively, with religion on the Northern and Southern
shores of the Mediterranean, and the mix of Christian, Islamic, and
Jewish traditions among us, our sense of academic community and
shared scientific interest never flagged. On the contrary, if our
experience suggests a general conclusion, it is that religion in
Mediterranean society is an exciting subject, the study of which
offers indispensable insights into how life is lived there. Hence
we hope that these books will stimulate others to continue the work
of improving our understanding of religious observance and commitment, and its significance for social existence, in the modern
world.

Jojada Verrips
Daniel Meijers

Table of Contents

Introduction

Eric R. Wolf, Herbert H. Lehman College of the City of New York

The anthropological interest in religion is generally associated with writings on primitive peoples and their 'exotic' practices. A collection of anthropological studies of religion in the region of the Mediterranean may therefore evoke a sense of surprise, even among anthropologists. Yet some of the earliest and most important anthropological insights into religion were first gained in the study of the 'complex' societies and religious traditions of the Mediterranean. Two books were of special significance in this development. These were *The Ancient City* by Numa Fustel de Coulanges, published in 1864, and *The Religion of the Semites* by W. Robertson Smith (1889), based on lectures that brought about the author's removal from his professorship at Free Church College in Aberdeen. *The Ancient City*, in examining the religious principles and rules that governed Greek and Roman society, prefigured Durkheim's approach to religion, while Smith's account dealt with the transactions between men and gods in ways that became familiar to social anthropologists after Hubert, Mauss, and Radcliffe-Brown. However, among the major anthropologists of the next filial generation only Westermarck concerned himself with Mediterranean religion, in his studies of Moroccan marriage (1914) and rituals and beliefs (1926). Thereafter social anthropologists went on to study religion in Chiapas or Borneo, leaving the fields of Mediterranean religion to be plowed by others. This book, then, marks an attempt to return to an earlier and fruitful area of study.

This return may allow us to reflect on the nature and identity of our topic, to ask what the realm of religion may be about, in contrast to the realms of local-level law, economics, or politics. Since the advent of functionalism anthropologists have learned a good deal about what religion *does*, what its functions are or can be for people in general and for particular people under specified circumstances. They have traced these functions in provocative studies of religious phenomena around the world. Yet we are still far from understanding what religion *is*. One seeming difficulty lies in our inability to replace the terms of religious 'common-sense' drawn from our own religious traditions with culture-free constructs. Such polarities as natural/supernatural, visible/invisible, profane/sacred, and ordinary/extraordinary merely restate, in altered form, the opposition of body and spirit that is ancient in the Mediterranean world and the religions that originated there, but would seem singularly alien to - say - natives of the South American Tropical Forest.

A second basic difficulty in understanding religion anthropologically lies in our views of how human beings convert the universe into a humanly usable habitat. It is now common to say that human beings 'construct' their world; but one must hasten to qualify that overly rationalist, conscious, voluntarist metaphor. Surely, if people construct their world, they do so as much under the impact of necessity as out of choice and free will. They are creatures of their circumstances, even when they strive to master them.

The religious enterprise is, moreover, a paradoxical undertaking, drawing human beings into contradictions which they then struggle vainly to resolve. Religion strives to contain and encapsulate the thrust of human drives and interests within a .fixed grid of symbolic thought and action. Its predilect mode of communication eschews the discursive and propositional semantic forms of everyday speech, and substitutes for these formalized sequences and configurations of vocal acts, kinesic motions, and sanctified objects (Bloch 1974). In religious communication "the medium is the message", not the message the medium. This religious mode of communication does not discuss and explain; it asserts and commands assent. Its aim is not information but certainty (Wallace 1966: 234). Yet this certainty is achieved at a price: it installs Tertullian's *credo quia absurdum*, a truth neither falsifiable not verifiable, but owing its existence entirely to active belief or passive acceptance (see Rappaport 1979). It is, moreover, always predicated on uncertainty and cannot exist without it. Its truths can only be asserted by holding them up against untruths and drawing distinctions between them. Every religion 'constructs' its truths against the background of untruths, erecting its order upon chaos. Hence certainty is always accompanied by uncertainty; behind the facade of faith lurks the demon of doubt. Thus history becomes a veritable graveyard of discarded paradigms, each alternative or successive symbolic grid bearing witness to the insufficiencies of its predecessors. When human activity threatens to break through the dam of certified assurances, religion can only insist stubbornly on the proper performance of the activities that created its 'truth' in the first place, or call on force to aid in its maintenance. In neither case is it concerned with meaning or explanation as such. When it seeks to undergird meaning, it does so by grounding it in ineffable and impenetrable mysteries that 'demand' things from men. To paraphrase Lévi-Strauss, the religious mode thus requires myths "to think men", before men can think myths.

At the same time, this anchorage of sense in no-sense always depends on "the willingness of the recipients of symbolically encoded messages to accept the messages they receive as sufficiently reliable to act upon" (Rappaport 1979:229). Sanctified structures may be desanctified, and other structures substituted for them. One set of unquestionable, unfalsifiable, and unverifiable propositions can come to be treated as misrepresentations or lies by non-believers; one man's sanctity may turn out to be another man's lie or at least his malevolent choice to remain ignorant about the truth. There may exist a dialectic between truth and falsehood, orthodoxy and hetero-doxy, consent and dissent, just as there is a dialectic between secularization and mythification (Bolle 1970). Yet this dialectic does not work itself out through a logical process of thesis and antithesis. Sanctity is not strong enough to ensure its own defense, and criticism not strong enough to overthrow sanctified truth. Clearly religion, in order to remain true, must be able to compel or coerce assent.

Whatever the ontogenesis of religion, it plays a signal role in placing human persons within their specific social and cultural matrix. It does so by specifying them as symbolically constructed selves in relation to the symbolically constructed world. Religion is thus 'ideology' in Althusser's terms, and its guiding function is the mental constitution of the human subject, the individual conceptualized as an agent within a symbolically imagined whole of which he is himself a symbolically constructed part (see Feuchtwang 1975). This formulation incorporates Durkheim's insight that the individual personality embodies a portion of the collective *mana*, as well as Marcel Mauss' insistence that the self is a socially constructed category. Arguing from a quite different perspective, Yehudi Cohen (1964) has made a similar point in saying that 'selfness' depends upon the development of social-emotional anchorages in socially bounded groups, such as families or descent groups, and that individuality will be culturally variable as social-emotional anchorages to different bounded groups vary. Religion is eminently concerned with the boundedness of social groups and with the anchorage of individuals within them. At the same time, it defines the human agent by relating these points of anchorage and these boundaries to the sacred. Ernest Becker has attempted to make this point by arguing that

In traditional and primitive societies the family was essentially a religious group, a priesthood, because of its sacred ritual duties to the departed ancestors. This is hard for us to grasp today. Every adult member of primitive or traditional society had a personal and family contract to help uphold the workings of the invisible world, in this visible one. All of nature and all the spirits were *watching* you. Every important thing that you did in

life - marriage, children, career had repercussions in the eternal
dimension. Even the small daily tasks were part of a larger scheme,
with ramifications not confined to earth. Everything a person did
was done, in other words, *partly in heaven* (1971:122-123).

Whatever may be the case in other societies, the major religious
traditions found around the Mediterranean have evinced an enormous
interest in the anchorage-points and boundary markers of the self, as
links to the holy.

Pre-eminent among these links have always been distinctions of
gender. In this collection, Anton Blok explores the symbolic templates
of masculinity and femininity and their changing evaluations over time.
His initial formulation has an almost 'neolithic' ring, and suggests
that later constructs had to be mortised, sometimes awkwardly, to
pre-existing tenons. John Davis, in turn, explores the differential
participation of women in 'sacred work' among Latin Christians and
Muslims. He seeks an explanation for this contrast in essential
differences between Christianity and Islam in their treatment of
sexuality, marriage, and procreation.

To underline this theme it may be useful to recall the paradigmatic
Christian myth of the Fall. Against God's express instructions, Eve
in paradise allows herself to be tempted by the serpent to offer the
fruit of the Tree of Good and Evil to Adam. The serpent is none other
than Lucifer, God's predilect angel cast into hell for rebelling
against God's will. Eve's transgression implicates Adam. Disobeying
God by eating the tree's fruit, he too rebels against God. This act
of rebellion initiates original sin. Previously unashamed, Adam and
Eve now experience shame and cover their nakedness with fig leaves.
God, noting their fig-leaf aprons, curses them and all of nature with
them; He condemns men to unremitting toil in a corrupted world and
women to painful parturition. Human kind has come to know (sexual)
good and evil, but the price of this knowledge is death. Yet God so
loves human kind that He sends His son to redeem the sinners. Christ
enters the world to bring life, where Adam brough death: "For as in
Adam all die, even so in Christ shall all be made alive" (I Corinthians XV:22). Able to choose between good and evil, humans can set
aside sin and strive for redemption. That striving for redemption is
to be managed by the Church, under the leadership of the Vicar of
Christ on earth, through its 'economy of salvation', including the
administration of the sacraments by an ordained priesthood.

This paradigmatic tale clearly does not apportion guilt for
original sin equally between the sexes. It was Eve who proffered the
fateful fruit to Adam, and Eve is stigmatized as a result. "Ever
since Eve, women have been seen as temptresses, slaves to passion,
the cause of man's downfall" (Christian 1972:153). Moreover, the
knowledge of good and evil is equated with sexual shame. As an outcome
of the Fall, Adam is granted command over Eve, and names her 'life',

supposedly for her procreative life as mother of human kind. As Elaine Pagels (1979) has shown, this interpretation of the Fall and of the role of woman in it was by no means the only one available to early Christendom. There were alternative versions that portrayed multiple principles at work in structuring human kind, upheld the quality of men and women as believers, and stressed the personal search for truth and knowledge. These lost out to versions that portrayed God as the sole supernatural master, ruling heaven through a celestial hierarchy and earth through the hierarchical Church, with priests superior to laymen, and men to women.

Although Davis stresses the participation of women in Church activities, this participation remains auxiliary by definition. The members of the ecclesiastical hierarchy are male and celibate. Their celibacy is the mark of their preference over ordinary men, who must marry if they are not to burn. (In Portuguese Estremadura, Joyce Riegelhaupt notes, villagers are especially resentful of this qualification of the priesthood as setting them apart from other men). Women are not allowed to serve Mass at the altar. They may not touch chalice, paten, or corporal, the linen on which host and chalice are placed at Mass. Women may make liturgical responses from outside the sanctuary (Attwater ed. 1961:528), ornament the priests' apparel, and tend to church linen other than the corporal (Hirn 1957: 95). Only by taking religious vows can women escape the predicament of sexuality in marriage, and even then their role is secondary to that of priests. As William Christian put it, "the implication that sex is somehow less holy than celibacy is inescapable" (1972:154). Thus, the active role of women in the Latin Church is anchored in women's sexuality and their responsibility for the Fall, and involves them in recurrent cycles of pollution and purification.

In Islam, the concept of original sin is absent. The Koran reproduces the story of the Fall, but both Adam and Eve succumb to the angel Iblis' advice to eat from the tree. They experience sexual shame, and are assigned to earth to live and die. But their children are not tainted with the consequences of the Fall, as long as they follow "what has been sent down to you from your lord" (Koran 7-1-24). In consequence,

> they did not fall sinful to the core, corrupt in their essence, laboring under the metaphysical consequences of a Fall. No original sin had to be expunged. They were not in need of salvation through divine self-sacrifice, they needed information as to the true God and as to the behavior he demanded. Islam has never developed sacramental mysteries; it has remained faithful to the impulse of its origin by showing man the path to paradise in a purely rational, almost technical, manner. But man, rewarded or punished, remains man - God does not descend to earth to lift man beyond himself (Von Grunebaum 1955:3).

The Prophet transmits God's will and stipulates the terms of the correct life. Islam does not attack sexuality as such. Nevertheless, there is evidence from some parts of the Islamic world that sexuality is viewed as a source of personal and social disruption. As Lawrence Rosen noted in writing of Sefrou on the western edge of the Moroccan Middle Atlas, men see women

> as possessing extremely intense sexual desires which, untempered by an equally well-developed reasoning ability, are capable of wreaking havoc on the established social order. Men, in turn, are extremely vulnerable to this feminine sexual onslaught, simply because the best among them still possess passions of their own (1978:568-569).

Thus, women's flesh-centered desires and tensions (*nifs*) must be restrained by men through the exercise of reason (*'aqel*). Such a view of women as more 'nature-bound', and men as possessed of greater powers of reason, dovetails with the assignment of women to the sphere of childraising and domesticity, while men operate as 'cultural actors' in the public sphere (see Vinogradov 1974). This corresponds neither to the view women have of themselves nor to the observable ways in which the spheres of household and public may interact (Rosen 1978:569-571; Nelson 1974). Writing of the Roudanyin of Taroudannt in the Souss Plain of Morocco, Daisy Hilse Dwyer (1978) observed that Roudanyin women regard men and women as equally intensely sexed and consider women to be as capable of exercising self-control as men.

The view of woman as *habl el-Shitan*, the towline of Satan, is consistent with social arrangements that render women perpetual dependents of men. Islam may not have attacked sexuality as such, but it did little to challenge the contexts of agnatic lineage con- stitution within which the relations of husbands and wives must go forward. The Koran indeed described and circumscribed the conjugal tie, but placed it securely within the boundaries of wife-giving and wife-receiving groups. As a result, to paraphrase Paul Vieille (1978:468), sexual politics - control by elders over the sexuality of juniors - is joined to matrimonial politics, alliance-making between families and lineages. In these politics, women are assigned to their stations by men.

This contrast between Latin Christianity and Islam raises questions about the specific role of religion in the processes of incorporating or subjecting kin groups to the superior power of the state. One is led to inquire into the specific legal and political advantages of conversion to Christianity during the European Middle Ages. Latin Christianity fell heir to the decaying structures of the Roman Empire. One of its characteristics was its maintenance and development of Roman law, especially in the sphere of kinship and marriage. Such ecclesiastical influence was by no means sovereign or uniform. Yet over time it worked to enhance the conjugal bond, to decrease polygyny, to widen the claim of women to property, and to lessen the claims of kinship upon the conjugal pair. It fostered what Jack Goody has called "diverging devolution" or "the woman's property complex", especially through the institution of dowry,

> part of a familial or conjugal fund, which passes down from holder to heir, and usually from parents to the daughter ... a process of transfer that includes women as well as men; that is male property is transmitted to women as full heirs, semi-heirs or residual heirs (1973:17).

The dowering of women may be seen, in turn, as part of a larger complex of interests fostered by the Church. The Church insisted on monogamy, strengthening the distinctiveness of the conjugal pair and its offspring. It punished adultery and prohibited divorce. It forbade incest between relatives by blood to the third degree and by marriage to the second, and even more stringent prohibitions applied to persons related through ritual co-parenthood. The Church advocated virginity at marriage, thus strengthening the hands of parents in pursuing marital strategies. It fostered individual testation, by which a testator could alienate resources from his family and kinship group. It upheld the bonds of feudal contract against the ties of kinship. It also worked against the blood feud, thus enlarging the sphere of state law at the expense of legal self-help by kindreds. In these several ways ecclesiastical intervention reduced the solidarity of local kin and furthered "the vertical entrenchment of authority in a state society" (Cohen 1969:661). Some of this legislation was clearly self-interested, in that it raised the scale of donations to the Church by individual men and women. More importantly, however, it promoted the diffusion of "imageless legal relations arising from acts of agreement" between individuals (Smith 1964:258) in the sphere of kinship, marriage and heirship.

While the Church was thus involved in spreading contract law from early times on, it was not until the Council of Trent and the onset of the Counter-Reformation that it began to penetrate into households themselves. The Counter-Reformation, variously interpreted, can also be seen as a large-scale attempt to reduce the influence of larger kin networks in order to subject households to ecclesiastical influence. John Bossy has suggested that the successes of Lutheranism caused the Church to regard "household religion" as a "seedbed of subversion" (1970:68). To counter the dominance of domestic arrangements over ecclesiastical affairs, the Church sought roots in the local parishes: not until the Council of Trent did it become "a parochially grounded institution" (Bossy 1970:53). The Council formalized the conduct of marriages, instituted rapid baptisms, formalized godparenthood, institutionalized the confession box, reduced the role of vigils and wakes, curtailed autonomous religious confraternities, and initiated the catechization of children. It also intensified the cycles of purification and redemption, which William Christian saw as the abiding legacy of the Council in the Nansa Valley (1972:181). The wife/mother was exalted as the center and 'soul' of the home (Lisón 1966:307). John Davis similarly notes, towards the end of his paper, the more salient role of women in Church affairs after the Counter-Reformation. Re-affirmation of the Virgin Mary not only attracted women, but also served to re-orient husbands and sons away from the external arena of dubious politics and marketing towards the morally sublimated household.

All of these trends, promoted by the Church Militant, aimed at altering the anchoring points and boundary markers that articulated the religious individual with the sacralized portion of the world. Such a re-setting of markers and stakes dovetailed with political efforts to consolidate and strengthen state power. These combined efforts can thus be interpreted in the Gramscian sense, as attempts to erect a 'civil society' under ecclesiastical hegemony to correspond to the structure of the Counter-Reformatory absolutist 'thin' state.

At the same time, this new centripetal re-anchoring of religious subjects in the Christian family was supposed to take place under the spiritual guidance of the clergy. The clergy was also charged with the guidance of lay associations and their subjection to canon law. It is thus not surprising that many of the issues raised and adjudicated during the Council of Trent reappear in old or new guises whenever the boundary between the rights of the clergy to administer laymen is challenged. Riegelhaupt notes the persistence of Tridentine arguments in Portuguese Estremadura, while near Córdova, according to Henk Driessen, the class war is fought out "by other means" between class-based confraternities. The higher-class brotherhoods of landowners, shopkeepers, and artisans display more formal and pious behavior, while the proletarian brotherhoods engage in a rival 'raucous' Christianity. The different expressive styles serve to divide the community, rather than to integrate it.

At all times the clergy is confronted with "rituals of reversal", such as the *mafia* Mass discussed in this volume by Jane and Peter Schneider, or by blasphemies in common usage in Spain. Yet one suspects that there is some economy of effort involved both on the part of the Devil and in the clergy's response to such provocations. Clearly the Devil never sleeps, but some of his sallies are more serious than others.

Only further research can tell us whether the sexual patterning of religious labor in Christendom and Islam might have been more similar before the Counter-Reformation than after it. On the other hand, we shall also be required to take a closer look at the participation of women in Islam. Fernea and Fernea (1972) have discussed the contradiction between public female participation in worship and the prevalent sequestration of women, but they noted also that men and women frequently pray together in the Umayyad mosque in Damascus, while in Cairo this is common on special feast days or days marking the death or life of prominent saints. Among Shi'a in Baghdad, women may visit shrine-mosques, though not regular mosques. Saints' tombs are frequently tended and visited by women throughout the Islamic world, and both men and women go on the pilgrimage to Mecca. There is also evidence, mostly from Shi'as in Iraq, that women develop separate ceremonies and leaders, and in Egypt *zar* possession ceremonies are attended by both men and women (see also Saunders 1977). As the Ferneas concluded, what is needed is "more attention to popular Islam, not neglecting religious practices among women" (1972:401). Such an inquiry could well go hand in hand with a more finely-grained look at the interactions and interrelationships of women and men across the boundaries of the domestic and public spheres, as in information-gathering or reputation-building upon which the more obvious public displays of men depend (Nelson 1974).

Since the Counter-Reformation in Southern Europe and the decline of the Ottoman caliphate, the states of the region have undergone constitutional changes internally and relocation within the system of international politics. The 'world' religions and the organizations that embody them have realigned themselves to face these shifts and changes. Latin Christendom especially has had major changes forced upon it. Some of these changes have been due to the secularization of states and the growth of plebiscitarian politics. The internal bastions of ecclesiastical influence have been challenged by rationalist middle-class parties and anti-religious parties of the Left. On the international plane, the Counter-Reformatory states that once granted great power to the Church were displaced by capitalist powers often in league with Protestantism. Since 1917, moreover, an alternative Socialist system of states has developed in Eastern Europe and East Asia, which has weakened the power of the Church still further.

The resulting struggle against the internal Left and against godless Communism has taken the concrete form of fiercely contested elections and of political mobilization around religious symbols. The rise of the several fascisms in Latin Europe brought Church and State into renewed conjunction. In Italy, the *concordato* of 1929 and the alliance between Church and State that followed the Fascist victory of 1922 were seen by many leaders of the Church and of Catholic Action as a means of regaining their control of civil

society. "The crucifix in the schools, religious teaching, the
recognition of the Catholic university, the banning of freemasonry
were immediately seen not as final concessions, but as the first
steps towards the return of the Catholics in society, towards a
reconquest that would annul the effects of sixty years' absence"
(Mario G. Rossi, quoted in Lyttelton 1976:138-139). Salazar's New
State in Portugal (1926-1974) was explicitly pro-clerical, while the
fascist insurgency in Spain in 1936 took on all the characteristics
of a religious crusade against infidels. This made the Church hierarchy down to the local priest allies of state power, hence targets
of local dissatisfaction. In our collection Riegelhaupt discusses
how villagers in Estremadura in the 1960s viewed and challenged the
priest's functions as a continuing mediator of the moral order.

With the defeat of the Axis powers in 1945, political and moral
defense against the Communist threat inside and outside received a
further impetus. Jeffrey Pratt examines the pro-Communist and anti-
Communist electoral politics of a Tuscan village in Italy. He shows
how Church-sponsored politics turned the structure of the family
into the privileged battleground with the forces of moral dissolution,
and illustrates how political propaganda strove to portray Communism
as "an attack on this most Christian of institutions". William
Christian, in turn, utilizes an 'epidemiological' approach to apparitions of the Virgin, tracing out the nature and incidence of these
visions in relation to the intensified politics of the Cold War.
While the visions could never be wholly controlled by the clergy and
often served to bring the faithful together without clerical
mediation, their end effect was to intensify religious solidarity by
focusing on the anti-religious enemy. Even in Malta, as Adrianus
Koster shows, changes in the role of the parish priest in relation
to his parishioners, and changing relations among the Vatican, the
bishops, and the local priests after Vatican II must be understood
in the context of pro-clerical and anti-clerical politics.

All kinds of internal and external political change have also
affected the Islamic states of the Middle East, but "the family and
personal status aspects of Islamic law and custom ... have been held
onto most tenaciously" (Keddie and Beck 1978:27). Until the middle
of the nineteenth century, Islamic law -- the Shari'a -- reigned
supreme, and its essentially moral rules were enforced through
courts presided over by *quadis* with little motivation to qualify the
basic pronouncements of the Koran, especially in such matters as
women's structural dependence on men, the institution of polygyny,
and the disability of women as heirs, as witnesses before the law,
and as partners to divorce. Since then courts have begun to evidence
greater flexibility in drawing on different Islamic schools of law,
in exempting cases from the jurisdiction of the law, and even in
admitting re-interpretation of the law (Anderson 1971). Yet "Islamic

society has been more conservative in its maintenance of old law and traditions in this area than have other societies" (Keddie and Beck 1978:27-28).

At the risk of oversimplification, one may perhaps seek an answer by looking at the differences in structural form distinguishing Christian and Islamic societies. In the Islamic world Church and State were not separated; moral injunction and political rule were closely intertwined. At the same time, such societies were marked historically by a recurrent inability of the political center to command the constituent segments, while the segments continued to compete with each other and with the center for a larger share of available power and resources (see Vinogradov and Waterbury 1971). Islam as a hegemonic ideology thus worked in contradictory ways. On the one hand, it underwrote and extended the power of the ruler, as 'commander of the faithful' who leads the society in prayer and 'orders Good and prohibits Evil'. On the other hand, it imparted to the segments the corporate strength that depends directly on the power of agnatic affiliation. Thus, claims to religious purity or accusations of corruption and heterodoxy feature prominently in the competition between the constituent units of society. This disjunction and competition may indeed have intensified during the last centuries, when the realms of Islam were weakened politically and rendered dependent on the West.

In this perspective one cannot avoid the ironic observation that religious boundary-making on both sides of the Mediterranean may have received reinforcement from the changed integration of the region into the world system that developed from the 16th century on (Wallerstein 1974). The Counter-Reformation penetrated kin networks on behalf of centralizing states, but these states were themselves losers in the race for capitalist accumulation. Within the world of Islam, religion served both rulership and agnatic dominance; yet it did so in a context of diminished autonomy and power on the part of Islamdom in general.

BIBLIOGRAPHY

Anderson, J.N.D.
    1971   The Role of Personal Statutes in Social Development in Islamic Countries. *Comparative Studies in Society and History* 13(1):16-31.
Althusser, L.
    1971   Ideology and Ideological State Apparatuses. *Lenin and Philosophy and Other Essays*. London: New Left Books, pp. 121-173.

Attwater, D. (ed.)
    1961   *A Catholic Dictionary*. New York: Macmillan.
Becker, E.
    1971   *The Birth and Death of Meaning*. New York: Free Press.
Bloch, M.
    1974   Symbols, Song, Dance and Features of Articulation: Is
            Religion an Extreme Form of Traditional Authority?
            European Journal of Sociology 15:55-81.
Bolle, K.W.
    1970   Secularization as a Problem for the History of Religion.
            Comparative Studies in Society and History 12(3): 242-259.
Bossy, J.
    1970   The Counter-Reformation and the People of Catholic Europe.
            Past and Present 47:51-70.
Christian, W.A. Jr.
    1972   *Person and God in a Spanish Valley*. New York: Academic
            Press.
Cohen, Y.A.
    1964   *The Transition from Childhood to Adolescence*. Chicago:
            Aldine Press.
    1969   Ends and Means in Political Control: State Organisation
            and the Punishment of Adultery, Incest, and Violation of
            Celibacy. *American Anthropologist* 71(4):658-687.
Dwyer, D.H.
    1978   *Images and Self-Images: Male and Female in Morocco*. New
            York: Columbia University Press.
Fernea, R.A. & E.W. Fernea
    1972   Variation in Religious Observance Among Islamic Women. In:
            N.R. Keddie (ed.), *Scholars, Saints, and Sufis*. Berkeley:
            University of California Press, pp. 385-401.
Feuchtwang, S.
    1975   Investigating Religion. In: M. Bloch (ed.), *Marxist
            Analysis and Social Anthropology*. Association of Social
            Anthropologists Studies 3. London: Malaby Press,
            pp. 61-82.
Fustel de Coulanges, N.D.
    1956   *The Ancient City*. Garden City: Doubleday (orig. 1864; first
            English translation 1873).
Goody, J. & S.J. Tambia
    1973   *Bridewealth and Dowry*. Cambridge Papers in Social Anthro-
            pology 7. Cambridge: Cambridge University Press.
Grunebaum, G.E. von
    1955   *Islam: Essays in the Nature and Growth of a Cultural
            Tradition*. Comparative Studies in Culture and Civilization
            4, American Anthropological Association Memoir 81, vol.
            57(2), part 2.

Hirn, Y.
    1957   *The Sacred Shrine: A Study of the Poetry and Art of the
            Catholic Church*. Boston: Beacon Press.
Keddie, N.R. & L. Beck
    1978   Introduction. In: N.R. Keddie & L. Beck (eds.), *Women in
            the Muslim World*. Cambridge: Harvard University Press,
            pp. 1-34.
Lisón Tolosano, C.
    1966   *Belmonte de los Caballeros: A Social Study of a Spanish
            Town*. Oxford: Clarendon Press.
Lyttelton, A.
    1976   Italian Fascism. In: W. Laquer (ed.), *Fascism: A Reader's
            Guide*. Berkeley: University of California Press, pp. 125-
            150.
Nelson, C.
    1974   Public and Private Politics: Women in the Middle Eastern
            World. *American Anthropologist* 1(3):551-563.
Pagels, E.
    1979   *The Gnostic Gospels*. New York: Random House.
Rappaport, R.A.
    1979   *Ecology, Meaning and Religion*. Richmond, Cal.: North
            Atlantic Books.
Rosen, L.
    1978   The Negotiation of Reality: Male-Female Relations in
            Sefrou, Morocco. In: N.R. Keddie & L. Beck (eds.), *Women
            in the Muslim World*. Cambridge: Harvard University Press,
            pp. 561-584.
Saunders, L.W.
    1977   Variants in Zar Experience in an Egyptian Village. In:
            V. Crapanzano & V. Garrison (eds.), *Case Studies in Spirit
            Possession*. New York: John Wiley, pp. 177-191.
Smith, J.C.
    1964   The Theoretical Constructs of Western Contractual Law. In:
            F.S.C. Northrop and H.H. Livingston (eds.), *Cross-
            Cultural Understanding: Epistemology in Anthropology*. New
            York: Harper & Row, pp. 254-283.
Smith, W.R.
    1957   *The Religion of the Semites*. New York: Meridan Books
            (first published 1889).
Vieille, P.
    1978   Irian Women in Family Alliance and Sexual Politics. In:
            N.R. Keddie & L. Beck (eds.), *Women in the Muslim World*.
            Cambridge: Harvard University Press, pp. 451-472.
Vinogradov, A. & J. Waterbury
    1971   Situations of Contested Legitimacy in Morocco: An Alterna-
            tive Framework. *Comparative Studies in Society and History*
            13(1):32-59.

Vinogradov, A.R.
   1974   French Colonialism as Reflected in the Male-Female
           Interaction in Morocco. *Transactions of the New York
           Academy of Sciences* 36:192-199.
Wallace, A.F.C.
   1966   *Religion: An Anthropological View.* New York: Random
           House.
Wallerstein, I.
   1974   *The Modern World System.* New York: Academic Press.

Overviews

The Sexual Division of Labour in the Mediterranean

John Davis, University of Kent, Canterbury

1. OUTLINE OF THE ARGUMENT

The problem requiring explanation is that men and women have got
different religious roles in the Catholic countries of the north
shore and in the Islamic countries of the southern shore of the
Mediterranean. Consider these two descriptions:

'They are often women with a great deal of charity, with incred-
ibly scrupulous attention to the smallest detail of their lives
... Their faults might be due to their lack of education or their
age, but they are often people who live in the presence of God.'
... They are assiduous not only at public church functions but
also in the reading of prayer books, the performance of novenas
... and private meditations. Some of them make virtually total
effort to live up to what they think a Christian should be. And
in the process they have a good time. For [one such woman]
religion is no morose waiting thing. It is quickened with joy and
discovery. Reading the *Guide for Sinners* of Fray Luis de Granada,
her eyes light up with pleasure. For her and some of her friends,
religion is poetry, drama, mathematics ... The older women
become, in their own way, mistresses of a vast body of arcane
lore and tradition, philosophers and technicians of the sacred,
consultants to their daughters and grand-daughters, to whom they
pass on their personal patrons and their techniques for contact-
ing and consulting with God (Christian 1972:160-161).

The times of prayer ... regulated and ritualised the daily flow
of time. Prayer [was] also [the culmination of] the week. On
Friday mornings men made their weekly visit to the public baths
in anticipation of the noon prayer. Work came to a halt while
they bathed and put on their best clothes. At the same time their
wives busily prepared the special meal to be served at home after
the prayer. Just before noon the gates of the city were locked,
and the governor began to lead his entourage to the mosque ...
During the time of prayer there was a deeply felt sense of the

equality of all Muslims. Informants repeatedly stressed that at
these moments every man experienced an awareness that he was
God's servant, and that in His house no social distinctions
existed...

Every adult male used to attend the meetings of one of the
religious orders regularly. Fifteen orders had lodges in the
city... In the evening many of the townsmen went to lodges to
perform the evening prayers ... followed by liturgical recitations
and litanies specific to each order... Some informants stated that
at moments of crisis in their personal lives they would go to
their lodge to speak with their saint (Brown 1976:88, 110, 112).

The reader will of course wish to introduce nuances into the picture
before it is generalised; and he will be right to do so. But the
pattern holds good: on the whole Catholic women are expected to be
more devout than Catholic men; and Muslim men are expected to be more
devout than Muslim women. Religious work is chiefly entrusted to
women in the Catholic countries, to men in the Islamic ones. Moreover,
this difference in the division of religious labour, corresponds to
no other difference in the division of labour, and you cannot explain
the division of religious labour by associating it with some other kind.
You cannot say, for example, that the religious pattern plays superstructure to any political or economic or familial infrastructure.
So you may be led to look at religious ideas. That is extraordinarily
difficult because on the one hand religious doctrine is never
unequivocal; and on the other, the sets of local religious practice
and ideas are linked to the variably authoritative and variably
central bodies of doctrine in ways which anthropologists have not yet
specified very clearly. So the outcome will be speculative in the
highest degree; but the tentative conclusion is that differences in
religious ideas are not directly the causes of differences in
religious practice. The source of explanation probably lies in the
historical relations of religion and politics.

2.

The contrasting sexual differentiation of religious roles is not
uniform: in some Catholic countries men are publicly and approvedly
pious; and there are reports of the vigorous spiritual exercises of
respectable Muslim women. Spiritual activity is not constant throughout an individual's life, but has periods of greater and lesser
intensity. And in what may perhaps be called deviant religious practice women are predominant in both Islam and Catholicism.

Consider first the accounts which suggest that Catholic men and
Muslim women are not equally excluded from devotion in every community.[1] In Ramosierra "the cult of the Virgin Mother ... has its

greatest supporters among the men and should not be confused with mere religious practice, at which the women excell" (Kenny 1961:79). In Malta, Boissevain says, when the Angelus rings "work and conversation stop whether in a government office or a village cafe, men remove their hats, and someone among them leads them in a short prayer". "Most girls and women and many boys and men attend one of the three or four daily masses", and "virtually everyone" attends on Sundays (1965:55). In this respect the Maltese are unique, and that may be because Catholic observance was so politically charged. For the most part women far outnumber men at daily masses[2], are much more likely to fulfill the obligations to attend mass on Sundays[3] and make confession and communion on the days of precept[4]. Moreover, women are much more likely to undertake superrogatory devotions[5], to guard the spiritual welfare of their households[6] and to express emotion[7] than men are. While men do not participate as much as women in regular and superrogatory devotions they do walk in processions in all the Catholic communities, and attend the mass in basilica, church or chapel which is invariably part of the celebrations. Women also participate, although men are responsible for organising the procession and the *festa* of which it is a part[8] and men also generally carry the statues[9]. Processions are unlike the daily devotions of *las beatas* because they are occasional and take place on holidays when all men except shepherds and daily farmers are freer than usual. They are also generally reported to be not merely religious events but in some sense celebrations of community[10]: this is said of patronal festivals as might be expected; in some cases it is said also of celebrations of the major holy days of the Church, Good Friday and Easter[11]. Participation of men in processions depends in part on their social roles and status. 'The authorities' are often prominent[12], as are members of confraternities who may have the right to carry the statue of the saint or devotion of their association[13]. Confraternities themselves may be open, or restrict membership to particular social groups[14]. In general, on the matter of processions, it does not seem to be utterly impossible to argue that men participate to the degree that the celebrations are secular and not religious: is it because *festas* symbolise aspects of community that men are so prominent? At least, you might argue that when men publicly express their spiritual lives they do so to protect the community for which they are also politically responsible; women do so too -- but in their daily devotions and participation they are concerned mostly with the spiritual welfare of their households.

Anthropologists have not provided much evidence about the spiritual life of Muslim women. "The religious activities of Muslim women have varied considerably from place to place. This is in large part because the segregation of the sexes ... does not accord well with public acts of worship"[15]. Moreover, many ethnographers of North

Africa have been men, and have not had access to the private religious gatherings of women. Public religious activity is perhaps an even more important component of the spiritual life in Islam than it is in Christianity: celebration of the community of the faithful, of the *'umma*, at the very least is the camaraderie of the lineage group at prayer in its mosque; that it can be much more is clear from, say, the work of K. Brown, part of which is one of the epigraphs to this paper. But women are excluded from nearly all mosques[16], and from some of the Orders[17]. So it is not simply that women are privately devout: public devotion is an aspect of spirituality which is not open to women[18].

Women do practice religion inside their houses, and some accounts suggest that their spiritual exercises are strenuous. They pray at the obligatory times[19]; they may hold or attend special meetings at which they recite religious poems or read the Qur'ān[20], and they may also be the main religious actors at times of crises in their households[21]. Some women may have reputations for special learning and piety, but since they cannot express them publicly they appear not to acquire a following nor generally to become saints[22].

Turn now briefly to a slightly different point. Piety, a spiritually active life varies, at least in Catholic countries, with the age of the individual[23]. Most of the evidence for this is in the footnotes to the preceding page. It is clear that women become increasingly active in religion as they get older: Christian's type, the progressive approach to a state in which God is immanent in every moment and activity, seems to be general: old Catholic women, old Muslim men are those most likely to achieve it. Catholic men are more likely to have an active spiritual life in late adolescence and early manhood.

It seems appropriate to reserve to a special category those practices which anthropologists call religious, or at any rate class with religion, but which are not accepted as such by the doctrinal experts of Catholicism and Islam: cures for evil eye, love potions, charms, amulets, magical bindings and the like. These are nearly always the speciality of women; one exception is the charms or philtres involving paper with the written word in Islamic countries, which require a literate scribe; another is that men may turn to male witches for aid in securing their hearts' desire[24]. But in general women have, as it were, appropriated the local, the idiosyncratic unofficial domain of religious belief and practice. In Catholic countries you might wish to associate control of this domain with women's control of the minor and local saints, some unrecognised by the Church, even by the parish priest (see esp. Christian 1972:101). When Christian discusses seers (*divinas*) -- 'older women' who are 'relatively benign supplements' to officially accepted or approved figures, he seems to suggest that women have a

sphere of religious action which is below the threshold of ecclesiastical perception: all women "have a tap on the unknown" -- but
those who are married and under control lose their access: *divinas*
and witches, who live alone, can still draw on the occult and on the
local sources of "*mana*" (ibid:191-194). Cutileiro makes the point
rather more elaborately: women are experts in the evil eye and in
blessing the sick. "These old women officiate in the same religion
of which the vicar is priest. They do not celebrate masses, hear
confessions or administer sacraments, but in the day to day struggle
to propitiate God ... when a human mediator is needed they and not
the priest are called in... They are unordained priestesses ..."
(1971:275).

Perhaps it is mistaken to put such emphasis on these subliminal
activities? But this seems to be the one area of religious activity
in which Catholic and Muslim women have similar roles -- contact
with the occult, the feared and the unofficial powers. The women's
markets of the central Rif are associated (by men) with sorcery:
"Men do not know what may go on in women's markets, but they usually
fear the worst and ... invariably allude to women's purchases of
herbs and potions" (Hart 1976:87)[25]. Akhdari women are said (by
other women) to bewitch their husbands with potions and spiritually
dangerous substances in their food[26]. The consequence of that would
be that whereas women in general bring sanctity and spiritual well-
being to Spanish houses, they are spiritually dangerous in Akhdari
ones: polluting, in possession of potions and charms, able to
administer them most easily in food, Akhdari women appear threatening. It is hard to say how widespread that might be. In Kerkanna[27]
and in Kufra it is men who are responsible for the spiritual and
economic well-being of their households, but there is not enough
information to judge whether women are commonly regarded as a
spiritual menace. Nevertheless, it is in this area that the spiritual roles of Catholic and Muslim women most closely resemble each
other. And it should not pass unnoticed that these depressed
religious areas are also often enough associated with midwifery and
other practical treatments of women's particular problems -- *sub
rosa* birth control, and abortions, as well as washing the dead:
lying-in and laying-out[28].

Although these variations undoubtedly exist, and are undoubtedly
important, you may agree they do not alter the fundamental picture.
In the Catholic countries women are pious in public more than men
are; and, although this is described only by one writer, they appear
to achieve an intensity of spiritual awareness greater than that of
men[29]. In the Islamic countries it is men who constitute the '*umma*
-- the public community of the faithful. Men secure the well-being
of the Muslim communities, women that of the Catholic ones --

although men play a major part in patronal festivals. In Muslim
communities men watch over the spiritual security of their households,
and it may be that women threaten it; in Catholic communities it is
women who are responsible, and who urge men to fulfill their
religious obligation. Catholic women are chiefly concerned with the
peace of the souls of the dead, whereas it is Muslim men who conduct
the public memorial readings for their dead men and women. In both
Muslim and Catholic communities women look after women in a practical
way, and are the main experts in the ritual or spiritual care of
women during the crises, pains and illnesses they are heiresses to.

Perhaps it is appropriate to point out that these patterns are
not mirror images of each other, nor do they contrast in any symmetry.
It does seem right to refer to the religious position of Muslim women
in terms of religious disability -- they are excluded by their
secular seclusion from full participation in spiritual life. They
appear to be devout and faithful, but they have no part in the public
demonstration of surrender. On the other hand, Catholic men often
enough proclaim their anti-clericalism[30] and, while they may be
involved in religious affairs when the reputation of their community
is at stake, or when as in Malta they are involved in political
struggle, they have to be persuaded to care for the safety of their
own souls. So while there is a rough symmetry in the roles and
spiritual activity of those who are more devout, there is no corres-
ponding symmetry in the activities of those who are less devout: it
is not as though men are chiefly concerned with charms and potions
in Catholic societies, for example; nor are Muslim women in any
sense anti-clerical. So, a straightforward structuralist account of
the differences seems not to be on the cards.

3. THE SEXUAL DIVISION OF OTHER LABOUR

It is not necessary to retail every nuance of the sexual division of
secular labour. The patterns show considerable variation, but always
a fundamental consistency: men are concerned with politics, with
major economic undertakings in production, with the education of
adolescent boys and young adult men; women are concerned with minor
productive tasks, with nearly all processing, with the organisation
of consumption, with the education of girls and of small boys. Women
are also ultimately responsible for keeping track of kinship
relations (though men are in control of lineage relations in
societies with lineages) and seem to be responsible, too, for the
initial moves in arranging marriages. That is the broad pattern, it
is not undifferentiated, and the exceptions have little bearing on
the issue because they do not correspond to exceptions in the
religious sphere[31].

The point is this: if it could be shown that differences in the division of religious labour between Muslim and Catholic countries coincide with differences in the division of other kinds of labour, there could be grounds for an anthropologist of particular ideological predispositions to argue that the explanation of the religious difference resided there. Indeed, if it were the case that, say , agricultural labour was entirely confined to women in Catholic countries, to men in Muslim ones, many people would seek no further for explanation, nor perhaps even bother to elaborate an argument to show there was more than correspondence of difference. "It is no coincidence", they might say, and let their minds come to rest. But in fact it is not the case that there is any difference in the division of secular labour which matches the differences in religious roles in spiritual life[32]. So it seems appropriate to consider the other term in the equation: if the division of labour can provide no clues, perhaps religion can. Does religious doctrine about sex, sexual relations and sex roles contain any possible explanation?

4. RELIGIOUS DOCTRINE ON SEXUALITY, VIRGINITY AND COPULATION

This is the most difficult part to write. Even Catholic doctrine is hard to discover, for it is a palimpsest of ancient and modern, of administrative control of the faithful and apologetics for the unconverted, an evolving and diffuse body of teaching and speculation over which practitioners continue to argue[33]. The doctrines of Sunni Islam are in some ways even harder to identify because there is such freedom of speculation within the poly-doctrinal communion. An attempt to produce an account of *the* doctrines of Islam and Catholicism on any subject, let alone one so fraught with interest as men and women and their relations, is impossible. Nevertheless an explanation for the differences between the Catholic and Islamic divisions of religious labour may lie somewhere in this area. There is a strong incentive to venture into the uncomfortable world of theology even if naivety is the only tool to hand. The three areas of doctrine which seem most likely to yield understanding are: doctrine about the spiritual natures of men and of women; doctrine about the Virgin Mary; and doctrine about the spiritual value of copulation.

The spiritual natures of men and of women. It is an occluded area in Catholic thought at the present time; the Church does not make clear statements which would imply the spiritual inferiority of women, although that inferiority is entrenched in the exclusion of women from the priesthood, and, for example, in the provision of special rituals for the purification of women from impurities which result not from voluntary actions but from the involuntary natural condition of women. The belief in spiritual inferiority is ancient, and seems to rest on two pieces of revelation. The first is the bisexual creation, and the manner of it; the second is the fall of man, and the part played by Eve in it.

Why are there men and women in the world? Men are created in God's image, and most of the things they do, they can do quite well on their own; worship, conversation, football or poetry require no sexual differentiation: it is not necessary for these things that the image of God should have a sex. Women therefore exist for sexual and procreative purposes: that is what distinguishes a sexed companion for Adam from an otherwise equally possible unsexed one. The finality of woman is instrumental: it is the sexual reproduction of the species[34]. In Aristotle and Aquinas men are drawn by their nature to intellectual knowledge and that is their purpose. Women are not so led: they have rational souls, but the purpose of women is reproduction. The manner in which Eve was created is indicative of her relative status in the divine economy of salvation: Adam is alone in the world (in the Genesis 2 version) until God creates animals and Adam names them. Then God takes Adam's rib, and Adam names the creature "woman" (Genesis 2:23) and later -- after the Fall -- "Eve" meaning "mother" (Genesis 3:20). Adam is superior to woman because he has priority in time, and in matter; his end also is superior -- it is his rationality; whereas the end of woman is reproduction[35].

The prelapsarian subordination and spiritual inferiority of women was firmly accepted by Christian theologians in the Eastern and Western traditions[36]. While Paul's revolutionary theology[37] asserts the irrelevance of social barriers that divide the Christian community, he also asserted the natural and spiritual weakness of women -- who are attacked by fallen angels unless they are specially protected, and who reflect the glory of man, in contrast to men, who reflect the glory of God (1 Corinthians 11:7).

The Fall accentuates the prelapsarian inferiority of women: woman was primarily responsible; the punishment of Adam and of Eve was sexually differentiated, and was attributed by Aquinas to the bisexuality of human kind (McLaughlin 1974:218). Eve was to bear children in pain (Genesis 3:16); and the fact that women continued to do so, even after the second Eve had borne Jesus, was taken from very early times as a sign that women's responsibility for the Fall was not cancelled by their contribution to redemption[38].

Catholic doctrine is much less determined, much more changing, much less centralised than is sometimes supposed: so any attempt to state what it is, in a few paragraphs, undoubtedly does violence to a rich and complex intellectual field. These difficulties and dangers are compounded in the case of Islam, where the doctrine is established

by the reputation and life of the doctrinal expert and his pupils,
rather than by any formal procedure: by prestige, rather than by
authority. The problem of maintaining a distinction between doctrine
and what people actually do and believe, by no means absent in
accounts of Catholic faith, is particularly acute in North Africa
with its florescent and estatic cults and orders, and has indeed
defeated some scholars, both Christian and Muslim. In fact any
attempt to move from a description of practice to an account of
doctrine can be greeted with the rejoinder, not infrequently angry,
"this is a false picture of Islam (and is motivated in the most
damnable ways)". Doctrine, defined by rejoinder from more than one
Muslim, becomes more elusive. In this paper, which is intended to
be inoffensive, it is not possible to offer a solution; but a
prophylactic device is used: *Islam* refers to such doctrines as it
is reasonable to suppose are doctrines; *Muslim* refers to the human
practice of religion, doubtless often coincident with Islam, but
apparently open to rejoinders of the sort described above[39]. In
Islamic doctrine women are ritually impure from month to month, for
reasons which do not depend on their will[40]. Women's spiritual
status, their part in the divine economy, depends in part on an
almost unqualified obedience to their husbands, a condition of
salvation which does not apply to men. When God warns Mohammad's
wives that they are liable to divorce for good cause, he describes
how they ought to behave: "... It may be that if he divorces you
his Lord will give him wives better than you, submissive, believing,
obedient, repentant, devout in worship, observers of the fast, both
widows and virgins"(66:2-6)[41]. Adam has priority over his mate in
time: "He created you [mankind] from a single soul and from it
created its mate and from the two created and spread many men and
women" (4:2, cp. 39:6).

So, Islamic doctrine disqualifies women on grounds of intermit-
tent impurity (not sin) from important religious actions; in most
circumstances spiritual health depends on obedience to husbands --
it is the spiritual nature of women to be subordinate. On the other
hand, the Qur'anic account of the fall ascribes equal responsibility
to both human parties: "Satan caused them both to slip from their
stand of obedience by means of that tree, and thus drove them out"
(2:36 ss). Both Adam and his wife plead for forgiveness from Allah
(7:24). And salvation is expressly assured for both men and women:
"I will not suffer the labour of any labourer among you, male or
female, to perish" (3:196)[42].

The conclusion -- tentatively based on a necessarily inadequate
understanding of a complex and disparate literature by an amateur --
seems to be that in Catholic doctrine women have a slightly inferior
position in the economy of salvation than they do in Islam: that is

because they are secondary in creation, instrumental in their finality, and unremittably culpable for the fall of man.

That is an awkward conclusion to come to because, if you are inclined to be fairly commonsensical about these matters, you might have expected the opposite: in those communities where women are the spiritual athletes, in continual training, you might expect a doctrine which gives them a superior nature to that accorded them in communities where they are disbarred from undertaking some of the most important exercises. But that is not the case: relatively lower spiritual status seems to go with relatively greater spiritual activity.

The Virgin Mary. It might be that women in Catholic communities play a more active role in religious life, and have fuller spiritual lives than they do in Muslim ones, because they have the image, the model of Mary: the marian cults and devotions propose an *imitatio* of a female who was chosen by God for really quite exceptional favour, who is Queen of Heaven and who intercedes against the severity of Judgement. From the middle of the last century, at least, theologians have argued that the cults of Mary have had beneficial effects on the position of women. On the other hand, it is quite clear that feminist Christians do not find mariology a fruitful source of theological justification for their criticism of the 'androcentrism' of the Church: "... the mediaeval cult of the Virgin ... rather than deep-ening an appreciation of the bipolarity of God's creation ... under-lined the weakness, inferiority, and subordination of real females" (McLaughlin 1973: 246)[43].

You do not have to be a feminist to accept that if there is mile-age in mariology, feminist Christians were the most likely to have found it; and the fact that they have not seems to lead to a first conclusion: devotion to Mary is not now a liberating force for women in any political or economic or indeed theological sense: it does not create an equal nor a parallel spirituality for women, but a sub-ordinate one (see note 1 above). Indeed, reading the seventy or so columns of the *Dictionnaire de spiritualité* on Mary it is difficult to ignore the fact that most mariological literature is written by men, and the cults and congregations mostly created by men. At least one consequence is not so much that women have become dominant, as that celibate priests have become more tender, more sensitive than they might otherwise have been[44].

The history of mariology[45] confirms the argument from intuition: it was a movement led by an increasingly celibate and ascetic clergy. Devotion to Mary was not a feature of the canonical Church. Women were certainly present and vocal in the early congregations: Luke's gospel has parallel parables -- one example for men (e.g., the shepherd's lost sheep) and one for women (e.g., the woman's lost silver), and was written for a mixed audience. Women are prominent

in Acts; but there appears no special emphasis on Mary. Paul was much
concerned with the spiritual status and religious behaviour of women,
but does not mention the Virgin, who indeed is not called that until
the middle of the second century. The first great impetus to marian
devotion is said to have been the end of the official persecutions
of the Church in 313: asceticism replaced martyrdom as the chief
witness to saintliness; and virginity, chastity, obedience, submission were modelled on the qualities of Mary. That was also the
time at which the Gnostics were defeated, and the masculinity of God
established for orthodox believers[46]: some few years before 350 Mary
was called *Theotokos*, Mother of God; and it is not wholly misleading
to see the subsequent history of mariology as a struggle by ecclesiastical authority to prevent the deification of Mary: both in form
and theology and in popular devotion there were constant pressures
to exalt Mary to a higher place in the economy of salvation than is
compatible with the doctrine of the Trinity[47].

Marian devotions were spread in Western Europe in consequence of
Charlemagne's attempt to standardise liturgy in the worship of his
empire -- a response to the threat of Islam. There was a considerable florescence of devotion, of literature, sculpture, painting and
buildings portraying or dedicated to Mary in the monastic revival of
the eleventh and twelfth centuries, with its accompanying emphasis
on asceticism and on combatting Islam. In the years before the
introduction of printing, wood-cut pictures of Mary were widely
circulated; and after the introduction of the press, popular
devotional literature about Mary was marketed throughout Europe.
Although Luther seems to have especial respect for Mary (while
condemning what he considered exaggerations) the Reformation was
(among other things) anti-marian[48]; and in the Counter-Reformation
there was renewed popular devotion to Mary, increasingly controlled
and co-ordinated by the Church. The French Revolution similarly
stimulated the growth of popular devotion: congregations were
founded, miraculous apparitions approved, the Rosary promoted, and
dogma altered, partly in response to the anti-clerical movements
which recur throughout the century and a half after 1789; partly in
response to the growing positivism and secularism of the expanding
middle class. In 1854, six years after the Year of Revolutions, two
years after Cavour became prime minister of Piedmont, the Immaculate
Conception of Mary, disputed for nearly fifteen hundred years,
became dogma of the Church.

Devotion to Mary, and the development of dogma, is not independent
of the events and tendencies of the real world; the work of Lisón-
Tolosana and Christian further show that theological and devotional
changes have effects in remote parishes[49]: perhaps they are a response
to the excesses of popular devotion; perhaps they are also attempts
to control and stimulate popular piety during the historical crises

of the Church. Nevertheless it remains true that marian devotion
and theology was largely a product of ecclesiastical speculation
and elaboration -- that at the beginning it was designed in large
measure for the spiritual exercises of a celibate clerisy[50]; and
that the chief emphasis was on those aspects of Mary which make her
least like McLaughlin's 'real' woman.

That is to say, Mary -- at roughly the turn of this century -- is
a virgin generated without passion, vowed to chastity, who was
approached by God; who from pure faith consented to be the vehicle
of redemption, Mother of Jesus -- and -- Logos; who suffered no pain
in childbirth, and remained virgin. She may or may not have suffered
a mother's sorrow at the crucifixion of her Son; she (at that time)
may or may not have been often pictured as crowned and anyway sitting
enthroned beside her Son, interceding on behalf of the hundreds of
thousands of Christians who are devoted to her. She is the Mother
of Virtues, for her humility and obedience to God's will, a model,
variously interpreted, for those who are devoted to her in her
various aspects. In particular her relation to Jesus is the prototype of all human relations to Him; and she is the prototype of the
perfection which is human finality[51]. From time to time she makes
well-authenticated and officially certified apparitions in which she
gives advice and warning; and these in turn stimulate new devotions
and pilgrimages.

How to assess the import of Mary on the spiritual lives of
Catholic women of the Mediterranean? Part of the answer lies in the
contrast between -- on the one hand -- the highly theologised prototype of relations to Jesus, exemplar of celibate chastity, object of
subtle and tender *placement* in the economy of salvation, who is the
creation of ecclesiastical and usually celibate speculation; and --
on the other hand -- the Mother of *Gesù Bambino*, who washes the
nappies of the Logos, whose statues speak, weep, while welcoming
penitents who crawl on their knees and lick the floor. The two
virgins are connected -- they overlap and they are mutually respon-
sive in the long term. For while popular devotions, folk mariology,
often belong in the category of 'deviant' religious practice in
which pious women are 'unordained priestesses', official devotions,
introduced by priests or by the order of ecclesiastical authority,
do penetrate the parishes. It is not clear that the congregations
and confraternities admitted women in great numbers until say
roughly 1800: but after that date women seem to have been officially
encouraged by their celibate priesthood to standardise faith and
liturgy, and to stand, albeit in a subordinate position, against the
forces of revolution and change. Similarly, in the long term, popular
devotion can stimulate condemnation or codification at levels above
the threshold of official perception.

Apart from that possibility it seems that Mary, in terms of

official doctrine, ought to create spiritual activity in men rather
than in women (as in fact Kenny says she does, in Ramosierra). For
the example which Mary sets to men is one of fulfilment of their
rational finality; it is the purpose of men to achieve rational
movement of the soul towards God, and Mary is the prototype of that
achievement. But Mary was conceived without sin, and herself conceived without sin, vowed to virginity, giving birth without pain.
Mary, mariologically speaking, is not a typical woman, for women's
finality is not mainly rational: the bisexual creation implies that
the finality of women is their fruitfulness. Of course, women have
rational souls, and they can, do, achieve perfect union with God:
but that appears to be at the cost of their particular finality, not
in fulfilment of it. The example Mary sets to Catholic women is one
of self-abnegation[52].

Relations of men and women. In Catholic doctrine original sin is
transcribed by sexual generation; priests should be celibate, and
chastity is the best path to sanctity. After the resurrection, people
do not marry for they are like the angels. In Islam a spouse is the
half of religion; vows of chastity are limited to four months duration,
and people in paradise are really or allegorically sexual.

The Catholic doctrine on sexuality is founded on two notions. The
first is that it is sexual passion which transmits original sin:
people are conceived in sin. In the Garden of Eden, Aquinas said,
copulation was rational and without passion; there was no lust, no
pain in labour, and hymens remained intact. Augustine could not admit
that Mary was untouched by sin because he did not admit that her
conception was immaculate. Sin is a consequence of the bisexual
creation, and that is its propagation. The second leading notion is
that the resurrection entails loss of sexuality (Matthew 22, 30;
Mark 12, 25; Luke 20, 35-36). The preference for virginity is based
on these doctrines: "virginity doubtless reveals better than marriage
does, what our life will be in its eschatological phase... That does
not imply that, in the future life, married persons will be linked
only by the link of divine charity which will unite all the saved,
... but that we shall have no other occupation than serving God and
praising him... Of course, marriage is also service to God and the
Kingdom. .. But this service takes a less direct, less exclusive and
absolute form" (*Dictionnaire de spiritualité* s.v. Marriage, col. 384).
God is spirit, and he who wishes to approach close to God should
disengage himself as much as possible from material things. Aquinas,
still cited by contemporary authors (e.g., *Dictionnaire de spiritualité* s.v. Chasteté), said "I consider that nothing so casts down
the manly mind from its heights as the fondling of women and those
bodily contacts which belong to the married state". Copulation and
its inevitable post-lapsarian accompaniment of concupiscence is irrational and degrading. It follows that vows of chastity crown those

who have the prime virtue of faith. That is the justification for
the regulars; and it is one justification for the seculars: celibacy
permits a priest to devote himself more closely to God. But a priest
also serves man, and celibacy ensures that he is free from personal
attachments: "He who found a family belongs to it; but the priest
belongs to everyone". "A priest needs moral authority, respect, the
confidence of others, if the gift which he makes of himself is to be
useful. If he is married his moral authority can be compromised by
the shabby tricks ... or misconduct of members of his family". "To
hear Confession and to direct consciences requires a limitless filial
veneration for the confessor which becomes extremely difficult if the
priest is known to be coupled with a companion" (*Dictionnaire de
spiritualité* s.v. Chasteté).

The contrast with Islam is almost complete. The bisexual creation
is not casual: "We have created ... in accordance with the require-
ments of truth and wisdom" (15.86)[53]. "He has created mates for you
of your own kind so that you may find peace of mind through them, and
he has but love and tenderness between you. In that surely are Signs
for a people who reflect" (30.22; also 42.12). There is a Qur'ānic
emphasis on the purposefulness of the bisexual creation, on amity[54],
on marriage and legitimate copulation[56] which justifies Bouhdiba's
description of sexual relations as sacramental, an outward and visible
'Sign'[56]. The *hadith* "To marry is to accomplish half of religion" has
a quite literal meaning. In this context the carnalities of Paradise,
literal or allegorical and in any case elaborated on rather few
Qur'ānic verses[57], do not appear absurd nor profane. Celibacy and
chastity are not celebrated and virginity has a purely secular and
temporary value.

5. LAST PARAGRAPHS

The problem was to explain why men and women have different religious
roles in the Catholic countries of the northern Mediterranean, in the
Muslim countries of the southern shore. On the whole, broadly speaking, laymen in Catholic countries are less religious than women are;
in Muslim countries, men are more religious than women are.

Two possible kinds of explanation are discarded summarily. First,
if the pattern were symmetrical it could be attractive to try to
produce some kind of structuralist argument -- to say that Catholic
and Muslim patterns are mirror images of each other. That avenue
need not be explored further, because the pattern is not symmetrical:
women occupy the 'deviant' grounds of charms, potions, witchcraft,
midwifery, abortion, in both Catholic and Muslim communities. The
pattern would be symmetrical if this were the province in each case
of the people who have the diminished religious roles. Second, if
differences in the sexual division of religious labour coincided with

differences in sexual divisions of any other kind of labour, you
might feel inclined to explore that coincidence more fully. But
there is no such coincidence, hence no possibility of finding an
explanation there.

Both those paths are impasses. So the possibility arises that the
patterns of roles are related to ideas about the nature of men and
women, and their respective places in the divine economies of Islam
and Catholicism. Unfortunately that path too turns out to be a no-
through road. For any argument of this kind should try to demonstrate
a consistency of ideas and action: it would be a refutation of an
intellectualist explanation if it were found that ideas were
generally inconsistent with actions. If the Book and its glosses say
that women have an inferior position, and in reality women play a
dominating part, that is a refutation of any argument from the
relation of ideas to actions.

The conclusion therefore must be that the discrepancies exclude
any simple explanation in terms of ideas. The discrepancies are:
that women in Catholic doctrine have a relatively lower place than
they do in Islamic doctrine, and yet in Catholic life they play a
more dominant part than Muslim women do in actually existing concrete
communities. Similarly Catholic men -- all men, not just priests --
have a theological position which is more elevated above that of
women than an Islamic male's is -- and yet in Muslim communities it
is men who play the major religious roles. Because of these incon-
sistencies the intellectualist position also turns out an impasse.

The failure of the intellectualist possibility actually compounds
the problem. What started out as an apparently simple problem of
differences in religious roles seems now to subsume a further
dimension of intellectual discrepancy. For while Islam grants women
a relatively higher position in the divine plan than Catholicism
does, Muslim women appear to perform relatively diminished roles in
the spiritual life, compared to those of their Catholic sisters.
There is a similar though not symmetrical discrepancy which arises
if you contemplate the respective roles of men in spiritual affairs,
in Islam and Catholicism and in the practice of religion.

Three possibilities remain. The first is that the whole paper is
completely wrong from beginning to end -- the ethnography inadequate,
the doctrines misunderstood, the notions of what may constitute
explanation misconceived. Readers of papers are more likely to take
that line, than those who write them are. The second is that the
problem is wrongly cast. It might be more fruitful to compare
Catholic Mediterranean practice with that of Catholics in North or
South America, or North Europe, and with Greek Orthodoxy. It might
be more fruitful to compare North African Muslims with West African
or Indonesian Muslims and with Judaism. It is incontrovertible that
comparisons of that kind would increase understanding the social,

political, economic forces which shape and limit the interpretation
of religious doctrines, their translation from the Book into the
everyday spirituality of Christians and Muslims. Of course that is
so, and perhaps others may find the task intriguing enough to assist
in it. It is also the case that Catholicism and Islam derive from a
common Revelation; and that the Catholics and Muslims of the
Mediterranean have been in contact with each other, by conquest,
colonisation, commerce, for a millenium -- it is scarcely easy to
maintain, in these circumstances, that the problem is created by the
comparison of entities which are too unlike each other. So it still
seems sensible to regard the problem as one problem, not many to be
attacked severally and piecemeal: any explanation should explain the
totality of the pattern[58]. But it now seems that the explanation
must be sought not within the religious thought and religious
activity, nor within the general category 'the division of labour'.
Rather, and this is the third possibility, it seems to lie within
the history and the organisation of the religions. J. and P.
Schneider have argued that Islam and Christianity are centralising
forces set to undermine the autonomy of local groups, doing so
principally by undermining the dominance of men over women. "It seems
to us that in their confrontation with lineal descent groups both the
Church and Islam sought to buttress the position of women against
that of men. They granted women rights and status denied them by
their families... Familism and the code of honour ... defended the
family against the hegemony of Church and State" (1976:96). This
argument directs attention to the different consequences of interaction between local communities and supra-community organisations.
It is not without difficulty: neither religion in fact grants women
a superior nor even an equal status to men. And Catholic support of
women is at best equivocal: in the early theological battles between
Judaic and Hellenistic traditions, it was the more restrictive,
Judaic, view of womankind which prevailed. But so far as Islam is
concerned, the argument works: Islam *is* marginally more progressive
than the local communities which adhere to it: the fact that women
do not get their half-shares in inheritance; that they do not get
their place in mosques, do not have their spiritual individuality
recognised by their kinsmen and husbands therefore seems to suggest
that -- to use Schneider's terms -- local lineage groups were by and
large successful in resisting the hegemony of Islam: their success
is to be attributed at least in part to the weak organisation of the
centralising and liberating faith. The Catholic Church, always less
monolithic than imagined, was nevertheless more highly organised and
bureaucratised, more powerful than Islam has ever been: in a sense,
the conflict of Church and State (in theory absent in Islam) invites
the Church to acquire state-like characteristics. The difficulty
therefore is to explain how lay women, in defiance of religious

doctrine, came to acquire such prominence in religious practice. When did this happen? It seems to be in the period after 1750, perhaps as late as 1800. For example, while it is very difficult to tell whether or not women were members of lay confraternities and congregations before 1750, there were seven hundred such congregations devoted to Mary, founded and officially approved, between 1800 and 1950. This is the period, too, when the two important dogmas of the Immaculate Conception and the Assumption were finally agreed.

If this is so -- and it is by no means certain -- then it is possible -- and by no means certain -- that the discrepancy between Catholic women's formal spiritual status and their actual position is related to events and changes taking place in the secular world: the revolutions and secular, even anti-clerical governments, in France and elsewhere in Europe after 1789; the growth of rational-ising disciplines (economics, sociology) and of scientific discovery and theory; the changes in law which follow the Napoleonic invasions, and the establishment of bilateral inheritance; the growth of liberalism and of nationalism, most notably in Italy itself. These are the context in which women's spiritual activity increases (if it did increase) with the encouragement of the Church. In the battle for the survival of faith the Church calls in the reserves from the spiritually depressed areas of society.

APPENDIX

A brief chronology of doctrine concerning Mary and devotion to her. Note: The items are taken very selectively from *Dictionnaire de spiritualité* etc., fasc. LXIV, cols. 409-82, 1977.

Year

70	Mark, John do not mention the virgin birth; Matthew and Luke do, but make no necessary connection with Christ's divinity. Paul does not name Mary.
110	First patristic mention of Mary.
165 ca.	Mary called 'the Virgin' for the first time.
220	Irenaeus of Lyon draws parallel between Mary and Eve: Virgin and betrothed, Mary achieves salvation for herself and all mankind by her obedience to God. Eve, by her dis-obedience achieves the Fall.
222	Tertulian admits virgin conception, denies virgin birth. Clement of Alexandria (+214) asserts *virginitas in partu*.
300 ca.	First known invocations of Mary.
313	End of persecution of Christians. Martyrdom replaced by asceticism as the ideal type of the Christian life:

	consequent idealisation of virginity.
350 ca.	Mary called *Theotokos*.
388	Mary appears in baptismal catechism.
390	Jovinian excommunicated in Rome and Milan for saying that virginity carries no special premium over married life. St. Ambrose (Milan): "Mary brought us not only a stimulus to virginity; she gave us God Himself" and hence our redemption.
392	Gregory of Nysse asserts that Mary had taken a vow of chastity before the annunciation.
419	Jerome contests Helvidius' opinion that Mary and Joseph had normal marital life after the birth of Jesus.
430	Augustine the first Latin Father to assert that Mary took a vow of virginity. Augustine argues (against Pelagius) that Mary was not free from original sin because she was generated sexually (and original sin is transmitted that way).
431	Council of Ephesus: Christ had one nature only; therefore Mary gave birth to Jesus and *Logos* -- she is *Theotokos*.
440	Triumphal representation of Mary enthroned beside Jesus in S. Maria Maggiore, Rome.
800	Charlemagne attempt to standardise liturgy "but time elapsed before the four Marian feasts (Purification, Annunciation, Assumption, Nativity of Mary) were uniformly adopted".
1100	Cathedrals dedicated to Notre Dame. Marian Psalter of Pontigny, has 150 verses, each beginning "Ave ...". *Index Miraculorum B.V. Mariae* lists 1783 miracles.
1109	St. Anselm writes *Orationes sive meditationes*: there are more than 100 copies surviving in England and Paris.
1321	Dante portrays Mary as guide and intercessor.
1324	*Biblia pauperum* portrays Mary as Mother of Mercy, intervening with Justice.
1423	Feast of the (7) Sorrows of Mary established in Cologne. (Originally 5, they multiplied to 150 before stabilising at 7.)
1495	Confraternity of Mary of Sorrows established in Flanders.
1498	Michelangelo's *Pietà*.
1506	Cajetan opposes new feast "Spasmus B.V. Matris Dei".
1516	Council of Trent registers new feasts: Immaculate Conception, Visitation, Presentation of Mary in Temple.
1522	Luther condemns use of Mary as advocate.
1536	Michelangelo begins Last Judgement in Sistine Chapel (?Mary portrayed as helpless at the act of judgement?).
1550 ca.	'Slaves of Mary' becomes an important form of devotion. In 1673 Clement X forbids the use of chains and other

	practices incompatible with human and Christian liberty.
1587	Standardised constitution laid down for lay congregations of the Holy Virgin.
1588	F. Arias writes first 'imitation' -- De la imitación de Nuestra Señora.
1611	Foundation of Order of Mary Immaculate.
1622	Foundation of Order of the Visitation.
1638	France officially recognises patronage of Mary. (Ireland and Portugal 1646; Austria 1647.) In the many new churches built in this period, Mary and Christ often depicted with crowns.
1650-1900	"L'histoire mariale de cette période peut être caractérisée par une tendance ... à passer d'une diversité de dévotions à une attitude globale qui accentue et unifie la place de la Vierge Marie dans la vie chrétienne."
1671	Michel de Saint-Augustin writes *Vitae Mariaeformis*.
1708	Feast of Immaculate Conception established by Clement XI.
1716	Feast of the Rosary established by Clement XI.
1725	Dionisi publishes *Il mese de Maria* (i.e., special dedication of May to her): 18 editions by 1825.
1747	Muratori condemns common propositions:
	i) that Mary can forgive sins
	ii) that God forgives only on Mary's intercession
	iii) that devotees of Mary cannot be damned.
1800	Foundation of Congregation of Hearts of Jesus and Mary; 1804 - Sisters of Notre Dame; 1816 - Oblates of Mary Immaculate; 1817 - Brothers of Mary. (Between 1800 and ?1954 about 700 women's organisations devoted to Mary are founded. In 1972 Molette publishes a list of more than 150 extant.)
1830	Apparition of the Miraculous Medaillon; 1846 - Apparition of La Salette; 1858 - of Lourdes; 1871 - of Portmain. All these give rise to congregations and pilgrimages.
1851	Joachim Ventura argues that Mary desired the condemnation and crucifixion of Jesus.
1854	Dogma of Immaculate Conception. This is the doctrine that Mary was not generated in sexual passion and was therefore free from original sin: cp. the note on S. Augustine above, anno 430.
1866	Leo XIII publishes 12 encyclicals on Mary, especially on Rosary. Marian congress at Livorno: the first of 'hundreds'. 1900 - Lyons congress launches petition that Assumption should become dogma.
1917	Apparition at Fatima.
1932	Apparition at Beauraing.
1933	Apparition at Banneux - the most recent officially

recognised.

1950   Dogma of the Assumption of Mary.
1954   Proclamation of royalty of Mary.
1965   Vatican II - debate on the schedules on Mary (approved by
        1114 votes to 1074). As a result, in the following ten
        years:
          i) feasts of Transfixion of Mary, of Our Lady of Mercy,
             of the Holy Name of Mary are abolished
         ii) feast of Annunciation to Mary becomes Annunciation of
             Our Lord; Purification of Mary becomes Presentation
             of the Lord (at the temple)
        iii) encyclical *Cultus Marialis* of 1974 says that devotion
             to Mary must be part of devotion to the Trinity -- it
             must be Christological and Pneumatological.

NOTES

* The paper has benefitted considerably from criticisms offered at
  the conference itself, and from those offered at seminars at the
  Universities of Kent, Sussex, Stanford, and U.C. San Diego. It
  was also presented to the evening seminar of the Anthropology
  Department of U.C. Berkeley where wide-ranging comparative
  criticism was given in a convivial atmosphere. It is a great
  pleasure to recall these occasions on which colleagues made real
  contributions to the improvement of the text. In addition to
  these, particular thanks to Dr. Michael Gilbert of the University
  of Kent and to Drs. L.D. Meijers of the Vrije Universiteit,
  Amsterdam, who offered comments (some of which are incorporated)
  and information on the doctrine and practice of Judaism (alas,
  excluded to keep the paper wieldy). To all these, renewed thanks.
1. The most obvious point is that Catholic men may become priests.
   They are not much discussed here, for two reasons. First, they
   are not clearly male, as laymen may expect to be: they achieve
   their spirituality by sacrificing one of the most valued
   Mediterranean characteristics of masculinity (legitimate descendants). Secondly, although it is attractive at first sight to
   attribute laymen's low participation in spiritual life to their
   antagonism to a celibate and authoritarian priesthood, the pattern
   does not hold, and seems to contain no possibility of explanation.
   For in the Eastern Mediterranean, where Orthodox priests may
   marry, it appears that laymen are also less dutifully active in
   religious matters than lay women are.
2. But it is not the case that all women always attend daily mass.
   Lisón-Tolosana (1966:293-294): "militant Christians" are the
   twenty women who go to mass daily. Gower Chapman (1973:42): "Piety

and devotion to the church are also virtues shared by both sexes. As in most other European societies, however, women are more faithful in their religious practices than men", who do not attend weekday mass. The nucleus of women who attend church daily, and do odd jobs for the priests have taken "informal vows of chastity" and are referred to a "housenuns" (this data refers to the late 1920s). Schneider and Schneider (1976:95-96): "Women in contemporary Sicily are more religious than men. Unlike men they attend church regularly and are more likely to vote for the party of the priests". Cutileiro (1971:251) says that a few old women attend daily mass, but they stay away in bad weather.
3. Lisón-Tolosana (1966:293-294) gives figures. Cutileiro (1971:251): "Afternoon mass is said every Sunday and is attended by school-children ... and by a few women mostly young and single ... [whose presence] has attracted a few young men, but by and large men stay away from mass. Attendance by married women is also infrequent".
4. Lisón-Tolosana again gives figures: about 10 per cent of women and 20 per cent of men do not fulfil the precept. Christian (1972: 151) quotes an old woman: "We always have to push the men to get them to go to confession". Cutileiro (1971:264-265): school-children and those about to wed have to confess "but apart from these not more than a dozen women ... and even fewer men go to confession every year. The women are mostly old and have unfortu-nate lives".
5. Lisón-Tolosana (1966:307). Men take no part in most of the devotions to Mary. Gower Chapman gives examples of vows by women, including the vow to visit a saint *'lingua strasinnuni'* (1973: 160), while men vow to carry a saint in procession, or to let off fireworks in honour of a saint. In the last weeks of Lent mission services are attended "almost exclusively" by women (ibid.:166). May rosaries are held in the streets but not in those streets where there is no devout woman (ibid.:173). Cutileiro reports that pious women rescued statues of saints threatened in the anti-clerical period of 1911 (1971:260-261); that 17 women were pros-ecuted in 1913 for holding an Easter procession. In the 1960s "some women develop a close and somewhat exclusive relationship with their favourite saints" (ibid.:271), and make vows far more often than men do -- men are usually persuaded to make vows by their women (ibid.:272). Christian's survey of visits to shrines shows that 98 women (of various ages) had made 124 trips to shrines, 68 men had made 40 trips (1972:124) -- and women over-whelmingly outnumber men in wearing habits (ibid.:127).
6. The most thorough discussion is by Christian: "the woman ... assumes control of all affairs pertaining to the spiritual well-being of the household" (1972:134). His informant José remarks:

"When masses are ordered it is the women who handles it, but that is like when you send a kid to the store to buy something for you, it is really you who buys it" (ibid.:148) -- a pretension which Christian convincingly qualifies (ibid.:151). Douglas appears to say that while men mourn for a year, sitting in the *luto banque* at the front of the church, women are responsible for the perpetual cure of dead souls -- it is always women who 'activate' the *sepulturie* (1969:32, 53). Cutileiro (1971:272): "The assurance of divine protection for the community is therefore almost entirely the task of the women".

7. Lenten mission preachers in Belmonte describe the sufferings of Mary: "The women break into tears and sobs; the men say as they leave the church: 'that is how to preach'" (Lisón-Tolosana 1966: 308-309). Women do seem to internalise the holy stories more than men: this is partly perhaps because they know them better (e.g., Cutileiro 1971:272); but also because they relive them more imaginatively. Gower Chapman recorded a lullaby, for example, from Milocca:

> "When the Beautiful Mother went to wash
> The diapers of Our Lord,
> She rubbed them on the stones and kissed them,
> And hung them to dry on roses and flowers"
> (1973:175).

Christian suggests that such concrete imaginative sensitivity is showed by priests who, sheltered in seminaries, do not have it drummed out of them by the grossness of ordinary life (1972:135).

8. Alcalá is an exception: in the five religious brotherhoods "the wives of the *senoritos* play a leading part... Their functions are the organisation of religious festivals and charity" (Pitt-Rivers 1961:133).

9. So much so that when seventeen women organised a defiant procession in Vila Velha in 1913 the anti-clerical authorities were able to arrest them for a monarchist conspiracy: if it were a religious procession it would not have been only "the feminine element -- and the lowest among it at that" which took part (Cutileiro 1971:266). Christian however reports that women carry the statues of saints in some processions (1973:70 e.g.).

10. Freeman (1970:92-93) writes of a distinction between *fiestas corriendas*, where such guests as may come are invited by individual households, and *fiestas des pueblo*, when the community (on these occasions wholly or partly commensal) seems to act host to all-comers.

Gower Chapman (1973:197) describes processions which seem to symbolise the internal structure of Milocca: "... the drum, band, society banners, the fratelli in full regalia, the local

authorities and the clergy. The priest carries the ostensorium
over which the mayor holds an embroidered silk canopy". Compare
the photographs of Tret and St. Felix processions which Cole
and Wolf (1974:facing page 275) say show not only the structure
of the communities but important aspects of their cultures
(roughly, order and disorder) as well. Lisón-Tolosana has a
moving account of Good Friday processions, in which men and
women carry different statues around the town in different
directions until suddenly they confront the image of Jesus
carrying his cross to Calvary with the image of the Mother
Dolorosa (1966:298). If you will lapse into Greek Orthodoxy for
a moment, note Campbell's account of the Sarakatsani Easter
Sunday: although men are normally hostile to all unrelated
Sarakatsani they visit each other's households. "Except for a
summer festival this is probably the only occasion ... that a
man penetrates into the house and receives the hospitality of
an unrelated shepherd." The milk of Easter Saturday is given to
the poor or to the villagers. One point it may be worth investi-
gating is that while all these actions symbolise 'community'
they do not do so in a uniform manner: it seems that the
community may be celebrated vis-à-vis others (Valdemora); or it
may be celebrated to itself (Milocca); or people may represent
the relations between the sexes (Belmonte); or they may simply
celebrate the underlying brotherhood of men in a society in
which they usually keep distance (Sarakatsani).

11. The most noteworthy case is described by Boissevain (1965:56 ss)
whose data is also the fullest. "Many families make pilgrimages
to the churches in the twelve other parishes which hold Good
Friday processions. At each one they offer prayers before the
sepulchre and pause to examine the statues and funeral hangings
of their rivals... All morning visitors from outside stream into
Kortin to see the church."

12. See note 10 above (Gower Chapman, Cole and Wolf). Kenny says
that the patronal *fiestas* are organised by the confraternities
and their officers; *pueblo* authorities have a "privileged
position at the side of the altar" at masses, and in the symbolic feast in the school hall they sit on a dais and are waited
on by the members of the confraternities. The wives of the
municipal and confraternity officers have important tasks in the
rituals (1961:95 ss).

13. The main exception seems to have been Malta, where the brothers
wore robes in processions, benefitted from indulgences granted
to the association, and may still have had some prestige: but
from Boissevain's descriptions they did not carry the statues.
In Kortin the ten men who carried the crucifixion on Good
Friday had done so for years, and had signed a contract with the

parish priest giving them the exclusive right to do so
(Boissevain 1965:19-23; 56-58). Milocca (where many men were
imprisoned during the period of fieldwork) also seems to have
restricted confraternities to walking in the processions. Men
who carried statues did so because they had vowed to (Gower
Chapman 1973:160).
14. In Belmonte the confraternity of Our Lady of the Rosary had 15
members, recruited by succession from the *pudientes*, the middle
class (Lisón-Tolosana 1966:297). Nobody else writes very much
about the social rank of confraternity members.
15. Fernea and Fernea (1972:386). They give an interesting survey of
a varied and all too scanty literature, with particularly graphic
accounts of sh'ia women's *qraya* in southern Iraq drawn from
E. Fernea (1965).
16. In Eastern Libya, for example, men sometimes said that they had
heard there was a mosque in Tripoli big enough to have a section
for women. Devout women entered a mosque for the first time in
their lives when they went on pilgrimage to Mecca and Medina,
where provision is made for segregated worship. Even in the Mzab,
where the precept that the equality of Muslims includes women is
institutionalised, women do not go to the mosque (Alport 1970:
239).
17. "Many women also visited some of the lodges individually,
especially those that also served as burial grounds. But here
again the religious orders differed in their practices: some
accepted burials and visits by women, others did not." When men
attended the public cemetery at *'Id al kabir* "a small number of
women ... sat far to the rear of the men" (Brown 1976:112).
18. Akhdari women dance the *hedra* both on general occasions, e.g.,
'id al kabir, and on occasions specially reserved to women (e.g.,
during Ramadan). The women who do so are all exceptionally
intelligent and independent and are marginal -- "they fail as
social beings according to the dominant ideology" -- (Maher
1975:94-97). With the exception of a few holy women from the
Murabiteen tribes, who may be regarded as performing certain
public functions, "women are ... excluded from ... public life"
(Mohsen 1967:221).
19. "Many, many occasions in Edremit call for a group of women to
have a religious gathering in a house; usually it is a *mavlud*,
a recitation of a poem on the life of Muhammad." Such groups
centre on a 'specialist' -- a woman with knowledge of Arabic
and skill in recitation (Fallers 1976:252). "A few girls learned
to pray and to read the Qur'ān at home or in the house of a
woman teacher. They belonged to families which had a reputation
for learning..." (Brown 1976:107). In the Mzab the order of
laveuses ("unpaid and highly respectable" women, appointed by

men), have access to every house, must be consulted on all
occasions, and regulate the dress, cosmetics and hairstyle of the
other women. They have the authority to 'excommunicate' and know
the Qur'ān, the prayers and history of their sect as well as the
laws of the city (Alport 1970:239).

20. But see Hart (1976:776) "Women in general pray much less than men
    -- older women pray more often than younger ones".

21. Maher again: "When a woman makes *sadaqa* [provides food for the
    poor at the funeral of a household member] she throws open her
    house, normally a secret hidden place, for inspection by her
    neighbours. They demonstrate their confidence and solidarity by
    eating liberally of her food" (1974:100). The more food the poor
    eat, the more *baraka* is acquired by the hostess (ibid.:99).

22. The rarity or otherwise of women saints is not often remarked in
    the ethnographies. The Seksawa have Lalla Aziza as a founding
    ancestress and saint (Berque 1955:237-322), but other groups
    which claim common descent from an ancestress do not sanctify
    her: the *hurr* tribes of Cyrenaica, descended from Sa'ada, spring
    to mind (Peters 1960). The saints visited by Akhdari women for
    special intervention in women's problems seem to have been men
    (Maher 1974:97). And it appears also to be the case that the
    women's *suqs* in the Central Rif were usually at or near the sites
    of men's *suqs*, although held on different days, and benefitted
    from the sanctuary of a male saint (Troin 1975:115-116; Hart
    1976:86-88). The Encyclopedia of Islam lists only one female
    saint, the mystic Rābi'a al 'Adawiya.

23. Also, undoubtedly, with rank. The part played by authorities is
    noted above (cf. note 10); but anthropologists have not said
    much more than that. Here are three references: Gower Chapman
    says "men of the upper class may be somewhat less regular in
    attendance at Mass and less overtly devout than other people"
    (1973:43). Cutileiro describes the worldly associations of
    priests and their identification with the latifundists, who are
    those most likely to observe days of precept, and who may use
    their power to insist that would-be clients should attend church
    (1971:258-69; 221-222). Pitt-Rivers (1961:134) "Men of the ruling
    group tend to consider more the political implications of
    religion, and to them anti-clerical is synonymous with 'Red'".

24. Maher (1974:103).

25. Anne-Marie Troin went to women's *suqs* to observe for her husband
    and reported sales of pottery, jewelry, perfumes, ointments,
    knick-knacks and some cloth. The volume was negligible except
    at the Azrhrar *suq*, which is close to a *Club Méditerranée*, and
    exchanges were "essentially social" (Troin 1975:117 and note 16).

26. Maher says that this is a consequence of women's powerlessness in
    in legitimate activities: "women are forced to turn to intrigue

and attempt to redress the balance of power, on a personal level, by means of witchcraft". It is often a man's female kin who accuse his wife of bewitching him, "which supports the hypothesis that witchcraft is a weapon presumed to be used in a power struggle between spouses" (1975:100-102). A power struggle of a different kind is suggested by Christian who adopts Le Roy Ladurie's description of women's participation in the occult and in obscure local devotions: they are a 'counter-cult' (1972:194). The same view is clear in Pitt-Rivers' epigram, that wise women are to the church what the black market is to government control of grain (1966:201). However, it is not at all clear that 'wise women' see themselves as in any sense an opposition to established orthodoxies and authorities (a view in any case not explicit in Maher's account) and a wise man might feel inclined to withhold the accolade of contrariness until more detail is available.

27. K. Platt, personal communication.
28. Cutileiro (1971:273): Midwives know "not only the technicalities of rural obstetrics, but also ... the religious rituals". Maher (1975:103) describes "an old black woman" who seems to have combined these activities. Milocca had thirteen female witches (*fattuchiere*), and a male 'Astronomer' "said to have diplomas in Theology, Astronomy and Magnetism" from Palermo. The boundary between them and healers (*dutturisse*) is not clear. Milocca at that time had a state midwife (Gower Chapman 1971:9). The important position given to *laveuses* in the Mzab has been noted above (cf. note 19).
29. The anthropologist is Christian. Cutileiro seems to hint at the same fact.
30. Vila Velha had a national 'anti-clerical' government from 1910-1926, and no parish priest from 1926-1944. The priests, when present, played important secular roles: these affect laymen's willingness to entrust them with details of their spiritual lives; but anti-clericalism is relatively muted because villagers depend on the priest's secular power (Cutileiro 1972:264-266). In Milocca priests as a category, and members of a class, are "proverbially lacking in charity and their supposed chastity is doubted": that does not conflict with admiration for particular priests, which is particularly likely to be granted if he is your son or brother (Gower Chapman 1971:43). The two priests were ridiculed, "the size of their hernias was discussed openly and without compassion" and people said: "As for priests, listen to the Mass and break their backs" (ibid.:193). The priests each had followers and were vigorously supported by them, but the cleavage did not follow party lines (ibid.:143, 193-194). "Not only in the doctrine that the priest espouses but also in the

mere fact that he intrudes at all into the sphere of the family
unit, he generates hostility among the men... In a sexist society
the priest is at a remarkable cultural disadvantage" (Christian
1972:151-152). Compare the Schneiders' argument that the cultural
code of honour is (among other things) an assertion of the
autonomy of households against interference by Church and priests
(1976:95-97).

31. For example, in Murelaga, where women have much greater political
and economic equality with men than in other Iberian communities,
where there is no double standard for moral judgement of sexual
activity, and where women speak in *auzoa* meetings, nonetheless
they are chiefly responsible for activating *sepulturie*, the
central religious act. Men take charge of festivals at which the
auzoa is represented to the community (Douglas 1969:109).

32. Some writers on Catholic communities hint -- no more -- that
women are more active in religion because they have more time to
spare from production than men do. "I go to mass; I like to when
I can. But when I can't, I don't. You have to wash up and dress
up and then change clothes back again before you can go off to
the cows ... I tell my wife I don't want to bother anybody about
it, and nobody should bother me about it" (Christian 1972:148-
149). Although it is of course true that "while her husband is
working in the field [a woman can] attend mass or make a quick
visit to the church" (Lisón-Tolosana 1966:309) the same is true
of Muslim women who do not have substantially more housework
than Catholic ones. The 'spare time' argument, if it were ever
elaborated, would not be satisfactory.

33. The main source used here for Catholic doctrine is the *Dictionnaire de spiritualité* published in parts since the early 1950s.
The most recent fascicules (XIV-XV) have reached Ma...-Marie,
Mariage. For a measure of the rapidity with which the language
of religious discussion changes readers are invited to compare
the articles on *Chasteté* (1955) and *Mariage* (1977). "It is often
difficult ... to know what in Scripture is truly revealed ...
and what does no more than reflect as an echo the cultural,
ethnic and ethical milieu in which the books of the bible were
composed" (*Dictionnaire de spiritualité* s.v. Mariage et vie
Chrêtienne).

34. McLaughlin (1974:217) "This ... is the only explanation Thomas
Aquinas can offer for the existence of a 'second sex'".

35. So, it is possible to construct the following statement of
relationship Man : Woman : Mind : Matter.

36. The tradition is now muted. For example: "In Woman, whom God
created by taking her from the man's side, *man* finds an alienated
part of *himself*... Their union should reconstruct the primitive
but disrupted unity" *Dictionnaire de spiritualité* etc., fasc.

LXIV, col. 361; this is published 1977).

37. "There is no such thing as Jew and Greek, slave and freeman, male and female: for you are all one person in Christ Jesus" Galatians 3:28. See Parvey (1974).

38. E.g., Tertullian: "best beloved sisters ... the sentence of God on this sex of yours lives in this age: the guilt must of necessity live too. You are the devil's gateway; you are the unsealer of that tree; you are the first deserter of the divine law; you are she who persuaded him whom the devil was not valiant enough to attack. You destroyed so easily God's image, man. On account of your desert, that is death, even the Son of God had to die" (cited Prosak 1974:105).

39. See Antoun (1968, 1970); Abu-Zahra (1970).

40. *Encyclopedia of Islam*, s.v. Haid: menstruating women "may not perform the *salat* nor the *tawaf*, nor fast, nor touch the Kur'an, nor repeat a verse from it nor enter a mosque". The only Qur'ānic prohibition is on copulation; the rest is derived from tradition and interpretation.

41. The Qur'ān gives examples of two unbelieving women, two believing ones.The wives of Noah and Lot are unbelievers: "They were married to two righteous servants of Ours, but they acted disloyally towards them". The believing women are Mary daughter of Imran "who guarded her chastity and ... fulfilled the words of her Lord and His Books and was obedient;" and Pharaoh's wife who prayed "deliver me from Pharaoh and his work, and deliver me from wrongdoing people" (66:11-13). You should say that obedience to husbands is not an absolute requirement: obedience to a wrongdoing husband is by no means a guarantee of salvation.

42. Cf. "Keep in mind the day when thou will see the believing men and believing women, their light running before them and on their right hands, and they will be greeted with: Glad tidings for you" (57:13). "Allah has prepared forgiveness and a great reward" "for men who are truthful and women who are truthful, and men who are steadfast and women who are steadfast [... humble ... alms givers ... fasting ... chaste ... remembering Allah]" (33: 36).

43. The encyclical *Cultus marialis* of Paul VI (1974) attributes to feminists the argument that the Virgin Mother is an unrealisable and therefore crushing example; moreover that it is degrading to present women with an example of passivity, self-effacement and silence. The encyclical therefore proposes a greater emphasis on Mary "comme la personnalisation de son peuple, fille de Sion, une type de lucidité, d'élan, d'initiative, de créativité prophétique et charismatique éclatante" as she appears in Mark and John. However, what the American feminist theologians objected to was rather different; and it is by no means utterly

certain that *Cultus marialis* remedies their distress.

44. That is almost too speculative to write. But see McLaughlin's reference to a "feminizing balance" in mediaeval Christianity (1974:248). Also Christian's comments (1972:135; sup. note 9) that priests share imaginative sensitivity with women because they are protected from socialisation into harder ways.

45. The sketch which follows is supplemented by a brief chronology appended. See also Warner (1976) and Graef (1963).

46. Pagels E., *The Gnostic Gospels* (forthcoming). Extracts published in New York Review of Books, October 22, November 8 and November 22, 1979.

47. In 1621, after the Reformation -- by and large anti-Marian -- N. Coffeteau wrote "As Our Lord was crucified between two thieves, so the doctrine of the Church balances between two heresies: it condemns the sacrilege of those who defer excessively to the Virgin, and it rejects the impiousness of those who steal all honour from the Virgin". In 1747 (see appendix anno 1747) it was considered important to attack the opinions that God would forgive sins *only* if Mary interceded. The existence of this struggle was revealed to Muhammad: "And when Allah asked Jesus son of Mary 'hast thou said to the people -- Take me and my mother as two Gods beside Allah?', he replied, 'Far be it ...'" 5:117s. (also inf.no. 55.)

48. O.E.D., for instance, records *mariolatry* from 1612. Newman's *Letter to Rev. E.B. Pusey* of 1866, "le meilleur document de la littérature mariale du siècle", is a response to the strength of opposition to marian devotion in the Anglican Church.

49. Lisón-Tolosana (1966: Ch. XI) gives an account of episcopal visitations to Belmonte, from the late sixteenth century. Among other things, the visitor tries to regulate the affairs of the four confraternities, two of which were dedicated to Mary. In 1619 the Mayor, jurymen and councillors of Belmonte "voted, confessed, believed and made a solemn vow" that the Virgin was untouched by original sin (ibid.:306). Christian has material of great interest on the introduction of devotions (1972:81-83; 87-88); in particular his is the only eye-witness account of the local consequences of the major shift in devotional emphasis formulated at the second Vatican council (ibid.:180-187).

50. It is difficult not to be touched by the tender piety with which St. Bernard addresses Mary, for example. It does not seem inappropriate to speak of love in some of these relationships. In other cases the femininity of Mary stimulated resentment rather than tenderness; for example, Bernardino of Siena tormented himself in blasphemous fantasy: "... one Hebrew woman invaded the house of the eternal King. One girl, I do not know by what caresses, pledges or violence, seduced, deceived, and if I may

say so wounded and enraptured the divine heart and ensnared the Wisdom of God". (Cited by McLaughlin 1974:249).

51. "Car Dieu aime réaliser en germe, au début de ses oeuvres, en le concentrant souvent en une personne, ... le prototype de la perfection qui sera réalisée plus largement ... au terme de l'oeuvre."

52. In a religion in which Jesus is not the Son of God, his mother cannot be *Theotokos*. But in Islam Mary is miraculously conceived, does conceive Jesus by the breath of Gabriel, and is said by Allah to be "elected above the women of all created beings" (3.42), but she was not deified (see note 49). She is said to be venerated in local cults in Iran; and to be the first candidate in discussions whether or not women can be prophets (-- the answer is generally no). See Abd el Jalil (1950); *Encyclopedia of Islam* s.v. Miriam.

53. And: "We did not create the heaven and the earth and everything between them in play. Had We wanted to find a pastime We would surely have found it in Ourself, if We had at all been inclined that way" (21.17s).

54. "It is made lawful for you to consort with your wives during the nights of the fast. They are as a garment to you, and you are a garment to them."

55. "Arrange the marriages of widows from among you and of the righteous ... under your control, male and female. ... Force not females under your control into unchastity by restraining them from marriage" (24.33s). A married man can make vows of chastity for a period of up to four months; at the end of that time spouses must agree to resume cohabitation, else the wife has the right to divorce (2.227-228).

56. "L'exercise coranique de la sexualité revêt donc une majesté infinie. Il est la vie véhiculée, l'existence multipliée, la création perpétuée. La fonction sexuelle est en soi une fonction sacrée. Elle est une de ses signes, auquels se reconnaît la puissance de Dieu" (Bouhdiba 1975:23).

57. E.g., 2.26 has "mates most pure" for the elect in Paradise. "Chaste maidens of modest gaze, untouched by man or jinn, ... good beautiful women, ... black-eyed, guarded in pavillions ... untouched by man or jinn, reclining on green cushions and beautiful carpets" (55.60-78).

58. It is for this reason, for example, that arguments based on the Virgin Mary have to be discarded: her example might be admitted to have some influence on the religious roles of Catholic women, so discrepant with their theological status: but Mary cannot be involved as a *Theotokos ex machina* to resolve the discrepancy between Muslim women's *placement* in the divine economy and their relatively lower position in actual religious practice. The same

kind of argument suggests that Christian's explanation of the
Catholic discrepancy is invalid. Christian thinks that the
hyperactivity of Catholic women's spiritual life is in part the
consequence of their inferiority in the plan of salvation. "It
seems likely ... that behind the ... religious activities of the
women lies a sense of impurity that has been laid on by the
Church and its ministers. Ever since Eve, women have been seen
as ... the cause of man's downfall. With an overwhelming
emphasis on female models who were pure and virgin ... adult
sexually active women ... feel ... they are unworthy, that they
have something to expiate" (1972:153). That argument could be
extended to include Muslim women: Women are active in Spain
because they are of low spiritual status, quiescent in North
Africa because they are secure in their sexuality. Moreover,
laymen are quiescent in Spain because they are secure in their
rationality. But there are two particular difficulties: the
first is that laymen in Catholic countries do not always feel
content about their wives' spiritual activities; and they resent
the intrusions of the priesthood into family affairs (e.g.,
Christian 1972:151-152): there is conflict between laymen and
the celibate clergy. Secondly, the schema does not fit the
intense sociable spirituality of Muslim men and therefore does
not meet the total problem. A more general difficulty is that it
seems a little facile when there is a problem in the anthropological or sociological sphere of discourse, to slip into
another field where the problem is resolved as it were by inversion. Of course it is true that if you are bad at arithmetic
then you may work harder for those exams than you do for others.
But does this model work when it is generalised to the majority
of populations for centuries, for the duration of individuals'
lives? Christian may be right: Catholic women may be spurred to
religious activity by a collective complex of religious inferiority. But the suggestion needs anthropologising: the mechanism
needs to be specified, as do the circumstances in which it will
operate for particular categories. At the moment it "seems like
likely", to Christian, that so many women's minds could work
that way for so long. Perhaps you will agree that it is not
sensible to rest explanation on intuition, however sympathetic
and grounded in long experience.

BIBLIOGRAPHY

Abd-el-Jalil, J.M.
    1950   *Marie et l'Islam.* Etudes sur l'histoire des religions 8.
            Paris: Beauchesne.
Abu-Zahra, N.M.
    1970   "On the Modesty of Women in Arab Muslim Villages". A Reply.
            American Anthropologist 72(5):1979-1987.
Alport, E.A.
    1970   The Mazab. In: E. Gellner & C. Micaud, *Arabs and Berbers.*
            From Tribe to Nation in North Africa (1973). London:
            Duckworth, pp. 141-152.
Antoun, R.T.
    1968   On the Modesty of Women in Arab Muslim Villages. A Study
            in the Accommodation of Traditions. *American Anthropologist*
            70(4):671-697.
    1970   Antoun's Reply to Abu-Zahra. *American Anthropologist* 72(5):
            1088-1092.
Berque, J.
    1955   *Structures sociales du Haut-Atlas.* Paris: P.U.F.
Boissevain, J.
    1965   *Saints and Fireworks. Religion and politics in rural Malta.*
            L.S.E. Monograph in Social Anthropology. London: Athlone.
Bouhdiba, A.
    1975   *La sexualité en Islam.* Paris: P.U.F.
Brown, K.L.
    1976   *People of Salé. Tradition and Change in a Moroccan City,*
            1830-1930. Manchester: Manchester University Press.
Campbell, J.K.
    1964   *Honour, Family and Patronage. A Study of Institutions and*
            Moral Values in a Greek Mountain Community. Oxford:
            Clarendon.
Christian, W.A.
    1972   *Person and God in a Spanish Valley.* New York: Seminar Press.
Cole, J. & E. Wolf
    1974   *The Hidden Frontier. Ecology and Ethnicity in an Alpine*
            Valley. New York: Academic Press.
Cutileiro, J.
    1971   *A Portuguese Rural Society.* Oxford: Clarendon.
Dictionnaire
    1955   *Dictionnaire de spiritualité, ascétique et mystique,*
            doctrine et histoire. Paris: Beauchesne (continuing).
Douglas, W.A.
    1969   *Death in Murelaga.* Seattle: Washington University Press.
Encyclopedia
            Encyclopedia of Islam. Leiden: Brill.

Fallers, M.C.
    1976   Sex Roles in Edremit. In: J.G. Peristiany, *Mediterranean Family Structures*. Cambridge: Cambridge University Press in association with Social Science Research Centre, Cyprus, pp. 246-255.
Fernea, E.W.
    1965   *Guests of the Sheik. An Ethnography of an Iraqi Village*. New York: Doubleday.
Fernea, R.A. & E.W. Fernea
    1972   Variation in Religious Observance Among Islamic Women. In: N.R. Keddie (ed.), *Scholars, Saints, and Sufis. Muslim Religious Institutions in the Middle East since 1500*. Berkeley: University of California Press, pp. 385-401.
Freeman, S.T.
    1970   *Neighbours. The Social Contract in a Castilian Hamlet*. Chicago: University Press.
Gower Chapman, C.
    1973   *Milocca. A Sicilian Village*. London: Allen & Unwin.
Graef., H.
    1963   *Mary. A History of Devotion and Doctrine* (2 vols.). London:
Hart, D.M.
    1976   *The Aith Waryaghar of the Moroccan Rif. An Ethnography and History*. New York: Viking Fund publications in anthropology 55 (Wenner Gren).
Ibn Tufayl
    1972   *Hayy Ibn Yaqzan. A Philosophical Tale*. New York: Twayne.
Kenny, M.
    1961   *A Spanish Tapestry*. London: Cohen & West.
Lisón-Tolosana, C.
    1966   *Belmonte de los Caballeros. A Sociological Study of a Spanish Town*. Oxford: Clarendon.
McLaughlin, E.C.
    1974   Equality of Souls, Inequality of Sexes. Women in Mediaeval Theology. In: R.R. Reuther (ed.), *Religion and Sexism. Images of Woman in the Jewish and Christian Traditions*. New York: Simon & Schuster, pp. 213-266.
Maher, V.
    1974   *Women and Property in Morocco. Their Changing Relation to the Process of Social Stratification in the Middle Atlas*. London: Cambridge University Press.
Mohsen, S.K.
    1967   Aspects of the Legal Status of Women among the Awlad 'Ali'. *Anthropological Quarterly* 40:153-166.
Parvey, C.F.
    1974   The Theology and Leadership of Women in the New Testament.

In: R.R. Reuther (ed.), *Religion and Sexism. Images of Woman in the Jewish and Christian Traditions*. New York: Simon & Schuster, pp. 117-149.

Peters, E.
1960   The Proliferation of Segments in the Lineage of the Bedouin of Cyrenaica. *Journal of the Royal Anthropological Institute* 90:29-53.

Pitt-Rivers, J.A.
1961   *The People of the Sierra*. Chicago: University Press.

Prosak, B.
1974   Woman. Seductive Siren and Source of Sin? Pseudepigraphical Myth and Christian Origins. In: R.R. Reuther (ed.), *Religion and Sexism. Images of Woman in the Jewish and Christian Traditions*. New York: Simon & Schuster, pp. 89-116.

Schneider, J. & P. Schneider
1976   *Culture and Political Economy in Western Sicily*. New York: Academic Press.

Troin, J.F.
1975   *Les souks marocains. Marchés ruraux et organisation de l'espace dans la moitié nord du Maroc* (2 vols.). Aix-en-Provence: Edisud.

Warner, M.
1976   *Alone of All her Sex. The Myth and the Cult of the Virgin Mary*. New York: Knopf.

Rams and Billy-Goats: A Key to the Mediterranean Code of Honour

Anton Blok, Catholic University, Nijmegen

Although anthropologists have dealt at length with the theme of honour and shame in the Mediterranean, the code of honour as such still awaits further unravelling. By combining structural with historical analysis, this article tries to demonstrate that the meaning of the horn-symbol as a disgraceful attribute of the deceived husband or *cornute* provides a key to an originally pastoral code of honour predicated upon virility and strength.

> My wish has always been to take seriously Durkheim's idea that the properties of classification systems derive from and are indeed properties of the social systems in which they are used (Douglas 1975:296).

The problem as to why deceived husbands in European societies have been referred to, derisively, as *cornutes*, men who wear horns, has never been solved (cf. Brand 1877; De Jorio 1832; Elworthy 1895; Cocchiara 1932; Onians 1951). A recent study of gestures in western and southern Europe and the Mediterranean rehearses no fewer than fourteen different 'theories' on the symbolism of horns and the vertical horn-sign (Morris et al. 1979). Although the authors have reasonable doubts about most of these explanations, they still believe that "one day, some new evidence will come to light that will favour one above the rest" (1979:121). As will be shown, however, the problem has less to do with a scarcity of ethnographic data than with the mistake of separating a code from its context.

Oddly enough, anthropologists writing on honour and shame in Mediterranean societies have fared no better than earlier folklorists and modern students of semiotics. Ignoring that "the elements of symbolism are not things in themselves but 'relations' organized in pairs and sets" (Leach 1973:48-49), their emphasis has been on horns as such, on horns as a phallic symbol, and on horns as attributes of the Devil (e.g. Pitt-Rivers 1961:116; 1965:46; Campbell 1964:152). This leaves the question regarding the implicit meaning of the *cornute* completely open.

In the Mediterranean code of honour we are not concerned with horns as such, but with the horns of a specific animal, namely the billy-goat -- a fact regrettably played down by Pitt-Rivers in his essays on honour and completely disregarded in the aforementioned study of gestures. The deceived husband in Italy, Spain and Portugal is identified with the billy-goat (*becco, cabrón, cabrão*). The Italian term *becco* is a synonym of *cornuto* -- husband of an unfaithful woman. In Spanish, too, *cornudo* and *cabrón* denote a man who consents to his wife's adultery. The Portuguese *cabrão* is likewise synonymous with *cornudo*, with the double meaning of billy-goat and deceived husband or lover.[1] We may thus ask: why of all horned animals just the billy-goat?

EXTERNAL ANALOGIES AND INTERNAL HOMOLOGIES

The answer may be quite simple for those familiar with certain characteristics of the behaviour of these animals. Like the deceived husbands, billy-goats tolerate the sexual access of other males to females in their domains, as I could observe when I lived for some years in a Sicilian mountain village. In his study of a Castilian rural community, Kenny (1966:83) writes:

> In popular terminology a wife's looseness is reduced to the level of mating among goats. I was assured by a shepherd that when two male goats fight over a female the winner covers her first and then allows the loser to do so. To call a man a 'buck' or 'he-goat (*cabrón*) is the worst possible insult, the important implication being that he consents to the adultery of his wife. When referring to a cuckolded husband, it is said that he has been given 'horns'.

In ancient Greece and Rome, the billy-goat was considered a lascivious and somewhat anomalous animal, epitomising unrestrained nature. Summarising the views of various classical writers, Keller (1909: 308) remarks that:

> already at the age of seven months, the billy-goat was able to procreate, and the extravagant voluptuousness, already visible in his eyes, uses the animal up so quickly, that he loses his strength in a few years, reaching senility before the age of six.

In several respects, the billy-goat differs sharply from another horned animal typical of the Mediterranean, namely the ram. Unlike the billy-goat, the ram tolerates no rivals. Shepherds must regulate the number of rams with precision according to the size of the herd

to prevent rams from fighting one another if the number of ewes de-
creases. Whereas two billy-goats are required to cover roughly fifty
goats, one ram will serve at least the same number of ewes (cf.
Keller 1909:308, 319).[2] From antiquity onwards, the ram has been
known for his virility, strength and fierceness. In various European
languages to verb 'to ram' still connotes the most striking feature
of this animal. Next to the bull, the ram was considered the most
procreative of all animals (Keller 1909:322). No wonder then that
these characteristics have qualified the ram as an appropriate
symbol of kings and the most powerful and prestigious gods, such
as Ammon, Zeus, Apollo and Poseidon, and that the Latin *aries* (ram)
is related to the Greek *aristos*, the best one (cf. Keller 1909:319-
326). Although in ancient Mediterranean myth billy-goats are also
associated with gods, these are nature-like gods, such as Pan,
Bacchus and Venus, known for their unrestrained behaviour.

In Mediterranean thought, rams and billy-goats form a distinct
pair. Their opposition reflects the differences between honour and
shame. In the Old Testament -- as in ancient Greece -- rams are
sacrificed to express gratitude to a god for his bounty, whereas
billy-goats are sacrificed by sinners to appease the god's wrath
(see Genesis 22, where Abraham sacrifices a ram instead of his
son Isaac; Leviticus 10 and 16 for the notion of 'scapegoat', better
rendered in the German word *Sündenbock*; and Numbers 15).[3] As a
symbol of honour and power, the ram formed the counterpart of the
billy-goat, the symbol of shame. This union of opposites replicates
and in fact stands in a homologous relation with the complementary
oppositions between sheep and goats, right and left, good and evil
(cf. Matthew 25).

In everyday language, Sicilians rarely refer directly to the
ram as a symbol of strength, virility and honour. Only once did I
hear a shepherd, pointing at the head and beautifully curved horns
of a ram, speak of *il vero maschio*, the real male. An implicit reference to rams is nonetheless contained in the standard expression
un uomo coi coglioni grossi ('a man with big testicles'), used by
Sicilians to denote an influential and powerful personage.[4] In
the village where I stayed, lived a woman forced by circumstance to
take care of many things which are usually men's affairs. She ac-
complished these tasks in a way which earned her wide approval. One
male informant described her, favourably, as *una donna a cui mancano
i coglioni*, that is, 'a woman who [only] lacked testicles [to make
it as a man]'. He illustrated this phrase with a charateristic gesture: he moved both fists downwards in a curve, holding them demonstratively in front of the lower part of his body -- the movement and posture evoking the image of a charging ram.

Although ethnographic material on the symbolic meaning of the
figure of the ram is scarce, there are nevertheless important clues

suggesting that in Mediterranean thought this animal has been since
Homer's time the symbol of strength, honour, manliness and power,
forming a complementary opposition with the billy-goat.[5] Both
animals differ in notable respects, but share enough features to
form a distinct pair: both belong to the category of small livestock producing milk, cheese and wool, which sets them off from
the bull, often and erroneously identified as the animal associated
with the vertical horn-sign (e.g. Morris et al. 1979:121-127).

Vestiges of classifications developed long ago by tribal pastoralists remain in the Mediterranean world. Since early times, sheep
and goats have formed a principal source of subsistence for Mediterranean people (Braudel 1972:85-94, 350-351; Finley 1977:60-61;
Houston 1964:117). Indeed, the importance of small livestock is
still carried in the word *pecunia* (from *pecus*, sheep, ram), meaning
both wealth and livestock (cf. Keller 1909:326, 432). The gradual
expansion of agriculture at the expense of pasturage led both to
the displacement of pastoralists to peripheral areas and to their
stigmatisation.[6] These long-term transformations could not but
erode the categories of thought in which rams and billy-goats formed
a union of opposites. In this way, the ram as one of the *imagines
symbolicae* largely disappeared from the mental world of the Mediterranean population -- as literally from the horizon of a growing
peasant and urban population. Although goats are still part of daily
village-life -- a circumstance which may account for their persistence as a symbolic image -- the study of gestures mentioned earlier
implies that none of the informants was aware that the vertical
horn-sign referred to the billy-goat.[7] This particular study clearly
suffers from an urban bias, since there is abundant evidence, both
linguistic and ethnographic, from rural areas attesting to the association between *cornutes* and billy-goats.

One may expect that the symbolism of rams and billy-goats is best
conserved in the surviving pastoral communities on the margins of
the Mediterranean region. Yet the excellent ethnographer Campbell,
who studied the moral values of Sarakatsan communities in northern
Greece, makes no mention of it. Is it possible, then, that the ram
as a symbolic image has become obsolete even among shepherds? Campbell's book contains evidence, however, that in Sarakatsan thought
rams and billy-goats do form a distinct pair of opposites, as part
of a more comprehensive symbolic representation hinging on the
complementary notions of honour and shame.[8]

Among the Sarakatsani sheep and men are opposed in a binary
fashion to goats and women. Sheep are milked exclusively by men,
while women usually milk the goats (Campbell 1964:31-32; cf. Földes
1969). Here Campbell refers to 'complementary oppositions'. But
he does not push his analysis far enough to realise that a key to
the code of honour lies within easy reach, as may be seen from the

following remarks:

> For the Sarakatsani, sheep and goats, men and women, are important and related oppositions with a moral reference. Sheep are peculiarly God's animals, and their shepherds, made in His image, are essentially noble beings. Women through the particular sensuality of their natures are inherently more likely to have relations with the Devil; and goats were originally the animals of the Devil which Christ captured and tamed for the service of man. It is consistent with these ideas that sheep and shepherds in their respective animal and human worlds display ideal moral characteristics. Sheep are docile, enduring, pure, and intelligent. When the shepherd carries out a small veterinarian operation or when the ewe gives birth, the animal suffers in silence. To match this purity and passive courage shepherds ought to be fearless and devoted guardians, and clean in the ritual sense. After sexual intercourse a shepherd must carefully wash his hands before milking sheep and it is generally preferable that the two shepherds of the flock of milking ewes should be unmarried men (Campbell 1964:26).

> Women and goats are conceptually opposed to men and sheep. Goats are unable to resist pain in silence, they are cunning and insatiate feeders. Greed and cunning are important characteristics of the Devil and Sarakatsani will often say that although Christ tamed these animals the Devil still remains in them. Sarakatsani keep some goats to exploit that part of their grazing land which is unfit for sheep. But as animals they are despised, and a *stani* with too high a proportion of goats to sheep loses prestige. Women are not, of course, simply creatures of the Devil but the nature of their sexuality which continually threatens the honour of men, makes them, willingly or unwillingly, agents of his will. It is consistent, therefore, that in the practical division of labour women rather than men care for the goats (Campbell 1964: 31).

> The ethnographic evidence thus reveals the following symbolic pattern which I take as specific to a Mediterranean code of honour:

rams	- billy-goats
sheep	- goats
honour	- shame
men	- women
virile men	- *cornute* (*becco, cabrón, cabrāo*)
virility	- femininity
strong	- weak
good	- evil
silence	- noise
pure	- unclean

Following Lévi-Strauss (1962a; 1962b), we can speak here of homologies, not just external analogies between social groups and
species of animals, but internal homologies between two systems of
differences: between animal species (nature) and between groups of
people (culture). The differences between honour and shame, and
specifically those between jealous husbands and *cornutes*, are homologously phrased in terms of the differences between rams and
billy-goats. As has long been recognised, men have used animals to
represent the internal differentiation of their society (cf. Douglas
1975). In this sense, the operations of Mediterranean pastoralists
have responded to the more general problem, "faire en sorte que
l'opposition, au lieu d'être un obstacle à l'intégration, serve
plutôt à la produire" (Lévi-Strauss 1962a:128).

Only in this context can the symbolism of the horns and the
cornute be fully understood. The deceived husband is dishonourable,
and in more than one regard. His wife's adultery raises doubts not
only about his sexual capacities but also about his capacity to
protect her from the advances of other men, that is, his ability to
control and monopolise his wife, to ensure her chastity and thus to
guarantee the immunity of his domain.[9] Successful claims on a
woman entail domination of other men, both from the point of view of
the husband who jealously guards his wife, and of the adulterer, who
shows himself to be more powerful than the husband. Hence the
'domestication' of women, which has often been regarded as one of
the most striking features of all Mediterranean regions (cf. Schneider 1971). Since they lend themselves to anthropomorphic symbolism,
the differences between the habits of rams and billy-goats (rather
than any other pair or set of opposites) have been seized upon to
express the differences between strong, virile, courageous men and
the weaklings, those who fail to meet the demands of a pastoral life
in which, according to Campbell's apt phrase, "reputation is impossible without strength" (1964:317).

There is thus no need to speculate about horns as such. It is not
enough to point to the analogy between the billy-goat and the deceived husband, because the meaning of the symbol only becomes clear
in relation to the symbol of its counterpart, the ram.[10] Honour,
too, acquires its meaning only in relation to shame.

Homologously to the complementary oppositions already mentioned,
the Mediterranean code of honour includes those between the right
hand and the left hand (e.g. Höeg 1925:20), pastures and home, outside and inside, public and private spheres (e.g. Bourdieu 1979a;
1979b; Wolf 1969), healthy and ill, and the complementary opposition between cheese and milk. Sicilian men rarely drink milk. In
fact, they regard it as abominable. Nor do women expect them to
drink it. When it comes to dairy products, men prefer cheese. It is
widely believed that milk (and *ricotta* to a lesser extent) is only

good for women, children, the aged, and those who are ill, that is,
people who belong to the category of the weak. It should be noted
that milk from sheep always has to be processed into cheese, while
goats produce milk that can be directly consumed. The differences
between cheese and milk are thus a particular instance of those
between culture and nature, and both correspond to the social differentiation between men and women, between strong and weak.[11]
This brings us to the subject of the next section.

HONOUR AND THE PHYSICAL PERSON

In spite of its erosion by the expansion of agriculture, the growth
of towns and the rise of national states, the concept of Mediterranean honour is still primarily contingent on physical strength
and bearing, especially so in small-scale rural communities in
peripheral and mountainous areas, such as the Barbagia in central
Sardinia, Sicily's western interior, the Zagori in northern Greece,
the Andalusian sierras and Kabylia in northern Algeria.
    The case of the *cornuto* neatly exemplifies how closely the
notions of moral and physical integrity are interwoven. First, the
chastity of a woman has been violated, which damages both her reputation and that of her husband and family. Second, the deceived
husband cannot, without having rehabilitated himself through violence,
easily show up in the public domains dominated by competitive men.
According to a popular saying in Sicily, to appear in public would
'hurt his horns'. Therefore *cornutes*, like women, try to avoid the
public realm, thus aggravating their disgrace. Writing on public
and private spheres among the Kabyles in Algeria, Bourdieu remarks:

> All informants spontaneously give as the essential characteristic
> of the man of honour the fact that he *faces* others ... (1979a:128).

> A man who spends too much time at home in the daytime is suspect
> or ridiculous: he is 'a house man', who 'broods at home like a
> hen at roost'. A self-respecting man must offer himself to be seen,
> constantly put himself in the gaze of others, confront them, face
> up to them (*qabel*). He is a man among men. Hence the importance
> attached to the games of honour, a sort of theatrical performance,
> played out in front of others (1979b:141).

Metaphors and gestures expressed in the idiom of the human body
(in West-European languages still implicit in the saying 'loss of
face' and in the German *Ansehen*, which means both 'appearance' and
'reputation') abound in everyday conversation among Mediterranean
men.[12] As the case of adultery suggests, the discourse of honour
invariably bears on notions of physical integrity and strength. In

Andalusia, the popular term *hombría*, manliness, refers to courage and the capacity to resist claims and encroachments on what a man considers his property. *Hombría* implies a direct reference to the physical basis of honour: those who live up to this ideal have *cojones* (testicles), while those who fail to show fearlessness are lacking in manliness and are considered *manso*, that is, castrated, tame. *Manso* is derived from the animal world, and is used to indicate a castrated ox or mule, which, as a consequence of the operation, has become more tractable (cf. Pitt-Rivers 1961:89-91). In Sicily, too, the concept of honour is bound up with notions of virility and physical strength. As noted before, a powerful patron is called 'a man with big testicles', while a person who tolerates encroachments on his domains is called *manso*, with the same meanings as in Andalusia. The idea of physical integrity is also implied in the expression *in gamba* (from *gamba*, leg), meaning 'stalwart'. Likewise, the Sicilian phrases *omu di ficatu* and *omu di panza* (derived from the words for liver and belly), symbolise courage and endurance, qualities also contained in the well-known concept of *omertà* (from *omu*, man, rather than from *umiltà*, humility), the hallmark of *mafiosi* and bandits, who are specialists in the use of violence (Alongi 1886:74-75; Blok 1974:211-212; Schneider & Schneider 1976:192-194). As in other European languages, the current expression *fare bella figura*, to cut a good figure, and the reverse, *fare brutta figura*, carry connotations of the physical person, while referring to a man's public image and reputation.

In Sicilian society honour is at stake whenever property rights are wilfully infringed: when the chastity of a woman is violated, when livestock or crops have been stolen, when part of the harvest is damaged, when cattle, sheep or goats are driven through another man's pastures or fields (*pascolo abusivo*) or when fruit-trees or vines have been cut down. In all these cases the honour of the owner, proprietor or guard is impugned. Sometimes, these infringements are denoted by the term *sfregio*, affront. Again we are concerned with the idiom of the human body, since *sfregio* literally means the disfigurement or mutilation of someone's face by cutting his cheek with a knife so as to leave a long, visible scar as a lasting mark of dishonour. *Un furto per sfregio* is thus a special kind of theft (sheep or cattle), carried out not to ruin the owner but to jeopardise his honour in revenge, to damage his reputation. This may explain the excitement and the violent encounters that even 'little' damage or a 'small' offence can bring about. There is a parallel here with the so-called *point d'honneur* in western Europe under the *ancien régime*: on account of an 'insignificant' incident, men demanded satisfaction, and challenged their opponents to fight it out in a duel. (These were, of course, by no means bagatelles for the people concerned, since an affront could imply

that doubts had been raised about the group membership of the offended. Therefore nobles in early modern Europe were to some extent immune to offences from those who did not belong to the
'good Society', and who consequently lacked *Satisfaktionsfähigkeit*,
that is, the right to provoke a duel.) Very similar attitudes are
prevalent among the Kabyle, where *nif*, point of honour, literally
means 'nose' (Bourdieu 1979a:99-103). For the Sarakatsani, physical
perfection is an important ideal, both for women and men. Campbell
writes that "Maidens must be virgins, and even married women must
remain virginal in thought and expression" (1964:270); while "a
youth ought to be tall, slim, agile, and tough. Any kind of physical deformity is fatal to the reputation of a young shepherd"
(Campbell 1964:278). Adult males must be *barbatos*, literally 'provided with a beard', but metaphorically,

> well endowed with testicles and the strength that is drawn from
> them. The word also describes a certain ruthless ability in any
> form of endeavour. Here again we see the 'efficient' aspect of
> manliness. ... The manliness that is related to honour requires
> this physical basis, yet it must discipline animal strength and
> passions to its own ideal ends (1964:269-270).

In such Mediterranean pastoral communities the notion of honour
hinges directly on manly, self-assertive values (cf. Schneider 1971;
Herzfeld 1980). Reputations can only be made and maintained on the
basis of physical force and courage. The moral and physical existence of transhumant shepherd families depends on the capacity and
readiness of men to defend themselves physically against thefts,
insults and offences. Among the Sarakatsani,

> although aimless violence is dishonourable there is no missing
> the pleasure it gives when a man is forced to kill; nor the
> prestige which it brings him. For there is no more conclusive
> way of showing that you are stronger than by taking away the
> other man's life (Campbell 1964:318).

Pitt-Rivers has pointed to this intimate relation between honour
and the physical person (1965:25-29; 1968:505-506). He writes that
honour is linked to the physical person "in terms of the symbolic
functions attached to the body: to the blood, the heart, the hand,
the head, and the genitalia" and that "any form of physical affront
implies an affront to honour", while "the ultimate vindication of
honour lies in physical violence". Yet he does not pursue the
question *why* honour is symbolised in terms of the physical person
and *how* this code has developed over time. Why, indeed, has the
English word *cornute*, along with its equivalents in other West-
European languages, become obsolete -- together with much of the
vocabulary of honour (cf. Pitt-Rivers 1965:39; 1974:7; Berger 1970)

-- while in southern Europe, particularly in peripheral rural communities, these notions are still very much alive?

HONOUR AND STATE-FORMATION

The strong emphasis on physical integrity and strength in the Mediterranean discourse of honour suggests that the people who think in
these terms cannot depend on stable centres of political control
for the protection of their life and patrimony. In the absence of
effective state control, they have to rely on their own forces --
on various forms of self-help (Steinmetz 1931; Black-Michaud 1975).
These conditions of the wider power fields put a premium on self-
assertive qualities in men, involving the readiness and capacity
to use physical force in order to guarantee the immunity of life
and property, including women as the most precious and vulnerable
part of the patrimony of men.[13] The extremes of this sense of
honour are reached when even merely glancing at a woman is felt as
an affront, as an incursion into a male domain, touching off a
violent response. When might is right, women's virginity and
chastity can become men's dominant concern, the physical integrity
of women forming the linchpin of male reputation. Hence the intimate
relation between honour and strength as expressed in the idiom of
the human body and symbolised in terms of a specific set of animals.
Moral and physical integrity can be related to the point that

> to maintain one's honour is so much a duty, that one derives
> from it the claims to the most frightful sacrifices -- not only
> self-inflicted ones, but also those involving others (Simmel
> 1968:405).[14]

During the past two centuries, the role of physical strength in
the West-European concept of honour has lost much of its significance. In everyday language, the term 'honour' and its various
derivations have acquired archaic and sometimes ironic overtones.
In fact, *cornutes* have become 'cuckolds', a term in which the link
with the physical person has gradually lost its explicit imprint,
while women have become less dependent on men for their protection
and immunity. With the growing pacification and democratisation of
western societies, cultural forms of homage and chivalry have
slowly eroded. Apart from some important exceptions, to be presently
discussed, the vocabulary in which differences of rank -- especially
those based on physical strength -- were expressed, is disappearing
from ordinary conversation. The notions of honour as a universal
element of social evaluation is now phrased in other terms. One
avoids the word honour. The impugned honour of yore has become the
hurt vanity of today. Giving evidence of pride and self-importance

is no longer appreciated. Those who indulge in it are now regarded
as pompous and condescending, while in former times they were merely
competing for points of honour. Insults are no longer felt to be
injuries. Without 'losing face' one can often simply ignore them,
the more so since insults have become more embarrassing and painful
to the offender than to the offended. It has been noted that in
our society "the *reality* of the offence will be denied" (Berger
1970:339).

In two widely different sectors of western societies, the notion
of honour is still very similar to those prevalent in early modern
Europe and the Mediterranean. One can understand why. First, it
thrives in certain peripheral subcultures of 'men in groups', in
bars, dockyards, prisons, and the premises of organised crime,
where rank and esteem are largely matters of sheer physical force.
Second, a code of honour intimately linked with the physical person
is still conspicuous in the army as well as among sportsmen and
certain members of the surviving aristocracy. In these sectors of
society, honour does not only concern the bearing and physical feats
of human beings, but also the power and prestige of the national
state to which they belong, and which they represent. Indeed, since
the French Revolution, the discourse of national honour has gradually appropriated the vocabulary of personal honour (cf. Cobb
1969; Hampson 1973; Pitt-Rivers 1974:7). In particular matches and
games, in diplomatic negotiations, and in wars, national honour
may be regarded as at stake. It has been rightly emphasised that
the *point d'honneur* "is still evident today in the intercourse
between sovereign nations" (Jones 1959:35). Since the end of the
sixteenth century, the functions of attack and defence and the cor-
responding loyalties and sentiments have step by step been transferred from local and regional levels to the national arena. Dynastic
states have grown into national states, and the armies with which
the European powers used to fight one another have become national
armies. For protection and security, people have become much less
dependent upon their own forces. Their self-help has given way to
multiple forms of state-control.[15] The extension and differentiation of social networks, along with pacification and democratisation, entailed a gradual subduement and 'refinement' of
feelings and increasing control of bodily functions -- specifically
the control of violent impulses in everyday social intercourse (cf.
Elias 1969b). Only in this context can we understand why and how a
person's bearing and physical strength have lost much of their
importance to his social position, self-esteem, personal identity,
pride and sense of honour. With the expansion of scale, moreover,
public opinion acquired other forms and functions: it became less
existenzbegründend, less a foundation of social existence, than in
the small-scale, relatively closed circles of herdsmen, peasants,

and aristocrats, whose sense of honour and personal identity were largely and sometimes completely dependent on membership in those communities.[16]

CONCLUSIONS

I have tried to argue that the symbolism of the horns of the deceived husband or *cornute* should be understood as an integral part of an originally pastoral code of honour, predicated upon virility and physical strength. The Mediterranean code of honour, to which the complementary opposition between rams and billy-goats forms a main key, emphasised the physical integrity of both men and women. In rural communities located on the margins of larger state-societies, women formed the most precious and vulnerable part of the patrimony of men, who were thus prompted to sustain self-assertive qualities. Under the impact of the wider process of state-formation and of the 'civilising' movement, the code of honour in western Europe -- once similar in its main features to the Mediterranean variant -- lost much of its significance. Leaving little room for the idiom of the physical person, the terminology of honour has largely become obsolete. Instead, the term 'civility', in which the connexion with the human body is much attenuated, has become more appropriate to denote honourable behaviour.

The anthropological literature on Mediterranean societies contains various fragments of the categories of thought with which this article has been concerned. This state of affairs is partly due to ecological and political discontinuities within the Mediterranean region -- the *monde conçu* of rams versus billy-goats does not agree any more with the *monde vécu* of people who have slowly turned away from pastoralism -- and partly to a lack of historical depth in most anthropological studies. Despite their attention to the so-called material basis of Mediterranean cultures, anthropologists have neglected the minutiae of the behaviour of domesticated animals. Moreover, as Davis (1977:9-10) has indicated, few anthropologists who have worked in this part of the world have dealt with the means of orientation, with religious forms of expression and other collective representations. Although structuralists -- such as Lévi-Strauss in his studies of myths and totemism -- have been concerned mainly with a formal analysis of classification systems, abstaining from the study of the sequential order of events and from 'thick description' by endorsing an ahistorical perspective, one may also consider the Mediterranean code of honour as a function of pastoral and peasant communities only nominally integrated into state societies. Therefore, if my interpretation of this code of honour is plausible, new light may be thrown on an old problem: how structural and historical analyses can be combined.

NOTES

* Earlier versions of this article were presented at the Conference on Religion and Religious Movements in Mediterranean Areas, Free University, Amsterdam, December 1979, and at the Conference on the Civilizing Process, Balliol College, Oxford, January 1980. I am much indebted to Jojada and Kitty Verrips for helping me to clarify the argument. For valuable criticism of earlier drafts I am grateful to Rod Aya, Jeremy Boissevain, Jan Willem Bennema, Henk Driessen, Florike Egmond and Johan Goudsblom. I also wish to thank Julian Pitt-Rivers for his extensive comments and criticism. Although we continue to disagree on several matters of fact and interpretation, I have learned much from his spirited response to my arguments. This article has previously been published in *Man* N.S. 16(4):427-440, 1981.
1. Cf. Zingarelli (1965); Pitt-Rivers (1965:76); Cutileiro (1971: 142); and De Morais Silva (1950). The Portuguese term *cabra* (goat) also means 'promiscuous girl or prostitute'. On the meaning of the Spanish *chivato* (billy-goat, spy), see Gilmore (1980:104).
2. In the ethnography of Mediterranean communities information on the habits of domesticated animals is almost completely absent. Apart from my own work regarding western Sicily, I have drawn on the report of Moyal (1956), which concerns transhumant shepherds in southern France, and the study of Keller (1909). I should indicate that my research interests were quite different when I conducted fieldwork in Sicily in the 1960s.
3. For ancient Greece, see Homer's *Iliad* (Book 3), where rams are offered to Zeus, and where Odysseus is compared with 'a thick-fleeced ram'. In the *Odyssey* (Book 9), the hero and his companians escape from the Cyclops tied under the bellies of rams. The biggest ram, which had carried Odysseus, was later sacrificed to Zeus.
4. An extremely powerful man is sometimes decribed as *un uomo con i coglioni fino a terra* ('with testicles reaching the ground').
5. See, for example, Herodotus, *History* (Book 2, chapter 2); and the passage on the ram as a symbol of a powerful ruler in Artemidoros, *Oneirocritica* (Book 2, chapter 12). A fifteenth-century edition of Fulgentius's *Mythologiae* contains a picture of Jupiter (Zeus) with the head of a ram above his own head and a billy-goat at his feet. Cf. the text of the fourteenth-century monk Ridevall in Liebeschütz (1926:78-79 and Plate I); also

Gombrich (1978:135-137 and Plates 144, 145, 147), to whom I owe
this reference. Further evidence concerning the opposition between
rams and billy-goats may be found in the astrological literature
on Aries and Capricornus.

6. Cf. Schneider (1971); Freeman (1970:177-184; 1979); Braudel
   (1972:94). On the stigmatisation of shepherds in central Europe,
   see Danckert (1963:174-180); and Jacobeit (1961:173-224).
7. The study *Gestures* is based on three years' research in 40
   localities in 25 European countries. The authors were assisted
   by 29 research workers and interpreters. Their research involved
   detailed interviews with 1,200 informants regarding 20 different
   gestures. (Morris et al. 1979:xiii).
8. The Sarakatsani, too, refer to the deceived husband as a man who
   wears horns (*keratas*), but Campbell misses this clue in following the lapsus of Pitt-Rivers (Campbell 1964:152).
9. For the relations between the notion of honour and immunity,
   see Bourdieu (1979a:115). Friedrich (1973) and Redfield (1975:
   160-223) discuss Homeric honour in terms of integrity and purity.
   The meaning of the medieval concept of *honor* ranged between
   'patrimony' and 'immunity' (cf. Niermeyer 1959). Of Sicilian
   mafiosi, men of honour *par excellence*, it is sometimes said that
   they are *intoccabili*, 'untouchable' in the sense of unapproach-
   able and awe-inspiring, a quality which underwrites the immunity
   of their person and patrimony (Blok 1974:146-147).
10. In his account of the Spanish expression *cabrón* and the English
    equivalent 'cuckold', Pitt-Rivers (1961:116; 1965:46) does not
    look for *sets* of animals. Nor does he point to the most obvious
    analogies. Instead, he regards the billy-goat as a symbol of
    sexuality (and horns as a phallic symbol), and then tries to
    explain the identification of the deceived husband with the
    billy-goat by means of what he calls 'a curious inversion'. He
    follows the same line of argument regarding the English ex-
    pression 'cuckold' (from cuckoo, the bird which lays its eggs in
    other birds' nests). Yet both animals -- billy-goats and male
    cuckoo -- have been considered anomalous, simply because they
    accept the wanton behaviour of their females. This matter is
    discussed in more detail by Mario Alinei in a forthcoming issue
    of *Quaderni di Semantica*.
11. Very similar oppositions have been described by Ott (1979) in her
    article on a French Basque mountain community, in which she
    deals with the analogy between the skill of making cheese and
    that of causing or preventing pregnancies.
12. Cf. Mauss (1954:38); and Goffman (1972:1-15), who also refers
    to the discussions of the Chinese conception of face. See also
    Pitt-Rivers (1961:114) on the notion of shamelessness in Anda-
    lusia: to be *descarado* or *cara dura* (hard-faced; cf. Italian

sfacciato, faccia tosta) is "a far more serious matter than to be 'thick-skinned', the nearest expression in English to it".

13. On this point, see the perceptive remarks in Schneider (1971:18). It has not always been recognised that women, at least in the peripheral rural communities discussed in this essay, form part of the patrimony of men, and that they, by implication, can have no honour. See, however, Black-Michaud (1975:218), who writes: "Women have no honour. But they do have 'shame' or sexual modesty, the feminine counterpart of and the complement to honour, which both they and their menfolk must do their utmost to defend".

14. In western Europe, the differentiation between moral and physical integrity is of recent origin. Until the early nineteenth century, the whole ritual of public torture and *post mortem* mutilation formed an integral part of punishment -- adding infamy to death (cf. Foucault 1975:36-72; Linebaugh 1975:65-117; Blok 1979; and Ranum 1980). The idea that honour can be more important than life itself, has been known since antiquity -- cf. Tacitus, who wrote in *Agricola* (chapter 33): "an honourable death would be better than a disgraceful attempt to save our lives"; Snell (1975:156); Walcot (1978:15-16); the Arab proverb quoted in Farès (1932:114); Ranum (1980:66); and Elias (1969a:145-146), who, writing on the French nobility under the *ancien régime*, also provides an explanation by stressing the relation between honour, personal identity and membership in the 'good Society'.

15. Steinmetz has emphasised the dialectic relation between self-help and state-control, when pointing out that self-help is the only device for people who are either abandoned (*im Stich gelassen*) or suffocated (*erstickt*) by central governments (1931: 522).

16. Cf. Simmel (1968:403-406); and Elias (1969a:144-151). How slowly this process took place, may be illustrated by the reception of the short story *Leutnant Gustl* by Arthur Schnitzler. Its publication in 1900 caused a sensation, especially in military circles, and the author, who had been an officer in the Austrian-Hungarian army, lost his military rank (see Scheible 1976:84). For Germany, see Jones (1959); and Demeter (1964:108-144, 260-286), who deals with the development of the jurisdiction concerning duelling. The fate of honour in Britain has lately been dealt with by James (1978).

BIBLIOGRAPHY

Alongi, Giuseppe
   1886   *La Maffia nei suoi fattori e nelle sue manifestazioni.*
          Torino: Fratelli Bocca.

Berger, P.
1970   On the Obsolescence of the Concept of Honor. *Archives
          européennes de Sociologie* 11:339-347.
Black-Michaud, J.
1975   *Cohesive Force: Feud in the Mediterranean and the Middle
          East*. Oxford: Blackwell.
Blok, A.
1974   *The Mafia of a Sicilian Village, 1860-1960: A Study of
          Violent Peasant Entrepreneurs*. Oxford: Blackwell.
1979   Theatrische strafvoltrekkingen onder het ancien régime.
          Symposion I:94-114.
Bourdieu, P.
1979a   The Sense of Honour. In: *Algeria 1960: Essays by Pierre
          Bourdieu*. Cambridge: University Press.
1979b   The Kabyle House or the World Reversed. In: *Algeria 1960:
          Essays by Pierre Bourdieu*. Cambridge: University Press.
Brand, J.
1877   *Observations on Popular Antiquities*. London: Chatto &
          Windus.
Braudel, F.
1972   *The Mediterranean and the Mediterranean World in the Age
          of Philip II*, Volume I. New York: Harper & Row.
Campbell, J.K.
1964   *Honour, Family and Patronage: A Study of Institutions
          and Moral Values in a Greek Mountain Community*. Oxford:
          Clarendon Press.
Cobb, R.
1969   The Revolutionary Mentality in France. In: R. Cobb, *A
          Second Identity: Essays on France and French History*.
          London: Oxford University Press.
Cocchiara, G.
1952   *Il linguaggio del gesto*. Torino: Fratelli Bocca. (Reprint:
          Palermo: Sellerio, 1977).
Cutileiro, J.
1971   *A Portuguese Rural Society*. Oxford: Clarendon Press.
Danckert, W.
1963   *Unehrliche Leute: die verfemten Berufe*. Bern & München:
          Francke.
Davis, J.
1977   *People of the Mediterranean: an Essay in Comparative
          Social Anthropology*. London: Routledge and Kegan Paul.
De Jorio, A.
1832   *La mimica degli antichi: investigata nel gestire Napole-
          tano*. Napoli: Fibreno.
Demeter, K.
1964   *Das deutsche Offizierkorps in Gesellschaft und Staat 1650-*

1945. Frankfurt am Main: Bernard & Graefe.
De Morais Silva, A.
1950 *Grande dicionário da língua portuguesa*. Lisboa: Confluência.
Douglas, M.
1975 Self-evidence. In: *Implicit Meanings: Essays in Anthropology*. London: Routledge and Kegan Paul.
Elias, N.
1969a *Die höfische Gesellschaft*. Neuwied and Berlin: Luchterhand.
1969b *Ueber den Prozess der Zivilisation* (2nd edition). Bern and München: Francke.
Elworthy, F.
1895 *The Evil Eye: the Origins and Practices of Superstitions*. London: Murray. (Second edition: New York: Julian Press, 1958).
Farès, B.
1932 *L'honneur chez les Arabes avant l'Islam*. Paris: Adrien-Maisonneuve.
Finley, M.I.
1977 *The World of Odysseus*. London: Chatto & Windus.
Földes, L. (ed.)
1969 *Viehwirtschaft und Hirtenkultur: ethnographische Studien*. Budapest: Akadémiai Kiadó.
Foucault, M.
1975 *Surveiller et punir: naissance de la prison*. Paris: Gallimard.
Freeman, S.T.
1970 *Neighbors: the Social Contract in a Castilian Hamlet*. Chicago: University Press.
1979 *The Pasiegos: Spaniards in No Man's Land*. Chicago: University Press.
Friedrich, P.
1973 Defilement and Honor in the Iliad. *Journal of Indo-European Studies* I:119-126.
Gilmore, D.
1980 *The People of the Plain: Class and Community in Lower Andalusia*. New York: Columbia University Press.
Goffman, E.
1972 On Face-work. In: E. Goffman, *Interaction Ritual: Essays on Face-to-Face Behaviour*. Harmondsworth: Penguin Books.
Gombrich, E.H.
1978 *Symbolic Images: studies in the Art of the Renaissance*. (2nd edition). Oxford: Phaidon Press.
Hampson, N.
1973 The French Revolution and the Nationalisation of Honour. In: M.R.D. Foot (ed.), *War and Society*. London: Elck.

Herzfeld, M.
1980   Honour and Shame: Problems in the Comparative Analysis
of Moral Systems. *Man* (N.S.) 15:339-351.
Höeg, C.
1925   *Les Sarakatsans: une tribu nomade grecque*, Volume I.
Paris: Edouard Champion.
Houston, J.M.
1964   *The Western Mediterranean World*. London: Longman.
Jacobeit, W.
1961   *Schafhaltung und Schäfer in Zentraleuropa bis zum Beginn
des 20. Jahrhunderts*. Berlin: Akademie der Wissenschaften.
James, M.
1978   English Politics and the Concept of Honour, 1485-1642.
Past and Present Supplement 3.
Jones, G.F.
1959   *Honor in German Literature*. Chapel Hill: University of
North Carolina Press.
Keller, O.
1909   *Die antike Tierwelt*, Volume I. Leipzig: Engelman.
Kenny, M.
1966   *A Spanish Tapestry: Town and Country in Castile*. New York:
Harper & Row.
Leach, E.R.
1973   Structuralism in Social Anthropology. In: David Robey
(ed.), *Structuralism: An Introduction*. Oxford: Clarendon
Press.
Lévi-Strauss, Cl.
1962a   *Le totémisme aujourd'hui*. Paris: P.U.F.
1962b   *La pensée sauvage*. Paris: Plon.
Liebeschütz, H.
1926   *Fulgentius Metaforalis: ein Beitrag zur Geschichte der
antiken Mythologie im Mittelalter*. Leipzig: Teubner.
Linebaugh, P.
1975   The Tyburn Riot Against the Surgeons. In: Douglas Hay
et al., *Albion's Fatal Tree: Crime and Society in
Eighteenth-century England*. London: Allen Lane.
Mauss, M.
1954   *The Gift: Forms and Functions of Exchange in Archaic
(1925) Societies*. Translated by Ian Cunnison. London: Cohen &
West.
Morris, D. et al.
1979   *Gestures: Their Origins and Distribution*. London: Jonathan
Cape.
Moyal, M.
1956   *On the Road to Pastures New*. London: Phoenix House.

Niermeyer, J.F.
  1959   De semantiek van *honor* en de oorsprong van het heerlijk
          gezag. In: *Dancwerc*. Groningen: J.B. Wolters.
Onians, R.B.
  1951   *The Origins of European Thought*. Cambridge: University
          Press.
Ott, S.
  1979   Aristotle Among the Basques: the 'Cheese Analogy' of
          Conception. *Man* (N.S.) 14:699-711.
Pitt-Rivers, J.
  1961   *The People of the Sierra*. Chicago: University Press.
  1965   Honour and Social Status. In: J.G. Peristiany (ed.),
          Honour and Shame: The Values of Mediterranean Society.
          London: Weidenfeld & Nicholson.
  1968   Honour. *Encyclopedia of the Social Sciences* 6:503-511.
          New York: Macmillan.
  1974   *Mana: An Inaugural Lecture*. London: London School of
          Economics and Political Science.
Ranum, O.
  1980   The French Ritual of Tyrannicide in the Late Sixteenth
          Century. *Sixteenth Century Journal* 11:63-82.
Redfield, J.
  1975   *Nature and Culture in the Iliad: The Tragedy of Hector*.
          Chicago: University Press.
Scheible, H.
  1976   *Arthur Schnitzler in Selbstzeugnissen und Bilddokumenten*.
          Hamburg: Rowohlt.
Schneider, J.
  1971   On Vigilance and Virgins: Honor, Shame and Access to
          Resources in Mediterranean Societies. *Ethnology* 10:1-24.
Schneider, J. & P. Schneider
  1976   *Culture and Political Economy in Western Sicily*. New
          York: Academic Press.
Simmel, G.
  1968   Soziologie. *Gesammelte Werke*, Volume 2. Berlin: Duncker
          und Humblot.
Snell, B.
  1975   *Die Entdeckung des Geistes: Studien zur Entstehung des
          europäischen Denkens bei den Griechen*. Göttingen:
          Vandenhoeck & Ruprecht.
Steinmetz, S.R.
  1931   Selbsthilfe. In: Alfred Vierkandt (ed.), *Handwörterbuch
          der Soziologie*. Stuttgart: Ferdinand Enke.
Walcot, P.
  1978   *Envy and the Greeks: A Study of Human Behaviour*.
          Warminster: Aris & Phillips.

Wolf, Eric R.
   1969   Society and Symbols in Latin Europe and in the Islamic
            Near East: Some Comparisons. *Anthropological Quarterly*
            42:287-301.
Zingarelli, Nicola
   1965   *Vocabolario della lingua Italiana.* Bologna: Zanichelli.

Case Studies

Religious Brotherhoods: Class and Politics in an Andalusian Town

Henk Driessen, Catholic University, Nijmegen

In many rural Andalusian towns the end of the social wintersleep
is heralded by hesitant shouts of cornets and rolling of drums.
These sounds are produced by the boys who belong to the bands of
the religious brotherhoods, which start their preparations for
the Holy Week celebrations with the arrival of spring. The
rehearsing bands accompany the renewal of the ceremonial cycle
throughout Lent.[1]
    In Mirabuenos[1], a small town in the undulating plains southwest
of Córdoba -- the capital of the Andalusian province of the same
name -- there are seven religious brotherhoods (*cofradías*), the
activities of which center upon the Holy Week rites. In addition,
there is a large brotherhood that focuses on the cult of the local
patron saint, Virgin Mary of the Valley, whose festival is celebrated at the beginning of September. As in most Andalusian towns,
the Holy Week and patron saint festivals constitute the high-days
of communal life.
    The large number of men organized into the *cofradías* and the
high degree of active and passive participation in the popular
festivals, form a sharp contrast with the attitude of the most
sizeable occupational group -- land labourers -- towards the Church,
the priest and the official Roman Catholic rites. This attitude
ranges from indifference to open hostility. The vast majority of
the male inhabitants of Mirabuenos only enter the church at special
occasions when a *rite de passage* is celebrated and even then most
of them remain at the back near the entrance or in the square in
front of the church, where the priest's voice gets lost in the
noise and bustle. They only come to fulfill a social obligation
and do not participate in official religious ceremony. The small
group of male devouts who regularly attend church and comply with
official religious duties, are drawn from sections of the local
middle and upper classes.
    Here we have two basic characteristics of religious practice in
Andalusian society which will be dealt with in this paper: the
opposition between Roman Catholicism as a universal institution and

a local, popular version centering upon saints; and religion as a
dimension for the expression of antagonism between landholding
and landless classes.

In this essay, religion will be examined as a resource of power
in the local class conflict. I will give a brief historical sketch
of the role of the Church and *cofradías* in Spanish society and in
Mirabuenos, in particular, and then concentrate on the post-Civil
War revival of religious brotherhoods and show their interrelations
and functions in the social configuration of Mirabuenos.[2]

In Spain, the intimate relation between Church and State dates back
many centuries and runs as a hardly broken line through its
national history. The Spanish State was built on a *Reconquista*
(718-1492) that was sanctioned by the Pope as a Holy War against
the infidel Moors. Religion provided the cement that held together
the heterogeneous Spanish regions. As participants in the struggle
against the Moors, the Church, religious corporations and priesthood were abundantly rewarded with landed estates and privileges
and so acquired a firm material basis for their sacred and secular
power. Religion became the main instrument for the homogenization
of the subject population in the evolving Spanish State. The
population was firmly controlled by the Inquisition and alien
elements, such as heretics, Jews and Moors, were expelled. The
position of the Church was consolidated during the reigns of the
Habsburgs who defended Her against the Reformistic movements.

At the local level, the Church deeply penetrated communal life.
In Mirabuenos, priests acted as mediators between local society and
the outside world when crucial issues, such as local autonomy, were
at stake. In the middle of the seventeenth century when the town
had to sell its jurisdictional and administrative autonomy, in the
face of poverty and decay, the local notables headed by some priests,
were persuaded by the bishop of Córdoba to sell it to a Cordobese
noble.[3] In the first half of the eighteenth century, a local
ecclesiastic landowner, officer of the Cordobese Inquisition and
benefactor of the poor, became the main spokesman for emancipation
of the town from seigneurial regime. He successfully defended the
town's plight before the Royal Council of Castile.[4]

Most of Mirabuenos' priests were born in the local community
(*pueblo*) where they owned land and performed various functions.
Corporate ecclesiastical lands amounted to 7.5 per cent of the
municipal territory.[5] This land was leased out under lenient
conditions to the landless peasants. The priests controlled
education, ran the hospital and dispensed charity to the poor. Three
of them were officers of the Cordobese Inquisition, licensed to
carry arms "during day-time as well as at night ... in order to
repress paganism and other delicts against Catholic faith". The

church acted as a meeting place when open, communal councils were celebrated. Important municipal decisions and events were sanctioned by a mass. The church bells announced important happenings in the communal round of life. Priests acted as mediators between God and the human community in times of crisis. In other words, the Church and its representatives fulfilled vital functions for the *whole* community. People of all estates accepted and respected ecclesiastic authority.

In was only in the course of the eighteenth century that the power of the Church began to erode under the impact of the centralizing and rationalizing policy of the Bourbons. Religious exclamations gradually vanished from the municipal records. The reforms of the anti-clerical liberal governments of the nineteenth century deprived the Church of its economic foundation through disentailment of its landed property. The State took over many of its social functions and so loosened the bond between Church and people. In the words of Gerald Brenan: "By cutting off the clergy and the monks from the possessions of land, it alienated them from the people, forced them to think of other methods of enrichment and so threw them into the arms of the wealthy classes, on whom alone through the greater part of Spain they have depended ever since" (1971: 44)[6].

This process involved a slow secularization of community life. Temporal crises like droughts and epidemic diseases, increasingly became matters to be handled by the municipal council and doctors. State-sponsored school-education was extended. In the second half of the nineteenth century, working-class ideologies and organizations spread over the countryside, offering viable alternatives for religion as means of orientation and organization. These developments culminated in the Second Republic (1931-1939), when civil and religious rites were finally divorced from each other.

In many Andalusian towns where a broad gulf separated the propertied classes from the mass of landless day-labourers, anti-clericalism took on violent forms. Adherence to the Church and church-attendance came to be identified as behaviour of the conservative landed elite -- *la gente de orden* (law-abiding citizens). For those who worked the land, the Church was the symbol of the existing power structure and religion the ideology that legitimated the status quo. It thus became one of the targets of class hatred in the class war that broke out in 1936.

One good indication of the scope of working-class anti-clericalism is the Church's failure to organize workers into catholic unions (Díaz del Moral 1973: 371-376). Another is the rate of baptism in the months following the occupation of Popular Front towns by the Nationalists during the Civil War, when the unbaptized were forced to undergo the rite of christianization. In Mirabuenos,

where the revolutionary government already fell a few weeks after
the outbreak of the war, the rate of baptism increased by 145 per
cent in 1936, and 55 per cent in 1937.[7]
     The Nationalists phrased the Civil War as a "crusade against the
Red Hordes" and the mass executions were sanctioned in the name of
Roman Catholicism. Most executions took place at the walls of the
cemetery. The festival of the Virgin in the middle of August turned
into a day of blood in the various parts of Spain that were controlled by the Nationalists (Frazer 1979: 164). The followers of
Franco's revolt displayed an often excessive piety while at the
same time acting like beasts towards their political opponents.[8]
     Religion, then, took on a strong political load. As during the
Reconquista, it acted as a source of identification and cohesion
among the rather heterogeneous Nationalists. Franco immediately
abolished the separation between Church and State and usurped
important competences regarding religious matters. Community life
was violently resacralized by the new ruling elite and the members
of the working class had to submit themselves to religious rites
for physical survival. Under the auspices of the parish priest,
the elite's wives were organized into supra-community associations,
such as "Catholic Action" and "The Daughters of the Blessed Virgin."
Display of religious devotion was required in order to be considered for charity.[9] As we shall see below, land labourers were
not completely powerless against severe political repression and
humiliating spiritual patronization. They took to the saints and
turned them into weapons against their oppressors.

The institution of religious brotherhood as voluntary association
is deeply rooted in Andalusian community life. In most *pueblos* it
is the sole corporate institution of popular religious practice.
     Some of these *cofradías* originated as military defense associ-
ations against the Moors during the *Reconquista*, others have roots
in the medieval *gremios* or guilds.[10] The majority date from the
sixteenth century when Franciscan and Dominican friars founded them
as bastions against the threat of Reformation (Luque Requerey 1980:
74-75). In the first century of their existence they were mainly
joined by priests and local notables. In the second half of the
sixteenth century, there were five such *cofradías* in Mirabuenos.[11]
Their activities centered upon propagating and sustaining Christian
cult -- organizing a feast on the day of the saint, maintaining and
decorating the chapel where the saint's image was, and saying masses
for deceased members. The most important and richest brotherhood
was the *Cofradía del Santísimo Sacramento*. This brotherhood organized
the festivities of Corpus Christi, one of the highlights in the
religious calendar. In the second half of the seventeenth century,
active participation of townsmen with "rustic professions" (Luque

Requerey 1980: 86) increased with the growing elaboration of the Holy Week brotherhoods. From the book-keeping of one of them we learn that money was spent on fireworks, tunics, and music bands, that there were at least two Holy Week processions -- on Maundy Thursday and Good Friday -- that the brotherhood acted as a burial society, contracted preachers, and sponsored the *fiesta* of the Holy Cross in May.[12]

In the eighteenth century, *cofradías* played a key role in the profanization of religious ritual. The increasing 'popularization' of Holy Week festivities led to serious conflicts between ecclesiastic authorities and the members of the brotherhoods (Luque Requerey 1980: 90-95).

During the last two centuries, the *cofradías* lived through well-defined periods of crisis and decay. Under Charles III, for instance, a Royal Decree was issued ordering a revision of brotherhood regulations, which in practice meant the suppression of many of them. Another period of decay followed the disentailment of ecclesiastic landed properties in 1836 that also affected the religious brotherhoods.[13] These crises coincided with general erosions of traditional authority. This also happened during the Second Republic.

Despite these temporal crises and the fact that only few *cofradías* survived without interruption into our days, they developed into the main carriers of the popular version of Catholicism. They have always been the only institutions at the local level in which strict democracy was maintained.[14] They strongly opposed interference by outsiders.

The majority of the contemporary *cofradías* were founded or refounded in the aftermath of the Civil War. In Córdoba-City, for instance, there are twenty-eight brotherhoods that center upon Holy Week celebrations and organize about 20,000 people. Seven of them were founded prior to the Civil War, thirteen during or in the aftermath of the War, four in the 1950s and four in the 1970s.[15] In Mirabuenos only one of the seven brotherhoods led an active existence in pre-Civil War times.

Most priests and bishops of Andalusia oppose the burlesque and boisterous cult of the saints, which is the core of popular religion. Many tried to eliminate popular cults, but all bumped their head against a wall of obstinacy.[16] The present parish priest was one of them. He came to Mirabuenos in 1963, when profound transformations were taking place. Until the end of the 1940s emigration of unemployed peasants and labourers was contained with the objective of keeping agrarian wages low. Consequently, workers were dependent on scarce local resources, a situation in which patronage could thrive. At that time, the parish priest was still a powerful patron. When don Gerardo came to Mirabuenos, Franco's new policy of modern-

ization was well under way and had opened new paths for the unemployed proletarians. Emigration to industrializing regions in
Spain and Western Europe was the most important of these new
opportunities. It lessened the dependence of workers on local
employers and patrons.

For years don Gerardo tried to banish what he considered to be
pagan customs of excessive drinking of spirits, dancing and
shouting during the Holy Week processions and the resulting disorders. The Good Friday climax of Holy Week processions openly
conflicts with the liturgical directives of the Church, which
stress inner penance and sobriety. Don Gerardo lacked the authority
of his predecessors who were still able to suppress excesses by
means of patronage. He only generated growing hostility among
townspeople of all classes. A few examples will illustrate this.

There is an old local saying expressing parochialism, 'As to
plains, chapel and church bell nobody can beat us.' It is said
that the old bell was so loud that it could be heard up to thirty
kilometers from the town. It broke down years ago and was finally
sold by don Gerardo, however, without the knowledge and consent
of his parishioners. This provoked a huge scandal among townspeople
of all classes and persuasions and the priest's obstinate action
sealed his fate in Mirabuenos forever. When asked why he did not
sell some valuable paintings in the church in order to finance
necessary repairs, he replied with a meaningful gesture symbolizing
the cutting of his throat.

That it is better not to meddle in the *pueblo*'s affairs was also
brought home to a Dominican friar whom don Gerardo had invited to
preach during the Holy Week. This man, who came from the north of
Spain where relations between Church and parish are different, was
shocked by the burlesque scenes of the processions. When he tried
to intervene, he was threatened with a knife by one of the drunken
members of a *cofradía* and had an untimely but mandatory departure.

The parish priest does not participate in the Holy Week processions. The official Lenten sermons he organizes are only attented
by some forty people. The majority of the local population boycotts
them. The priest is and remains an outsider (*forastero*) to those
born in Mirabuenos.[17] Most ecclesiastic authorities reluctantly
recognize the strength of popular religious expressions or "folk
Catholicism" as they call them. In 1975 the bishops of Southern
Spain declared that "they (the brotherhoods) are typical institutions of our region, extended over and rooted in all *pueblos*."
The bishop of Córdoba added to this, "the Cordobese Holy Week is
necessarily somewhat baroque and rich in expressiveness because
of its being Andalusian (...). It is faithful to the peculiar
Andalusian temper that should be as follows: serious, dignified
and profound" (Gutiérrez 1978: 20-23). These last three words tell

more about the bishop's wishes than about the reality of Holy
Week in Côrdoba. One of the very values embodied in the *cofradías*
is independence *cum* local patriotism, which openly conflicts with
bureaucratic authority and interference from outside in the *pueblo*'s
affairs.

In Mirabuenos local politics and religious brotherhoods are
like Siamese twins. They are fed from the same sources. Local
politicians usually play prominent roles in the brotherhoods. Men
who have been active in certain brotherhoods often run for
political office. There are numerous examples of the intertwining
of politics and religion to be found in the minutes of the town-
council. Let me give some examples from recent local history.[18]

In 1912 one of the two land labourers who sat in the town-
council for the anti-clerical Republican Party, caused a scandal
by frequently interrupting a Holy Friday sermon in church; for
this the mayor rebuked him in public. A year later, the three
Republican councillors accused the priest of abusing public funds,
while at the same meeting they actively supported a proposal to
subsidize the Holy Week processions; one of them, a blacksmith,
was *hermano mayor* (major brother) of one of the brotherhoods.

In 1919, at the height of labour agitation in the province of
Côrdoba, the mayor ordered the Civil Guard to oversee the Holy
Week processions in order to prevent political disturbances. In
the same year the priest's house was set on fire, the authors
remaining unknown. After three years of labour unrest that shook
the existing order to its foundations, the working class actions
were finally repressed. On the initiative of the mayor, a large
public ceremony was held in the square in front of the town-hall
during which the parish priest blessed two national banners. One
of the flags was granted to the local commander of the Civil
Guard. This event described at length in the council minutes, was
highly significant. All components of the challenged order played
leading roles in this spectacle: the national flag, representing
national unity; the parish priest as representative of sacred
authority in the *pueblo*; the mayor as the highest civil authority;
the commander of the Civil Guard as defender of public order; and
the town's patron saint, symbolizing the *pueblo*'s moral unity that
had been threatened. What was acted out was the restauration of
the pre-existing power structure and the unity of sacred and
secular authority.

In 1930, the socialist mayor proposed to change the name of
Church Street to Pablo Iglesias Street (P.I. was the founder of
the Spanish Socialist Party). The proposal was rejected by five
to three votes. A year later when five socialists had been elected
into the council, the same proposal was accepted.

In 1936 after the outbreak of the Civil War, the socialist mayor set a permanent watch over the church and priest's house to prevent anti-clerical attacks. Some months later, the mayor and several of his comrades were shot by the Nationalists. The language of the new rulers was interspersed with religious exclamations. The patronal brotherhood of the Virgin of the Valley was revived by the victors, who also held the offices in this *cofradía*. The parish priest became a member of several municipal committees.

In the 1940s and 1950s the town-councils provided funds for the celebration of the Holy Week, masses "in honour of those who fell for God and Nation", and mission work by Franciscan friars in the township. In 1952 the council decided to proclaim Virgin Mary mayor of Mirabuenos "as humble recognition of received benefits".

The brotherhood of the Virgin of the Valley is the sole association that can claim community-wide membership. It organizes about 600 out of 640 families living in Mirabuenos-town. Membership was required in order to receive municipal and religious charity in the harsh post-war years. The core of the brotherhood's executive board consisted of the mayor, the auxiliary municipal secretary and the president of the syndical organization of agrarian employers. Today, it continues to be controlled by the same few powerful men. Until recently, the brotherhood has been used as an instrument to re-impose the elite's paternalistic image of the moral community.[19] However, the leaders of the patronal brotherhood have increasingly come under criticism by the workers. The latter feel that *their* patron saint has been manipulated by a minority. Only after Franco's death do these feelings of class hostility come into the open. An analysis of the relations between brotherhoods during Lent and the Holy Week of 1977 and 1979 will show how class antagonism is expressed in popular religion.

During the Second Republic (1931-1939), the Holy Week celebrations in Mirabuenos were on the wane. Only the brotherhood of *Jesus Nazareno* was still active and patronized the Good Friday procession, the sole one held in those days. The land labourers who constituted the majority of the local population, had their Workers Society, their own social house (the *Casa del Pueblo*), festival (first of May) and more worldly things on their mind, such as how to achieve a social revolution. The small group of tenants and small land-owners was organized in a similar way. In the fall of 1936, these secular associations were wiped out along with their core members. When the Civil War came to an end, the brotherhoods of *Cristo de la Vera Cruz* and *Nuestro Señor Amarrado a la Columna* had been reorganized. The brotherhood of *Jesus Nazareno* was still by far the largest and owned five images of saints. In 1946 a group of small land-owners, shopkeepers and artisans branched off and founded a semi-autonomous *cofradía* that centered upon the image of *La Virgen de la*

Soledad, still property of the maternal brotherhood. The same happened a year later when eleven students, encouraged by the parish priest and Catholic Action, constituted a new brotherhood around the image of *San Juan Evangelista*, which was granted to them by *Jesus Nazareno*. The foundation of *Maria Magdalena* in 1950 occurred along similar lines. The seventh brotherhood, *La Veronica*, was set up some years later.

In the 1960s some of the brotherhoods lived through a serious crisis, their most active members being drained off by emigration. It was then that land labourers and construction workers took over the brotherhoods of *Veronica* and *Magdalena* and started to put their seal upon the Holy Week celebrations.

When I came to Mirabuenos in 1977, all brotherhoods fared well. In name still sub-sections of *Jesus, San Juan, Soledad, Veronica*, and *Magdalena* behaved as autonomous brotherhoods. The parish priest had lost control over them and all but one had ceased to present their book-keepings to the ecclesiastic authorities (which is still officially required).

By then, the configuration of brotherhoods had become a rough mirror of the local class structure.[20] Let us look at them individually. *Cristo* consists of members of the non-agrarian middle class: shopkeepers, civil servants, teachers, and professionals; almost half of its members are *forasteros*, people born elsewhere. Its most prominent members are a teacher who owns the local bookshop and who was mayor from 1977 till March 1979, and a teacher who holds the office of judge of peace. The seven core members are kinsmen.

Jesus is predominantly composed of agriculturists. The biggest local landowners are members, the most important of them is a young entrepreneur who controls 300 hectares of excellent land. He is also the president of the powerful syndicate that organizes twenty-three medium and large landowners.

Soledad is the most heterogeneous brotherhood as to occupation. Among its 'brothers' are small farmers, permanent and autonomous land labourers, artisans, shopkeepers, a civil servant, and an important local entrepreneur.

San Juan is a brotherhood of secondary and university students.

El Amarrado is composed of 117 members who belong to two family lines. It is a closed brotherhood, that is, its members are exclusively recruited from the two families. The core of this *cofradía* has dominated public life in Santaella throughout the Franco era by holding the important public offices. At a banquet that the brotherhood arranged for its members and official guests when its Holy Wednesday procession was over, one of its members, the then mayor of Mirabuenos, remarked to me: "as you may notice we are one united family; there are rich and poor among us, yet we are all

equal". He and his brothers own a medium-sized farm, a shop, and
are local agents of several national firms and a bank. Their grandfather who founded the brotherhood, made a fortune as a grainbroker.
La Veronica consists of skilled construction workers and some petty
ambulant traders who were once artisans. Most of its members have
recently joined the socialist or communist trade unions.
La Magdalena is exclusively composed of land labourers, except for
a shopkeeper whose father, however, was a day-labourer. It is nicknamed 'the brotherhood of the sugarbeet lifters', because the overwhelming majority worked as seasonal migrants in beet harvesting in
Northern France. Its members also make up the core of the recently
founded local branches of the Spanish Socialist Workers Party (PSOE)
and the socialist labour union (UGT), Two of them were elected into
the town-council in April 1979, one of them the new socialist mayor
of Mirabuenos. The membership of *Magdalena*, the socialist party and
trade union, and an agrarian cooperative is overlapping. It is the
sole brotherhood that admits female members, a recent innovation of
which only a few girls availed themselves.

Brotherhoods display the following structural characteristics.
They are male societies, a fact that might at first sight be in
contradiction with the widespread opinion among men that females are
'by nature' more devout than males. However, devotion is associated
principally with inner feelings, with what happens *inside* the church.
On the other hand, brotherhoods are associations which belong *par
excellence* to the public sphere, which is largely dominated by men.
Since a few years the question whether to admit female members has
become a topic of discussion in the *cofradias*. Occasionally, some
middle-class members bring their wives to the brotherhood's clubhouse on Saturdays or Sundays. The few girls who are 'sister' of
Magdalena do not enter these social houses. The overwhelming majority
of the 370 odd active members of the Holy Week brotherhoods oppose
any kind of female participation.

A second structural feature of brotherhoods is that they include
men of all age grades. The drumbands which are part of the brotherhoods, however, consist exclusively of boys and unmarried men.
Manliness is a basic value represented in religious brotherhoods. To
beat the drum for hours, to carry the heavy floats (*pasos*) on which
the statues rest through the steep and winding streets, to drink in
excess, requires considerable power of endurance. The Holy Week
processions are for most participants competitions in masculinity.

Thirdly, religious brotherhoods are, roughly speaking, organized
along class lines.[21] Class determines the attitudes toward Lent
and Holy Week. On the one hand, *Jesus* and *Amarrado* stress the collective and individual reaffirmation of the devotion to Jesus Christ
and the Virgin Mary as the primary meaning of Holy Week brotherhoods.
Their members are 'religious purists', who view the Holy Week as a

solemn and sober ceremony. They are backed by the parish priest, but like the other brotherhoods they oppose interference on his part in the *cofradía*'s affairs. They do not open drinking locales for their members during Lent and it is the traditional elite that puts its stamp on *Jesus* and *Amarrado*. On the other side are the brotherhoods of *Soledad*, *Magdalena* and *Veronica*, which underline sociability and festivity as the primary goals of *cofradías*. Consequently, they open clubhouses throughout Lent where their members socialize in the evenings. These brotherhoods are of working-class composition and their members are unambiguously anti-clerical. An intermediate position is occupied by *Cristo* in which middle-class men predominate. This brotherhood also runs a clubhouse, where its members meet, drink, eat and make fun.

The representatives of the former attitude condemn those of the latter as uncivilized peasants (*no tienen cultura*, i.e. they do not possess culture), who mistake the Holy Week for Carnival. In their turn, the latter see the former as conceited *ricos* (the rich) who 'creep under the priest's coat', as one of them expressed in juicy working-class jargon. Relations between *Jesus* and *Amarrado* on the one hand, and *Magdalena*, *Veronica* and *Soledad* on the other, are marked by hostile avoidance. When *Amarrado*, for instance, has its procession on Good Wednesday, most members of the working class do not go out, because they consider the procession as dull and without *ambiente*. In their turn, *Amarrado* and the local elite in general boycott the Good Friday procession, in particular the traject through the 'lower *barrio*' of town. In this proletarian *barrio* the main actors are the members of *Veronica*, *Magdalena* and *Soledad*, who are more or less delirious because of liquor, exhaustion -- the procession starts at five o'clock in the morning and ends between three and four in the afternoon -- and the monotonous rolling of drums. The procession finishes in total chaos.

Relations between the working-class *cofradías* involve strong competition, honour being at stake. It is the kind of competition that is characteristic among near-equals.[22] Issues at stake concern: which brotherhood has the best drumband, decorated image and float; the biggest quantity of Bengal fireworks, wine and brandy; and finally, which brotherhood can boast the finest clubhouse.[23] The hours-long processions are cheered on with hoarse shouts like: 'Long live Veronica, the prettiest of all', or 'La Sole is the best'.[24] At night, when the floats are parked in the parish church, members from one brotherhood try to steal as many carnations as possible from the rival brotherhood's float. The atmosphere is always stirring, but rarely does competition result in physical violence. One incident, however, is famous; it concerned a fight between *Veronica* and *Magdalena* inside the church just before the beginning of the Good Friday procession. The damage done was mainly material as drums, cornets and candles were used to beat up opponents. Such stories are probably overstated over a glass of wine.

This leads us to the main question of this essay: What is the role of religious brotherhoods in the town of Mirabuenos? All brotherhoods fulfill functions of cohesion and identity for their members. They are mutual aid societies. This is most dramatically expressed when a member dies: the men of the brotherhood to which the deceased belonged carry his coffin to his final resting place. Brotherhoods consist of clusters of intimate friends (*amigos de confianza*), who often have grown up as co-members of a brotherhood and assisted at each other's life crises. They regularly meet in the same café and often work together.

Seen from the level of the local society at large, brotherhoods and the Holy Week celebration acted as a vehicle for the expression of intra- and inter-class tensions within a political system that systematically denied and suppressed class conflict. In the Franco era, the working class was deprived of any formal means of political and economic organization, so they finally availed themselves of the only institution accessible to them and turned it to their own ends. This was the religious brotherhood, a respected association, which was even promoted by the local power elite. In this way the labourers 'took revenge' on those who during and after the Civil War had inflicted hardship and humiliation upon them. They did this in the very idiom and context that was used by their class opponents as a source of cohesion and orientation and put their own mark of working-class culture on the brotherhoods. As one member of *Jesus* remarked when he was refused admittance to *Magdalena*'s social house: "Formerly there was less politics (*politica*) between brotherhoods. This all started when they (the labourers) took over *Veronica* and *Magdalena*." The proletarian brotherhoods dominate the Lenten and Holy Week scene by acting the most expressive and loudest.

That the institution of *cofradía* was used as a means to express and celebrate class cohesion and identity was first brought home to me when I visited the brotherhood's clubhouses during Lent, 1977. At that time, public discussion of politics was still considered dangerous. However, in the locales of *Veronica* and *Magdalena* lively debates were going on about illegal pamphlets of the underground communist and socialist labour unions. Half a year later, when trade unions and political parties had been legalized, local branches were set up by the very men I first met in the *cofradía* locales. Thanks to the institution of religious brotherhood the workers did not have to start to organize themselves totally unprepared. The popularity of Holy Week is so widespread in Andalusia that the leftist regional and local politicians, who were elected into office just before the Holy Week of 1979, were quick to declare in public that shows of respect for the religious brotherhoods were 'manifestations of popular

Andalusian culture'.[25]
    The renaissance of *cofradías* in the aftermath of the Civil War,
should be viewed as a function of political developments in the 1930s.
The Second Republic and the violent class war had shaken the moral
and political order to its foundations. The power and authority of
the *caciques* (political bosses), priests and landowners had been
strongly affected by the collective actions and doctrines of the
proletarian class. Communities had been torn apart into opposing
camps. Blood had run through villages and towns. It is not surprising, then, that the victors of the Civil War revived an age-old
institution -- the religious brotherhood -- as part of their strategy to justify the restoration of the pre-Republican order.
Spiritual patronage and corporacy had to cover up the deep scars of
the war. The 'moral unity' of the *pueblo* had to be re-established.
We have seen that this was an impossible task.

CONCLUSIONS

In analyzing the functions of religious brotherhoods in an Andalusian
town, we had to look beyond the strictly religious at the total
configuration in which they operate. I started with a description
of the changing relations between Church, State and Community. I
argued that with the decline of ecclesiastic power and a concomitant
loss of social functions of the priests for the majority of the
community members, the Church became increasingly identified with
the small sector of landed interests in the *pueblo*. Having less to
offer to the people, the activities of the Church came to be experienced as an encroachment on local autonomy and the privacy of
the family.
    The opposition between official Roman Catholicism and its local,
popular version, may be viewed as a function of local patriotism.
Religious brotherhoods embodied the ideal of local autonomy vis-à-vis
interference from outside. With the increasing polarization of
classes in the first decades of the twentieth century, religion was
drawn into the political arena. Adherence to the Church and anticlericalism became catchwords in the struggle between landowning
and landless classes.
    The analysis of the post-Civil War revival of *cofradías* revealed
that they came to be organized along class lines. I maintained that,
given the specific political circumstances, competition between the
classes had taken on a ritualized form in the rivalry between brotherhoods. The tensions generated by the increasing differentiation of
the working class -- a consequence of the process of modernization
and migration -- find an outlet in the strife between *Veronica*,
Soledad and *Magdalena*. The institution of religious brotherhood

fulfilled similar functions, i.e. cohesion and identity, for the members of diverse occupational groups.

It has been recently argued that religion and ceremonial practices in Andalusian agro-towns provoke strong negative reactions, which ignite class conflict (Gilmore 1980:153). The class principle plays a dominant part in the social life of Andalusian towns. However, class loyalties are often cross-cut by territorial loyalties, i.e. the strong identification of Andalusians with their *pueblo* of birth. The principle of class is overridden by local patriotism when local day-labourers oppose the influx of outside labourers during the olive and cotton harvests. Class and territorial principles often go hand in hand. The following statement made by a day-labourer in the clubhouse of *Magdalena* illustrates this point:

> Here (referring to the men in the room) we are all agricultural workers. The people (*la gente*), who belong to *Jesus* are bad, they don't want to open a locale. They are *ricos* (wealthy) like those of *Cristo* and *Amarrado*. *Veronica* is of our class. They are the best. You were lucky to choose Mirabuenos, they are all good fellows here, I mean, in our class. The rich are different, you know, there are only few nice fellows among them. We could strike if we wanted, but we don't do these kind of things, we just work hard and that's it. Yes, you were lucky to have come to Mirabuenos. The very Civil Governor of Córdoba said that this is the most quiet (*tranquilo*) *pueblo* in the province. Yes, you'll find out that this is a noble town.

In this statement one may note the shifting of identification between class and local community. This is also expressed in the recurrent discussions about whether the statues of the saints are the exclusive property of the brotherhoods or of the *pueblo* as a whole.

It would, however, be misleading to argue that the Holy Week and the patron saint's festivals provide a stage on which communal unity is acted out. On the other hand, it would be equally fallacious to maintain that class antagonism is the strongest force in the *pueblo* society and that crosscutting community mechanisms are non-existent (Gilmore 1980:218ff). Most inhabitants of Mirabuenos agree that the Holy Week and other festivals enhance the *ambiente* of the town. One of my informants put it in this way: "The strife among brotherhoods serves to embellish the Holy Week". It also serves a centripetal function. It is one of the main occasions on which hundreds of emigrants return to their native town to participate with their kith and kin in the festivities. And these ceremonial activities are also the idiom through which inter-*pueblo* competition is expressed.

The rather strong crosscutting community mechanisms in Mirabuenos might find a partial explanation in two local idiosyncrasies.

Mirabuenos is the urban center of twelve village and hamlet settlements, which are mainly inhabited by agricultural fieldhands. Class
solidarity is cross-cut by the basic opposition between town and
country (*pueblo* and *campo*). Brotherhoods are one of the marks of
social life that differentiate town from country, townspeople from
country people. Mirabuenos is also a society with a long tradition
of *seasonal* emigration. The seasonal migrants' ties with their town
are reinforced abroad. Definite emigration of workers was and is
limited by the prospect of two large settlement *cum* landreform
projects in the municipal territory, the first of which was realized
in the late 1960s and proved to be a success in the eyes of most
agricultural labourers. These projects reinforce the bonds of
workers with their town.

Future research will have to show whether the religious brotherhoods will eclipse with the increasing organization of employers
and employees into class-based economic and political associations.

NOTES

*   I am indebted to Anton Blok, Willy Jansen and Huub de Jonge for
    their helpful comments on an earlier draft of this article.
1. Mirabuenos is a pseudonym for the town where I conducted field-
    work from March 1977 till March 1978. I revisited the town
    during Lent and Holy Week of 1979. In 1975 the total population
    living in the municipality amounted to 5,290, almost half of them
    living in the urban center, the rest distributed over twelve
    settlements scattered over the large municipal territory.
    Research also included detailed study of parochial and municipal
    records.
2. For descriptions of folk Catholic institutions see Pitt-Rivers
    (1971), Boissevain (1965), Riegelhaupt (1973:835-851), Christian,
    Jr. (1972); two excellent monographs on religious brotherhoods
    have been written by the Spanish anthropologist I. Moreno Navarro
    (1972 and 1974). Older publications on religious brotherhoods in-
    clude Foster (1953:1-28), Caro Baroja (1957:24-49). These authors
    have stressed the integrative functions of brotherhoods, but
    hardly paid attention to the functions of *cofradías* within the
    community at large. Since the preparation of my paper a mono-
    graph was published on the Holy Friday celebration in the south
    of Côrdoba, J. Luque Requerey, *Antropología Cultural Andaluza.*
    El Viernes Santo al Sur de Côrdoba. For a brief summary of the
    historical role of the Church in Spanish society see Pitt-Rivers
    (1971:132-134; 218-220); Brenan (1971:39-55).
3. Escriptura de Ventta de la Jurisdizion, Señorío y Vassallage de
    Mirabuenos, A.M.M., 1649.

4. Escriptura de Ventta Real y Judizial de Jurisdizion civil y natural de la villa de Mirabuenos, señorío, ofizios y vassalaje, A.M.M., 1734.
5. Elaborated from 'Interrogatorio, Catastro de Ensenada', A.M.M., 1752. Landed property of individual clergymen is not included here.
6. In the course of the nineteenth century the financial situation of the Church deteriorated quickly: the revenues of the parish church dropped from 289.282 *reales* in 1818, to 53.836 in 1829 and 35.937 in 1856; Libros de Cuentas de Fábrica, R.P.M.
7. From 1931 to 1935 the average rate of baptism was 124; it rose to 303 in 1936 and fell back to 190 in 1937; Libro de Bautizos, R.P.M.
8. Major Ibañez of the Civil Guard was in charge of public order in Córdoba. Under his regime mass executions and other atrocities took place. Writes Fraser (1979:163):
   He was also exceedingly pious, attending mass regularly. He advised the people that by all the means at his disposal he intended to 'exile from this holy earth' the vicious and irrational vice of blasphemy ... .
   This 'Don Bruno' as he became known was also responsible for the execution of several workers from Mirabuenos.
9. For similar forms of patronage in the south of Portugal see J. Cutileiro (1971:Chapter XXV).
10. See Peláez del Rosal & Quintanillo Raso (1977) for an example of a *cofradía* that served military functions. See Foster (1953:11) for the intertwined development of religious confraternities and guilds.
11. Libro de Visitas, I, 1553-1575, R.P.M.
12. Cuentas de la Cofradía de la Vera Cruz, 1624-1714, R.P.M.
13. Brotherhoods owned estate, which they used to finance the maintenance of chapels and statues, and the burials of and loans to their members. In 1788, for instance, the brotherhood of *Corpus Cristi* owned five olive groves, four irrigated gardens, and several houses. Bookkeeping conserved in R.P.M.
14. This is reflected in the minutes of official *cofradía* meetings. See also Moreno Navarro (1972:199-200).
15. Elaborated from Gutiérrez (1978).
16. Cf. *Alto Guadalquivir. Especial Semana Santa Cordobesa*, 1979. This is a special magazine issued by the overarching organization of Cordobese brotherhoods.
17. See Riegelhaupt (1973) and Christian (1972:151-154) for similar observations. The hostility of the traditional elite toward Don Gerardo is directed to his person not to the role of priest *an sich*, while the anti-clericalism of the working class involves both the person and his office.

18. All examples have been taken from the 'Actas Capitulares',
    A.M.M.
19. When Franco still lived, the mayor of Mirabuenos declared on
    the occasion of the patron saint's festival "We are one family
    in this *pueblo*, united in our love for the *patria chica*" (i.e.
    'small nation', that is the *pueblo*).
20. In 1975 the active population in town was distributed as follows:
    agriculture 71 per cent, commerce 3 per cent, civil service 7
    per cent, and professions/manufacture/services 19 per cent.
    Day-labourers and mini-holders accounted for 90 per cent of the
    people employed in agriculture. Source: padrón municipal,
    A.M.M., 1975.
21. In Estepa, an agro-town of 9,000 in the south-east of the pro-
    vince of Sevilla, two factions of the middle class are organized
    into separate brotherhoods, while the working class has its
    own brotherhood. Cf. Gregory (1978:210-211). In Puente Genil,
    a large town south of Mirabuenos, the upper, middle and working
    classes have their own brotherhoods. On the other hand, in
    Fuenmayor, an agro-town in the plains of Sevilla, there are only
    two brotherhoods, which are mainly joined by the rich. Cf.
    D.D. Gilmore (1980:152).
22. *San Juan* holds a marginal position among the local brotherhoods,
    because most of its members live as students outside the *pueblo*;
    Cristo is also placed a little apart. Its members' higher income
    is reflected in the extent of its ceremonial fund, so that the
    competition with the proletarian brotherhoods is uneven. More-
    over, it has its own procession on Maundy Thursday night.
    Amarrado's active participation in the Holy Week is restricted
    to its own procession on Holy Wednesday.
23. Cf. Boissevain (1965) for a similar description of competition
    between brotherhoods in rural Malta.
24. The relationship between the members of a brotherhood and its
    female saint has the erotic undertone of the relation between
    lovers. At the same time it also reflects the mother-son bond.
25. See *Diario de Córdoba*, 8-4-1979, 21. The Holy Week in the
    cities of Andalusia is also an important source of income, since
    processions are a major tourist attraction. Besides, ceremonial
    expenditures of Andalusians during Lent and the Holy Week are
    considerable.

BIBLIOGRAPHY

Boissevain, J.
    1965   *Saints and Fireworks: Religion and Politics in Rural
            Malta.* London: Athlone.

Brenan, G.
  1971   *The Spanish Labyrinth. An Account of the Social and
          Political Background of the Spanish Civil War.*
          Cambridge: Cambridge University Press.
Caro Baroja, J.
  1957   Semana Santa de Puente Genil. 1950. *Revista de Dialecto-
          logía y Tradiciones Populares* 13:24-49.
Christian, W.A. Jr.
  1972   *Person and God in a Spanish Valley.* New York: Seminar Press.
Cutileiro, J.
  1971   *A Portuguese Rural Society.* Oxford: Clarendon Press.
Díaz del Moral, J.
  1973   *Historia de las agitaciones campesinas.* Madrid: Alianza
          Editorial.
Foster, G.M.
  1953   Cofradía and Compadrazgo in Spain and Spanish America.
          Southwestern Journal of Anthropology 9(1):1-28.
Frazer, R.
  1979   *Blood of Spain. The Experience of Civil War 1936-1939.*
          London: Allen Lane.
Gilmore, D.D.
  1980   *The People of the Plain. Class and Community in Lower
          Andalusia.* New York: Columbia University Press.
Gregory, D.D.
  1978   *La odisea andaluza. Una emigración hacia Europa.* Madrid:
          Tecnos.
Gutiérrez, P.F.
  1978   *Semana Santa en Córdoba.* Madrid: Alpuerto.
Luque Requerey, J.
  1980   *Antropología Cultural Andaluza. El Viernes Santo al Sur
          de Córdoba.* Córdoba: Publicaciones del Monte de Piedad y
          Caja de Ahorros.
Moreno Navarro, I.
  1972   *Propiedad, clases sociales y hermandades en la Baja
          Andalucía.* Madrid: Siglo XXI.
  1974   *Las Hermandades Andaluzas. Una Aproximación desde la
          Antropología.* Sevilla: Publicaciones de la Universidad de
          Sevilla no. 24.
Peláez del Rosal, M. & M.C. Quintanillo Raso
  1977   *Priego de Córdoba en la Edad Media.* Salamanca: Kadmos.
Pitt-Rivers, J.A.
  1971   *The People of the Sierra.* Chicago/London: University of
          Chicago Press.
Riegelhaupt, J.F.
  1973   Festas and Padres: The Organization of Religious Action in
          a Portuguese Parish. *American Anthropologist* 75: 835-851.

OTHER SOURCES AND DOCUMENTS

Archivo Municipal de Mirabuenos (A.M.M.):
  1649   Escriptura de Ventta de la Jurisdizion, Señorío y
           Vassallage de Mirabuenos, Madrid.
  1734   Escriptura de Ventta Real y Jurizial de Jurisdizion civil
           y natural de la villa de Mirabuenos, señorío, ofizios y
           vassalaje, Córdoba.
  1752   Interrogatorio, Catastro de Ensenada.
  1975   padrón municipal.
  --   Acta Capitulares.
Registros Parroquiales de Mirabuenos (R.P.M.):
  1553-
  1575   Libro de Visitas, I.
  1624-
  1714   Cuentas de la Cofradía de la Vera Cruz.
  1818   Libros de Cuentas de Fábrica.
  1829   Libros de Cuentas de Fábrica.
  1856   Libros de Cuentas de Fábrica.
  1931-
  1937   Libro de Bautizos.

Popular Anti-Clericalism and Religiosity in pre- 1974 Portugal

Joyce Riegelhaupt, Sarah Lawrence College

INTRODUCTION

In the ethnographic works of Leite de Vasconcellos, which were
organized for publication after his death, there is a short section
on the 'Religiosity of the Portuguese'. It consists of a number of
unrelated anecdotes, tidbits of tantalizing insights, clippings from
newspapers of the time, and collected sayings. In a footnote to the
presentation, Orlando Ribeiro writes:

> It was the intention of [Leite de Vasconcellos] to treat the sub-
> ject in a condensed manner ... in order to develop a later section
> of the work. We are only publishing here, much as he left them,
> the notes and citations which we encountered under the rubric
> "Characteristics", given the delicacy of the subject and the fact
> that the author had not formulated in a definitive manner his re-
> flections about these notes. Part of the material clearly reflects
> the period in which it was collected; if [Leite de Vasconcellos]
> had been able to elaborate on these notes he would certainly have
> altered or omitted some things. (1958:508n).

The entries to which Ribeiro refers, were collected from the
eighteen-seventies through the first two decades of the twentieth
century. Their subject, religiosity, was certainly a delicate one in
those years which saw the rise of Republican anticlericalism and the
end of the Portuguese monarchy. In 1958, when the collected works
were published by the explicitly pro-clerical and authoritarian
Salazar government, the subject was still a delicate one.
Leite de Vasconcellos' notes begin with a series of observations
about which he advises himself:

> (Think about the following):
> Portuguese don't appear to be fundamentally religious. There is
> no doubt that the Catholic religion has had a great influence
> for a very long time. ... But among us there has never developed
> the type of mysticism which exists in Spain, and there has always

existed here a *strong spirit (espirito forte)* [author's emphasis] as in Gil Vicente[1] and Antonio Jose, which scoffs at the clergy, similar to what one encounters in medieval French literature, where at every step the *clercs* are castigated.

The Catholic among us is a formalist, as among the ancient Romans:

a) He goes to festivals primarily for entertainment, in order to sing and dance, in order to eat and drink -- festivals have a pagan character and are only for merrymaking.

b) He confesses during Lent in order to *desobrigar* (fulfil an obligation) and confession itself is even called 'the obligation'. This term suggests that he does not confess because of a religious feeling (*sentimento*), only because it is a duty and is imposed.

c) Frequently, in villages when he attends mass, he stands on the porch of the church, and when the priest says that he has not heard the mass, he says: Yes, I have, it's enough just to be there. ...

e) There are many songs about priests, and satirical stories and anecdotes about monks.

Frequently, and everywhere -- not only in one or another province, the degree of religious performance in the public life of a community (*um povo*) depends on clerical influence, and it is difficult to evaluate the sentiment. ...

In general, religion is diminishing. But there is more of it in the North and the Center, than in the South (1958:508, 509).

While today, the subject of 'religiosity' may no longer be 'delicate', the observations that Leite de Vasconcellos made about Portuguese religious behavior are still very pertinent for the student of that society. I am going to take up Leite de Vasconcellos' admonition and 'think about', one of the underlying issues to which he refers -- namely, the relationship between religiosity and, what I shall call, 'popular anticlericalism'. The meaning of religiosity in this Catholic community is one that I have pondered for several years and discussed in earlier papers (Riegelhaupt 1973, 1977). The relationship between Catholicism (whether it be questions of belief, faith or ritual) and anticlerical attitudes and actions is a theme which not only runs through the comments quoted above, but was also consistently evident in my own fieldnotes collected during the early nineteen-sixties in the rural, central Portuguese parish of São Miguel.[2] Within that parish, Catholicism as ideology and practice was communicated through the presence of the Church and the priest directly in the village, as well as through the dissemination of precepts and beliefs in the local school curriculum.[3]

SÃO MIGUEL: *'SOCIEDADE'* VS. *'SALÃO'*

Throughout the Estremaduran countryside, small villages are scattered at distances of three or four kilometers from one another. Stonewalls and the treeless fields worked by small peasant proprietors separate the villages and hamlets. Every so often one village has an impressive Catholic Church which marks it as the seat of a parish (*freguesia*, from the Latin 'sons of the Church'). Usually, the village with the Church is somewhat larger than nearby hamlets and villages, but otherwise it is indistinguishable. However, in the parish of São Miguel, some forty kilometers northwest of Lisbon, the parish seat (the village of São Miguel) not only houses the distinctive Church building, but also has two very large buildings which stand at opposite ends of the commons (*rossio*) around which the village is built. In a region where public buildings are few and far between, the presence of two in a village of less than 500 people is very surprising. On investigation one learns that the building next to the Church, on the north side of the commons, is the *'Salão'* (salon), and the building on the south side is the *'Sociedade'* (lit. society, fig. social club).

Each building contains an auditorium space, a stage, a television set, a balcony, and small rooms for various activities. The *sociedade* was financed by donations from all and built by the villagers in order to have a place in which to hold the weekly *bailes* (dances), watch TV and play cards. The *salão* was constructed by the priest, using funds he collected from the villagers, to draw the people away from the immoral environment of the *sociedade* and provide a place for watching TV, seeing approved plays and musicals, and participating in other social activities organized by the Church. In addition, the *salão* housed eight members of a female religious order who provided a range of social services to the parish.

The *sociedade*, the *salão*, and the commons, with its main fountain, constituted the public spaces of the village. In and around them were enacted the village *festas*, both religious and secular (Riegelhaupt 1973), as well as the public presentations of life events from baptism, communion and courtship to marriage and death. Only the *rio*, the public laundry house where women gathered, the football field, and the cemetery lay outside this square. The commons area was used primarily for social events, but, at one time, it was also a center for communal agricultural activities.

In the nineteen-sixties this spatial arrangement, Church and *salão* on one side of the commons and *sociedade* on the other, was virtually a 'symbolic' representation of a constant tension in São Miguel life: the antagonism between priest and parishioner, Church and society. This antagonism, manifested in anticlericalism, lay at the very base of local beliefs. Given the structure and organization of Catholicism, it created for São Miguelitos problems in access to religious ritual and validation. It raised, for the ethnographer, the question of whether Catholicism provided villagers with the "set of symbolic forms and acts which relate ... to the ultimate conditions of ... existence" (Bellah 1970).

DIMENSIONS OF 'ANTICLERICALISM'

Before beginning to discuss the relationship between anticlericalism and religiosity in São Miguel, it may be helpful to distinguish some of the different issues that have been subsumed under the concept of anticlericalism. Without much effort such an attempt could result in a virtual recapitulation of Church history, if not the very history of Christianity; for disputes over the proper role of the clergy, the proper relationship between Church and State, as well as the question of whether people 'need religion' have all, at times, been related to the issue of anticlericalism.

Let me set out some of the issues that underlie the different meanings of anticlericalism. It is necessary to distinguish negative attitudes and actions directed toward the institutional Church and by extension its agents (the regular and secular clergy) from those negative attitudes that focus directly on the position of the priest. Historically, it has been hostility directed against the favored institutional role that the Catholic Church has played in a given State that has most often mobilized anticlericalism. The Church's influence and power in economic and political spheres was challenged and the clergy, most often the regular clergy and the hierarchy, became the focus of anticlericalism.

Frequently, opposition to the worldly role of the Church included hostility to Catholicism as a religion. Here, too, the clergy were attacked as agents of a most pernicious institution, not only because of their misuse of economic and political power, but equally importantly because of their role as disseminators of an unacceptable ideology. It is not always possible to distinguish between those who opposed the Church's power in 'secular' affairs from those who opposed the very institution of religion since these often overlapped. However, we should analytically recognize a distinction between an anticlericalism that is fundamentally 'anti-Church' because of the Church's institutional position in a given state, and a broader anticlericalism that is equivalent to 'anti-religion'. In each of these dimensions, however, the attacks against the clergy are part of a larger attack on the Church as an institution.

Another set of concerns focus directly on the behavior of the parish priest and do not seem to question the larger socio-political

institutional structure within which the secular clergy acts as
local emissary, although the issues, namely, the priest's political
and economic activities, can be traced to the larger structure.
Finally, and again not always clearly separable from the above, are
a range of anticlerical criticisms that are explicitly directed
against the way in which a local priest handles his religious duties
and that often appear to question the sacerdotal structure of Catholicism. In both of these 'anticlerical' attitudes, the priest, *qua*
priest, is the target, not the institution of the Church nor religion. It is within this general range of anticlericalism -- the
antagonism of parishioners to their local priest -- that this
discussion shall focus.

Working within the southern latifundist region of Portugal, Jose
Cutileiro (1971:265-269) also encountered widespread local anticlericalism. In his excellent discussion, he distinguishes "pious
anticlericalism" (criticisms that focus on the way in which the
priest conducts the religious life of the parish) from "secular
anticlericalism" (criticisms that focus on the 'worldly' activities
of the priest). As in Vila Velha, the distinction between 'pious'
and 'secular' anticlericalism was also evident in São Miguel. There,
too, women were more apt to express 'pious' criticisms, while men's
criticisms were usually 'secular', although this distinction between
men and women was not as sharp as reported from the Alentejo. This
difference between men and women's concern becomes meaningful when
one recognizes, as Cutileiro does for Vila Velha, that within rural
Portuguese society religion is considered the woman's domain.

'POPULAR ANTICLERICALISM'

Cutileiro characterizes anticlericalism in Vila Velha as "luke-
warm" and "non-ideological and non-intellectual". He suggests that
these qualities serve to distinguish "popular anticlericalism" from
"elite anticlericalism". "Elite anticlericalism", he argues, was
concerned with the larger structural questions of Church/State relations[4], and explicitly against the economic and political power
of the Church. Cutileiro points out that although local "secular"
anticlerical issues were virtually indistinguishable from the anticlericalism of the Republican elite, they were of a different order.
Portuguese Republican and 'elite' anticlericalism fought against
Church power and restructured Church/State relations; Alentejan
(and Estremaduran) villagers during the nineteen-sixties objected
to *the priest*. Their criticisms arose from daily life and did not
seem to be "matters of principle" (Cutileiro 1971:267) questioning
the institutional and hegemonic role of the Catholic Church in the
Estado Novo.

However, under the pro-clerical Salazar government, it was not possible to publicly attack the Church. Given the Church's privileged position, such expression would have been tantamount to anti-State beliefs and as such, subject to repressive measures.

Consequently, what Cutileiro describes, and what I observed, namely, the 'non-ideological' or better, 'apolitical' character of anticlericalism may have been its only possible expression since, in the nineteen-sixties, 'popular anticlericalism' could not be mobilized into any other 'ism', religious or political. Nevertheless, the symmetry between villager conflicts with their priests and the issues of an earlier elite anticlericalism need not lead us to assume that the same political attitudes informed peasant 'popular anticlericalism'.

Although it was politically impossible to express anti-Church sentiments, as opposed to the expression of anti-priest statements, it does not necessarily follow that 'popular anticlericalism' was non-ideological. Rather, I shall suggest, that if we follow Cutileiro in recognizing that popular anticlericalism includes both a 'pious' and 'secular' aspect, then taken together we may be getting a series of village-level statements about what religion should be and -- by extension -- some very 'ideological' statements about the structure of society.

In each event that we shall examine the issues that triggered the antagonism and conflict between priest and parishioner were viewed by São Miguel villagers as having been generated locally. The State and Church dogma may have provided the structural position which the priest exploited, but the villagers' response, as far as I could judge, was not being manipulated from elsewhere nor informed by the massive literature of anticlericalism. Both 'pious' and 'secular' anticlerical attitudes in São Miguel were based on an evaluation of how the priest did his job. Implicit in both types of criticisms was a view that there was a correct way in which the role should be performed and what religion should be in São Miguel. Both types of criticisms were engendered by the multiple roles that the priest played in parish affairs.

By virtue of the sacerdotal and sacramental nature of the Catholic Church, the priest was the mediator of all rituals, both personal and communal. By virtue of State concession and Church ideology, he was the source of moral authority in the village. Combining his moral authority with the authoritarian political system and local social structure, he was also the chief agent of social control in the countryside. In addition, his institutional affiliation enabled him to operate as a political 'patron' (Riegelhaupt 1979). The particular power of São Miguel's priest resulted, thus, from an intersection of religious authority (universal to Catholicism), a

specific local agrarian social structure (the absence of a local
or landed elite), and a particular political system (a pro-clerical,
authoritarian state).[5]

POPULAR ANTICLERICALISM AND RELIGIOSITY IN SÃO MIGUEL

In sharp contrast to the acquiescence and submission that characterized São Miguelito attitudes and actions toward other powerful
institutions and individuals of the *Estado Novo*, the activities of
the priest (known as Sr. Prior) were constantly being evaluated
and criticized. Jokes and highly critical remarks permeated local
conversation, at least with the anthropologist. Outright hostility
was also evident although the mode was most often passive resistance and removal rather than confrontation. The issues that provoked
the conflicts were wide ranging and while it is possible to see
the issues of controversy as 'secular' or 'pious', these issues
fed one into another.
  São Miguel's priest was an activist priest, concerned with
'modernizing' the parish, and at the same time, monitoring both the
individual's and the village's practices and belief system. He had
no ties to the local community and the social structure of this
region of Portugal provided no resident upper class with whom the
priest was allied and identified. In São Miguel, the priest was
an 'outsider', an agent of the State. Rarely seen in the village
streets, São Miguel's priest was, from the villagers' perspective,
simultaneously a minister, a businessman, a patron, a policeman, and
a man, institutionally forced to deny his manhood. He was the
favorite subject of gossip, anecdotes, and at the same time a source
of fear.
  The very institutional ties of the Church to the authoritarian
Estado Novo created the potentiality for the priest to play the role
of both agent of social control and patron. In most Estremaduran
villages, there were no resident police or civil guard (*Guarda Re-
publicana*). While most of the rules and regulations of this tightly
controlled society were internalized by the people, thus maintaining
a high degree of order, the presence of a priest in a village was
also viewed as the presence of a police agent. São Miguel's priest
willingly informed on villagers when their activities violated his
(and the State's) regulations. He repeatedly objected to the social
activities that were associated with festivals and quasi-religious
celebrations. He acted upon those objections by reporting villagers
to the police for their failure to secure the proper permission and
licenses required to hold celebrations and gatherings.
  Despite his punitive actions, most villagers found at times that
they needed the priest's assistance as a patron. The *Estado Novo* was

a highly administered society, constrained and virtually strangled by bureaucratic rules and regulations (Riegelhaupt 1979). Receiving one's rightful social security payments, securing permission to build a house, getting a fine reduced, receiving permission to emigrate -- for all of these the peasant required the intervention of a powerful person. In São Miguel, only the priest could play that role. Within Portugal, the clergy historically played important administrative and political roles in rural parishes. Hence the role of priest as agent of the State was not a new one for the peasants, but it was considered an inappropriate combination. In São Miguel, the priest strictly avoided any 'political' identification, but to the villagers his ties to the regime were evident. The repressive nature of the *Estado Novo* prepared the villagers to accept, however much they disliked it, the fact that the 'outsider' (one of '*eles*') would have power over them. São Miguel's priest, as the one resident outsider, thus became the focal point of all antagonism directed against the elite of Portuguese society. The contradiction between the priest as one of 'them' versus the priest as source of all sacraments created one of the strongest areas of conflict.

Even less tolerable than the priest's political role were his activities as 'businessman'. To the São Miguelito, the priest (all clergy) got rich at their expense. "Look", they said, "who else drives a car in this village and has a vacuum cleaner; when he came here he only had a bicycle". "How do we know that all the money he collects from us to build the housing for the poor or the medical clinic really went for those things?" "Why should we give money to send the sons of the poor to seminary; no one from this parish has ever become a priest -- or even gone to high school". "The priest is just a businessman: priests don't work, their only profession is their tongue (*a lingua e a enxada dele*)".

To the villagers, the Church was not some abstraction but the living reality of the priest (*senhor prior*). They considered money given to the Church as money placed in the pocket of the priest. Power and money thus became the key focus of 'secular' anticlerical anger with sexuality a 'cover' for these more fundamental issues. São Miguel's priest denied any personal financial gain. He had, in fact, been primarily responsible for bringing many social improvements to the parish. Among these were: a medical clinic, a nursery school, a number of houses for the "worthy poor", a shoemaking establishment, and an expansion of the elementary school system. In each instance, villagers mocked his efforts as being inappropriate for a priest, obviously for his own advantage, and done with their money without their consultation. Like the *salao*, the priest undertook these *melhoramentos* (improvements) without asking what villagers wanted.

What was especially troubling to the villagers was that even though they had provided the money and the labor for the 'improvements', the priest could limit their access to them. That is, the priest in his role of religious authority decided who was 'worthy' -- and to be worthy one had to accept priestly authority over personal and communal religious life.

São Miguel peasants, both men and women, had a shared view of the proper domain in which the priest had the right to exercise authority -- within the Church. Despite the fact that they needed him as 'patron' and to a great extent benefited from his 'improvements', it was clear that these excursions beyond the Church were considered improper.

The delimited area to which the villagers wanted the priest confined was equally demonstrated in the next range of issues -- issues that relate directly to ritual and belief in Catholicism and the authority of a celibate male. These issues included conflict over a) the content and organization of communal festivals; b) the appropriate forms and times of worship; c) access and rights to sacraments; and d) who 'owns' the Church.

In the remainder of this essay I shall briefly examine each of these issues in order to highlight the manner in which anticlerical beliefs are in themselves statements about 'religion' and 'society'.

a) *Conflict over communal celebrations*

Despite a dogma which asserts that Catholicism is a religion of personal salvation, São Miguelito practices suggest a continuing concern with ritual activities that proclaim a communal basis of existence and seek validation of communal identity and concern through religious ritual (see Riegelhaupt 1973 for a full discussion). Four hundred years after the Council of Trent, which aimed, through its reformation of Church regulations, to turn collective Christians into individual ones (Bossy 1970), communal ritual still formed the basis of religious life in São Miguel. The Trentine reforms may have broken the larger kinship groups and structured the parish as the unit of social identity (cf. *Montaillou* and the question of 'community', LeRoy Ladurie 1977), but in so doing these reforms did not necessarily result in substituting a religion of personal salvation. In fact, one can argue that the Church, through the unit of the parish, ostensibly designed as a central place of worship to which individuals had to come as individuals, created in Europe the 'community' which anthropologists then went out and studied as a 'natural' unit. The feuds of rivalrous kin groups were ended only, it appears, to be replaced by the endemic rivalries which now take as their central focus one Church vs. another Church, made manifest in the Estremaduran countryside by the proliferation of chapels and local *festas* which almost always coincide with rivalrous units within and between parishes.

Priest/parishioner conflicts over communal events concentrated on three issues: 1) the priest's refusal to participate in community-wide, public prayer including the blessings of the fields, prayers for rain, the blessing of the houses and the cessation of numerous processions; 2) the priest's role in the selection of the *mordomos* of the festivals and his control of *confraria* account books; and 3) his condemnation from the pulpit, and to the police, of the social activities which accompanied festivals.

It is difficult to neatly categorize the different attitudes and actions expressed on these three issues as 'pious' or 'secular'. Both men and women were vociferous in their complaints, with women being more outspoken on the refusal of the priest to perform the community-wide prayers; men objecting to the priest's role in selection of the ritual leaders; and both men and women disagreeing with the priest's right to present himself as 'moral' authority.

These issues force us to look more deeply into the structure of festival organization and the differential participation of men and women. It might be possible to say that it is only in the organization and enactment of festivals that villagers were permitted to perform important roles in the community's religious affairs. Men collected the money, hired the priests, the bands, arranged the entertainment and conducted the auction. Women marched with their *promessas* in the procession, contributed the *carga* for the auction, bid actively in the auction, and were responsible for the cleanliness and displays of the village.

Thus, men managed the business of the *festa* and women performed the ritual activities. A good *festa* depended upon both sexes being mobilized and active. Just as there was no *festa* without organization, so a poor *festa* was made manifest in the limited participation of women. This differential male/female participation in religious rituals touches, of course, on the frequent observation in Mediterranean Catholic life that women are more 'religious'.

Examination of the spatial configuration of most *festa* celebrations reveals that none of the activities (organization, collection, procession, auction) required the participants to enter the Church; the saints' images left the Church and were then entrusted to the *mordomos*. But increasingly the priest was not entrusting the saint; rather he was selecting the men to carry the saint. Thus the issue became not merely one of accountability -- the conflict over the right of the *mordomos* to collect for a 'Church' festival and not hand over the receipts to the priest -- but literally over "whose festival is it?" São Miguelito men claimed that their refusal to carry the saints stemmed from their fundamental conflict with the priest's view that 'he' rather than 'they' 'owned' the saints. It was, in their words, "their Church and their saints", not his. The priest was granted some authority within the Church, but once one moved beyond the front door of the Church, they viewed the priest as subject to their authority.

This issue of the actual physical space within which a priest exercises authority is very consistent with Leite de Vasconcellos' observation about the peasant attending mass by standing on the porch of the Church. Spatially, São Miguel men demonstrated their antagonism to the priest's authority by the very distance that they placed between themselves and the altar. On the occasions when men did enter the Church, they barely got beyond the holy water font. More often they stood on the porch or further away just outside the Church wall. Men did come to Church; they did not go into Church. Once in the Church, the priest was superior; outside the Church, around the *rossio*, he was viewed as being subject to their requests. For most villagers there was no question that a good festival needed priests, but there was a very limited role for the priests to play.

This raises the question of the 'entertainment' quality of *festas*. São Miguel's priest, like other clergy over the centuries (cf. Zeldin 1970; Lisón-Tolosana 1966) was outspoken in his criticisms of the 'immoral' activities that followed the processions. Primarily, his hostility focussed on dancing and the expenditure of *confraria* funds for musicians and fireworks.

One must, however, go beyond viewing the social activities that occur at the *festa* as only 'entertainment' or 'immoral'. For there was an important social purpose to these activities, namely, the opportunity for young people to meet, to court, and for marriage arrangements to be concluded. Marriages in São Miguel were overwhelmingly endogamous within the parish; at most, partners came from contiguous parishes. It is not surprising, therefore, that women and young girls were very visible participants in all public phases of the *festas*, for it was at these *festas* that couples met. If one reviews the range of activities that accompany festivals from dances to games predicting mates and marriage possibilities, one begins to clearly see that beneath 'entertainment', the 'business' of the *festas* were very definitely marriage arrangements.

The issue of religion for the collectivity vs. religion as a means of personal salvation was equally demonstrated in the priest/parishioner conflicts over sacraments, attendance at the mass, and the importance of Holy Week activities. The priest was repeatedly criticized for the manner in which he controlled the ceremonies (and sacraments) necessary for individual salvation -- events which more broadly signify passage through 'life crises'. Here, too, the anthropologist wonders what transpired in Portuguese Catholicism for four hundred years as once more the issues of Trent (Bossy 1970) turn out to be among the issues of the mid-twentieth century:

the imposition of baptism as a ceremony which is to follow rapidly after birth; the right of the priest to establish appropriate standards for, and the limiting of, godparents; the restructuring of Holy Week celebrations with an emphasis placed on Easter communion rather than the communal celebrations which had proliferated on Maundy Thursday and Good Friday; and the assertion of the primary role of the priest as not only the mediator of rituals, but also the moral authority of the community.

As in the materials on priest/parishioner conflict over *festa* organization, each one of these issues can be discussed at length. Instead, in this essay I shall very briefly discuss a few selected issues, trying to focus on the insights that each case provides on the relationship between anticlericalism and religiosity.

b) *Appropriate form and times of worship*

Like other priests of his generation, São Miguel's priest had been instructed to change a variety of practices that no longer conformed with Church rules. It was about these changes that most of the 'pious' criticisms focused. On a range of issues including the ending of public announcements of marriage bans for three weeks before a marriage, the fact that the mass recited on the Day of the Dead no longer began with the priest reciting "This mass is for *all* the souls ...", the limitation on the ringing of Church bells, and the ending of the twenty-four hours of fasting before confession, the priest was viewed as undermining what villagers saw as 'their religion'.

These criticisms were most often heard from women who saw themselves, quite rightly, as unable to do anything about these changes except complain. However, both men and women, Church-goers and abstainers, were equally critical about the priest's newest innovation: the broadcasting of mass on Sundays, holidays and from Fatima over the loudspeaker which now occupied a prominent position in the Church's belfry. In fact, according to the villagers, the priest had refused to repair the Church's bells (the key communicator of parish affairs -- from mere time-keeping to the announcements of harvests, deaths and *festas*) and instead substituted the loudspeaker. The tensions over the use of the loudspeaker erupted clearly during Holy Week celebrations. In the following discussion, we shall see the particular pattern of Holy Week activities in São Miguel -- a pattern quite the contrary to the priest's expectation -- yet, a pattern quite in keeping with the villagers' view of the importance of communal ritual over personal salvation.

The two most important days of Holy Week from the villagers' perspective were Holy Thursday and Good Friday. On Palm Sunday, few people attended Church (as on Easter Sunday) and in the evening the

priest corrected for this abstention by broadcasting services over
the loudspeaker. It was, however, Holy Thursday that brought the
largest Church attendance of the year (Day of the Dead brought out
more people, but to the cemetery, not the Church).

Holy Thursday, the commemoration of the Last Supper, was still
seen by São Miguelitos as the communal day; formerly the celebrations, including feasting, would go through the night and only
end on Good Friday morning. Now Church celebrations lasted until
midnight and the priest needed two assistant priests to handle the
overflow of people (mostly women) who confessed and took communion.
Holy Thursday was still known in Portugal as *'Quinta Feira das
Endoenças'* (Thursday of Pardons), for it was on that day in pre-
Reformation times that the massive granting of pardons took place.
Even though the pardons ended long ago, the communal aspects, which
Trent also presumably ended, persisted.

Few people went to Church on Good Friday to perform the Stations
of the Cross. In fact, many villagers reported that the Church was
'closed' on Good Friday (apparently referring to the absence of the
daily mass). What was most characteristic and unique to Good Friday
was the fact that the village boys and men went off to the nearby
beaches and fished. Fishing, for these men who live their lives
with their backs to the sea and farm the land in an unending battle
against it, was not a usual activity. On Good Friday, husbands were
viewed as being responsible for providing the fish for family dinner
and the young men who went fishing often stayed at the beach and
prepared a communal supper. In fact, fishing success (the trapping
of octopus and squid in rock pools) was chancy and many men brought
home a catch that they had, in fact, purchased from the itinerant
fishmongers, who usually visited the inland villages to provide fish
for the Friday meals. In Lisbon, villagers reported, Good Friday was
a day of mourning. In São Miguel, it was a day in which men provided
the meal for the entire household.

Hallelujah Saturday brought once more the hostility between the
priest and the villagers out into the open. The customary way of
celebration was through the setting off of fireworks in different
sections of the village and parish. Now only a few surreptitious fireworks could be heard going off, for the priest had prohibited such
displays. Instead, the quiet of the night was shattered by the broadcasting of midnight mass over the loudspeaker. Curses and yelling
could be heard from many households as men and women complained
about the imposition of the priest and religion on them. Going to
Church, participation in the sacraments, and hearing the mass should
be *'libre vontade'* (free will), a personal decision; no one had the
right to compel attendance or impose 'religion' on unwilling adherents.

Again, what repeatedly came through from both 'pious' and 'secular'
critics was a strong sense that participation was a voluntary act and

that the priest had no right to compel, in the first instance, adherence, nor to set himself up as the arbitrator of correctness.
Thus, in issues concerning the festival calendar, participation at
mass, confession, and communion, São Miguel's priest was castigated
because he imposed and compelled. Villagers spoke warmly of other
priests "who just close their windows and let the people celebrate".

c) *Access and rights to sacraments*

The key to personal salvation within the Catholic Church is
through the receiving of the sacraments. The priest's authority as
the sole disseminator of these sacraments is built into the structure of the religion. Most villagers seemed willing to receive these
sacraments. But the echoes of Trent linger long in the countryside
as the continual conflict between the priest and the villagers was
over his right to decide eligibility and timing of baptism, marriage,
and the granting of last rites.

Promptness of baptismal ceremonies and the selection of acceptable godparents were constant issues. The priest had instituted
an impressive series of fines for parents who delayed in baptising
their child. However, to the parents, baptism meant not only the
admission of the child to the Church but also, as importantly, a
family celebration. It is interesting to note that at baptism and
marriages, men who may never go to Church accompanied their children
while their wives stayed at home. So, too, at the funeral ceremonies,
close female kin stayed at home. Moreover, at parish funerals it was
expected that each household would send one man as representative;
only if the deceased came from the village were women expected to
participate. Thus one is presented with the contrast, of women
going to mass, lighting candles, and being 'responsible' for the
safe passage of the family through life (in health and illness) and
men representing the family at each instance that it is called to
public accountability.

The required rituals from baptism to funerals, although participated in by the people, were enacted with resentment. Despite the
fines, parents delayed baptism until the proper social arrangements
could be made. Although the priest declared certain *compadres* of
baptism and marriage ineligible, villagers persisted in selecting
those individuals regardless of the priest's attitudes. Not infrequently, the priest was forced to choose between denying the
sacrament to the baby or the new couple -- thus reading those individuals out of the Church -- or accepting a 'godfather' or 'godmother' who was 'ritually' unacceptable. He usually acquiesced in
the direction of granting the sacrament, but the costs he extracted
from the parents (a fee for 'dispensation') only led to increased
hostility toward him.

Perhaps the most impressive communal stand against the priest's control of access to the sacraments occurred during a funeral for a young man who had committed suicide. Despite official statistics, suicide is not infrequent in this part of rural Portugal. Most suicides are by young men under thirty and the preferred method is drowning in a well (reverse baptism?).

Suicides are not eligible for final rites or Church burial. However, in a complex and controversial series of measures from the nineteenth century and into the Republic, cemeteries in Portugal became simultaneously State and Church ground. Hence, all are buried in consecrated ground, but the priest need not officiate at all funerals. Again through appropriate payments, it was often possible for a suicide to be treated as a normal death. Villagers assumed that through payments and their 'moral' acquiescence, the priest could be made to do their bidding. In one notable instance, however, the priest refused to perform the funeral for a suicide. No bells rang to announce the death nor did they ring to signal the entry of his coffin and accompanying procession to the cemetery. Despite 'official' silence, this was the best-attended funeral that villagers could remember. The cortege accompanying the body included not only the local men, but men and women from villages all over the parish. In the ultimate defiance of the priest, the cortege carried the coffin to the door of the Church before wending its way to the cemetery.

While villagers accepted the sacraments as necessary for life and after-life, they repeatedly, in action and in conversation, denied the priest the right to control access to these rituals. Certainly, within the structure of Catholicism it is the priest's right and duty to not only administer sacraments but to control access to them, for by its very nature the Church is episcopal, sacerdotal, and sacramental. Yet, in numerous ways, villagers demonstrated their opinion that their Church and its priest should be congregational and sacramental. Villagers were not willing to equate a heavenly model of hierarchy and mediation (Saint, Mary, Jesus/God) to an acceptance of power over them in secular or ritual affairs granted to the priest.

d) *'Ownership' of the Church*

In the course of discussing festival organization and communal activities, I have had occasion to mention the issue of who 'owned' the Church. Whether the question was the installation of the loudspeaker, the repair of Church bells, the painting of the Church building, or the removal of graves from the ancient churchyard cemetery, outspoken villagers felt that the priest was acting "as if he owned the Church" when, they would argue, it is "our Church". One

need only peruse the literature from nineteenth-century France
(cf. esp. Magraw 1970) to recognize the mulitude of petty squabbles
over Church property, pitting priest against villager, which animate
anticlericalism. In São Miguel, none of these issues were resolved
in the villagers' favor, for the priest exercised absolute control
over Church property.

It was the priest's callous removal of bones from the churchyard
in order to build the *salão* that was repeatedly referred to in
conversation as singular evidence for priestly hypocracy and un-
dependability. To build the *salão* on Church property, the priest had
had to use the churchyard which had been, until the middle of the
nineteenth century, the parish burial ground. Disinterment in this
part of Portugal occurs regularly as plots within the confined walls
of the parish cemetery are only purchased, with rare exceptions, for
periods ranging from five to twenty-five years. As in many Mediterranean cemeteries, the skull and crossboned gates opened on to
relatively recent graves, a very few new mausoleums, a small chapel,
and a *Casa dos Ossos* (charnel house) in which disinterred bones
were heaped. Disinterment has no ritual aspects, but the bones dug
up to make way for the *salão* were not placed in the *Casa dos Ossos*;
instead the priest had them reburied haphazardly under the local
football field, to the shock and dismay of both the devout and the
skeptical.

The removal of the bones thus highlighted the issue of continuing
responsibility of the Church to the dead. As in the 'pious' criticism that mass said on the Day of the Dead should be for 'all' and
not merely those who had paid the one or two *escudos* to have their
ancestors remembered, so, too, did those buried long ago retain
their rights as members of the community -- rights, in this instance, to remain buried in consecrated ground. The priest had
underestimated the villagers' definition of 'community'. He knew
that no one was a known direct descendant and assumed that therefore no one would care if these bones were disposed of. Yet, from
the villagers' perspective, these were the bones of people who had
secured their right to burial, regardless of whether or not they
were 'ancestors'; the priest had no right to move them. I suspect
also that the issue of 'death' and religion were also a factor in
the emotional reactions that still persisted in the community over
this event. Rituals celebrating life, although participated in by
most, could be considered optional; but as I have discussed, to be
denied access to a funeral brought out the most unanimous demonstration of hostility to the priest. Men and women alike expected
to be buried correctly, ritually (cf. Christian 1972). The action
of the priest in disturbing the dead was further compounded by
both his choice of reburial -- underneath the football field --
and his replacement of the graveyard with the *salão*. To many

village men and women, this act symbolized the moral inconsistency
of the priest, and all priests. It proved that he was 'a man like
any other'.

CONCLUSION

It had been my intention to devote a separate section to the
meaning of priestly celibacy and the way in which this attribute
of the priestly role came under constant criticism and skepticism.
However, it seems to me that in the range of conflicts and tensions
that I have presented the fundamental structure of sacerdotalism
and sacramentalism was being questioned. Thus, I find that the
debate over the meaning of celibacy is intrinsic to my conclusions;
for, it seems to me that within Portuguese Catholicism the fundamental issue is one in which São Miguel villagers were unwilling to
grant to any man, celibate or not, the priestly function of being
a "minister of God with the power to condemn or forgive" (Cutileiro
1971:265). In the words of one São Miguelito, "Why should we believe
priests and respect them; they are just like us; they are not
saints". The fundamental moral values of an essentially egalitarian
earthly community were not capable of being expressed through a
hierarchically defined religious community.
As one analyzes the villagers' complaints about the priest, jokes
and satirical stories about priestly seduction of women (and vice
versa), one can begin to see that what was being questioned was
explicitly the privileged position of the priest to mediate between
man and God, to have exclusive responsibility for ritual performance,
exclusive control of sacramental graces, and to be responsible to
the upper hierarchy rather than the local congregation.
In many ways, a priest who fulfils his vows of chastity and
lives a celibate life becomes a more controversial local figure than
the married priest -- or the priest whose housekeeper is his 'niece'
and clearly recognized as his mistress. The issue, especially for
male parishioners, was the right of the priest to present himself
as 'special', a specialness built on a superior moral character
(demonstrated through celibacy) which was then used to justify the
priest's right to be a 'moral authority'. The priest, through his
vows of celibacy and chastity, was presented to male and female
parishioners alike as a man who was like no other man. On the surface, an attack on sexuality, I think that similarly to what Ortner
(1978) reports for the Sherpas, priestly celibacy is in fact an
attack on the institution of marriage, and particularly on men who
are less 'special', precisely because they are involved in a marriage.
The issues that come through in São Miguel life whether we examine

conflicts over sacraments, *festas*, or morality rest on fundamentally
different views of the meaning of religion and hierarchy presented
in the person of the priest versus that accepted by both male and
female parishioners. With the exception of death rituals, the importance of the Church in daily life is almost exclusively as the
locale for communal/public activities. Even those individuals who
go to Church most often -- namely, women -- go not merely for their
personal salvation but to assure the health and success of the
other members of the family. The villagers saw religion, especially
through rituals, as defining community and placing individuals as
members of the community. All members of the community were entitled to the necessary sacraments; the priest was not to be the
arbitrator of the dispensation.

The issue of morality on which the priest took the strongest
stance was the question of 'dancing' -- an activity that was viewed
by him as leading to the release of unbridled sexual passion. In
São Miguel, the issues of birth control were rarely mentioned in
the Church. Villagers had little acquaintance with any contra-
conceptive devices, but family size was limited through abstinence,
coitus interruptus, and abortions (Riegelhaupt 1964). The immorality
of dancing was one of the key reasons cited by the priest for con-
structing the *salão*. In addition, he mobilized civil authorities to
refuse to grant permits for dances and he refused to participate
in *festas* associated with dancing, thus antagonizing most of the
villagers. When the villagers spoke against the priest's right to
legislate their morality, they most often invoked the unlikelihood
that any man actually remained celibate as ammunition supporting
their disavowal of his moral rulings.

In most of the preceding discussion, I have not distinguished
between male and female hostility to the priest. Unlike other
ethnographic reports, I did not find that anticlericalism was a
uniquely male attitude. Instead, in São Miguel I observed and
listened to tirades against the priest from both women and men. Yet,
as in most other Mediterranean communities, Church attendance was
overwhelmingly female.

Men, having expressed anticlerical attitudes and actions, used
their wives as religious proxies in much the same way as Christian
(1972) reports in Spain. Women who were anticlerical were often
much more conflicted, since their domestic roles made them responsible for the ritual well-being of their households.

Visitors to Portugal throughout the Salazar period repeatedly
commented on the sense of 'fatalism' and 'sadness' that seemed to
characterize Portuguese life. Village life -- black-clothed women
darting in and out among whitewashed houses, while peasant men were
isolated in their individual fields -- seemed to reassert the same
attitudes. If the confession lists were rolls of *'Desobrigar'*

(obligation) from the nineteenth century on, so, too, was the constantly expressed sense that life was to be endured and was under the control of God. The idioms of Roman Catholicism permeated the language. *"Se Deus quiser"* (if God wills) was interspersed as a constant litany in everyday conversation. Few events were seen as transpiring positively unless God willed. The unstated assumption also appeared to be that God rarely willed in your favor. Concurrent with the fatalism apparent in this view was the negativity that characterized the dialogue between individuals. Not only need 'God will' for any event to transpire, but at a parallel level in interpersonal relations one assumed a refusal of each request. One heard, repeatedly, the phrase *"pois não"* (of course not), particularly in the double negative (as in "you're not going to the store, of course not"). São Miguelitos saw no way to alter the conditions of their existence, either individually or collectively. Both locally, and nationally, the longing for some glorious past -- the Portuguese *'saudades'* and the mournful *Fado* -- became the national symbols in a country explicitly ruled through a Catholic ideology. How much of this sadness can be related to the inability of the Portuguese villagers to find solace and meaning in the symbols of Catholicism, I do not know. I do not find it inconceivable, however, that the conflict and tensions that separated parishioner from priest exacerbated the situation, particularly, I suspect, for village women.

Anticlericalism, at the village level, may thus be seen to contribute to a structural, emotional, and psychological ambiguity: both a need and desire to participate and a need and desire not to be subordinated, a balanced stand-off in the acceptance and rejection of Catholicism, the only available belief system in the *Estado Novo.* Analysts can argue endlessly about the symbolic significance of celibacy, about the place of women (Mary and Eve) in Catholic ideology (Warner 1976); yet all of that analysis, to be culturally significant, assumes a certain acceptance by the population about such issues.

São Miguel's priest saw himself as a missionary to pagan people. His secular and clerical actions contributed to an open and active anticlericalism among the population. Rituals, from baptism to funerals and festivals, although participated in by the people, were enacted with resentment. Parents were fined if they delayed a baptism and *compadres* of baptism and marriage were declared ineligible. Few men assisted voluntarily in the organization of festivals; most were coerced into their roles because of their dependence upon the priest as patron. *Promessas* and the carrying of *cargas* became less and less frequent and one rarely heard of people reciting *novenas.* Few homes had saints or madonnas or other religious art apart from a painting of the Last Supper or a picture

of the shrine of *Bom Jesus* in Braga and a cross. These pictures
often hung next to a portrait of the last Portuguese King and
were as significant of religiosity as the King's portrait was indicative of monarchist sentiments.

To the Church, São Miguel was one of many 'dechristianized' areas
of central and southern Portugal. But São Miguelitos were not anti-
Christian, nor did they see themselves as lesser Christians. They
just refused to be practising Catholics as demanded by the priest.
Since the *Estado Novo* severely limited forms of associability, the
only manifestation of anticlericalism possible in São Miguel was
the negative act of refusing to participate in Church rites and
rituals: to refuse to practise and to cut oneself off from belief.
Anticlericalism was in itself a belief. Among the villagers, however, it existed apart from any rationalistic questioning of faith.
Yet, given the organization of Catholicism, access to faith and
the required rites and rituals was only possible through the priest.
Thus, for many São Miguelitos participation as a Catholic became
unattainable and no other positive belief system was available.
Their 'anticlericalism' was intrinsically related to their un-
willingness to submit to the priest's hierarchical power, secular
and religious. Saints may be appropriate mediators to God and
patrons to communities, but on earth, "priests are not saints".

NOTES

* An earlier paper on a similar theme, "The Church, Anticlericalism
  and Religiosity: A Portuguese Perspective", was presented at the
  Social Science Historical Association meetings in October 1977.
  I am indebted to members of the panel for their constructive
  comments, and to Tom Bruneau, Muriel Dimen-Schein, Shirley Lin-
  denbaum, M. Filomena Monica, and Jaime Reis for their helpful
  criticisms of that earlier work.
1. Gil Vicente (1465-1537) is a pre-Trent Portuguese author whose
   works frequently attack "the worldliness of Rome, the sale of
   indulgences, the mechanical prayers, and the incompetency of the
   clergy (Serrão 1971:294).
2. Fieldwork in Portugal was undertaken in 1960-1962 under a grant
   from the National Institute of Mental Health (MF 12,360). Return
   visits were made in 1964, 1968, 1971 and 1976, but the bulk of
   the ethnographic material on religion comes from the first extended stay, and the present tense is used in describing events
   during that time. Consequently, this paper discusses Portuguese
   Catholicism pre-Vatican Council II and well before the Portuguese
   'Revolution' of 1974 which overthrew the *Estado Novo*. Under the
   Estado Novo, according to a Portuguese Jesuit, the impact of the

Council's actions on the Portuguese Church were minimal
(Dominguez quoted in Bruneau 1976:473). In the first two years
following the overthrow of the regime, the national Church
kept a very low profile and even the most radical provisional
governments "scrupulously avoided attacks on the Church" (Bruneau
1976:483). Since the summer of 1976, particularly at the parish
and diocese level, the Church has played an increasingly controversial and visible role. For an impressionistic report on the
role of the Church and a priest in a small central Portuguese
village in January 1976, see Jean Tavares' article in *Les Temps
Modernes*. A brief report on the status of the Church in Portugal
is to be found in Grohs 1976.
3. More than half of the second and third grade readings (only four
years of school were compulsory) were either biblical stories,
exemplary stories or explicit instructions in Christian doctrine.
One cannot say that the villagers were untutored; rather one
would have to say that they had strong disagreements with the
priest over what being a Catholic meant.
4. Although the terms 'elite' and 'popular' may not be the best, the
distinction between an anticlericalism which arises from an
ideological position and an anticlericalism which is focused on
everyday events is important. Thus in his review of anticlericalism, Jose Sanchez writes, "modern anticlericalism grew out
of the practices and attitudes of the cismontane and philosophi-
cal anticlericals, ... shaped by ... three dominating ideologies,
liberalism, nationalism and socialism" (1972:79). Moreover, in
his analysis, "the complete success of the secular revolution
in the twentieth century brought an end to anticlerical tensions
and conflict". While this may be true in terms of national
politics, it does not explain the persistence of 'popular anticlericalism'.
5. An analysis of the role of the Church in the Salazar regime is
beyond the scope of this essay. Yet, to understand the range of
'religiosity' that existed within Portugal -- the difference
between the 'religious' north and the 'dechristianized' south --
one must take into consideration a number of historical events
as well as state structure. At a minimum, to understand the
local issues that provoked anticlericalism one must recognize
the diversity in the structure of agrarian society in Portugal
as well as the source of recruitment to the priesthood. Whether
the priest is viewed as allied to the landlords (Cutileiro 1971);
as an outsider and an agent of the State (Riegelhaupt, this work);
or a local son who is one of us (Brettell 1978: personal communication; Tavares 1976); has important implications for the
way in which a given priest both exercises, and is seen as exercising, his political/religious authority.

BIBLIOGRAPHY

Bellah, R.N.
  1970   *Beyond Belief*. New York: Harper & Row.
Bossy, J.
  1970   The Counter-Reformation and the People of Catholic Europe.
          Past and Present 47:51-70.
Bruneau, Th.C.
  1976   Church and State in Portugal: Crises of Cross and Sword.
          Journal of Church and State 18(3):463-490.
Christian, W.A. Jr.
  1972   *Person and God in a Spanish Valley*. New York: Seminar Press.
Cutileiro, J.
  1971   *A Portuguese Rural Society*. Oxford: Clarendon.
Grohs, G.
  1976   The Church in Portugal After the Coup of 1974. *Iberian
          Studies* (Keele) V (1):34-40.
LeRoy Ladurie, E.
  1978   *Montaillou*. New York: George Brazillier.
Leite de Vasconcellos, J.
  1958   *Etnografia Portuguesa* IV:508-546. Lisboa: Imprensa Nacional.
Lisón-Tolosana, C.
  1966   *Belmonte de los Caballeros: A Sociological Study of a
          Spanish Town*. Oxford: Clarendon.
Magraw, R.
  1970   The Conflict in the Villages: Popular Anticlericalism in
          the Isère (1852-1870). In: T. Zeldin (ed.), *Conflicts in
          French Society*. London: Allen and Unwin, pp. 169-227.
Ortner, S.
  1978   *Sherpas Through Their Rituals*. Cambridge: Cambridge
          University Press.
Riegelhaupt, J.F.
  1964   In the Shadow of the City. Columbia University: Unpublished
          Ph.D. Dissertation.
  1973   Festas and Padres: The Organization of Religious Action
          in a Portuguese Parish. *American Anthropologist* 75(3):
          835-852.
  1977   The Church, Anticlericalism and Religiosity: A Portuguese
          Perspective. Paper presented at Social Science Historical
          Association Meetings, October, mss.
  1979   The Corporate State and Village Non-Politics. In: L. Graham
          and H. Makler (eds.), *Contemporary Portugal*. Austin:
          University of Texas Press, pp. 167-190.
Sanchez, J.
  1972   *Anticlericalism*. South Bend: Notre Dame University Press.

Serrão, J. (ed.)
  1971 *Dicionario de Historia de Portugal* IV:294.
Tavares, J.
  1976 Les paysans, l'église et la politique dans un village
      portugais. *Les Temps Modernes* 31 (360) :2234-2274.
Warner, M.
  1976 *Alone of all Her Sex: The Myth and the Cult of the Virgin*
      Mary. New York: Knopf.
Zeldin, T.
  1970 The Conflict of Moralities: Confession, Sin and Pleasure
      in the Nineteenth Century. In: T. Zeldin (ed.), *Conflicts*
      in French Society. London: Allen and Unwin, pp. 13-50.

Mafia Burlesque: The Profane Mass as a Peace-making Ritual

Jane Schneider, City University of New York, and Peter Schneider, Fordham University

Long dominated by an economy dedicated to the production of cereals on large estates in alternation with pastoralism, Western Sicily displays a settlement pattern in which peasants live clustered around urban nuclei, rather than dispersed in villages, hamlets or home- steads on the land. The resulting, widely spaced 'agrotowns' are compact and large, ranging in size from around 2,000 to over 50,000 inhabitants. In addition, they are sufficiently complex and strati- fied to contain within them a number of full-time, non-agricultural specialists such as merchants, artisans, bureaucrats and profession- als. In the late 1960s, we conducted field work in one such locality, an agrotown of approximately 7,500 population that we call Villamaura.

During our residence in Villamaura, the butchers' cooperative that monopolized the local retailing of meat entered into a truce with a family firm of meat wholesalers from Solera, pseudonym for another, slightly smaller, agrotown about an hour and a half drive away. A year before this event, the two parties had quarrelled over the Villamaura butchers' refusal to place an order for meat that, according to the Solera wholesalers, they were obligated to buy under a prior agreement. Instrumental in arranging the truce was a third group, the leader of which, also a butcher, brought the litigants together in the back room of a butcher shop in Villamaura. This third group, the initiators of the truce, lived in a small city, here called Palazzoverde, almost as far to the west of Villamaura as Solera is to the north, and having a population of about 31,000. The back room negotiation also included a fourth party, the merchant who had supplied Villamaura's meat since the quarrel. His home town, pseudonym Montebello, is one of the smaller and more isolated of West Sicilian settlements, its barely 3,000 inhabitants nestled in the shadow of a medieval castle on a high promontory that is visible from Villamaura, being a half-hour drive away.

The truce had a great deal going for it, especially the prestige of its organizers, who came from the most commercially developed center of the southwest Sicilian interior, and were well connected to the political machine of the regional Christian Democratic Party. The presence of the Montebello merchant also augured well for peace. This man was a dilettante in the commerce of meat, and had felt uneasy in his role as temporary competitor of the powerful wholesaler from Solera, fearing that he might in the end lose the affection of both sides to the quarrel. Yet no one present felt convinced that handshakes, hugs, and a round of toasts could guarantee the new agreement. Modern, capital-intensive processing plants were threatening to reorder the commerce of meat and, furthermore, some of the participants were mafiosi -- men known to settle disputes arising out of economic competition without resort to the law courts of the state, where necessary resorting to violence or its threat.

And so the Palazzoverde peace-makers proposed a *tavoliddu*, a feast to celebrate and cement the truce. As it turned out, five banquets materialized in four different places over a period of about three months, and Peter Schneider, having been present at the initial peace-making, was invited to each. As such he was witness to a pseudo-religious ritual that highlighted the banquets, becoming more and more outrageous as time went on. Performed the first time with apparent spontaneity, its main components were nonetheless familiar, having many parallels in Sicily and other European settings over the past several hundred years. This paper confronts the problem of how to account for such parallels without treating contemporary manifestations of a ritual theme as vestiges of an eternal, or 'primordial' tradition; and also without analyzing this theme in terms of an abstract function such as 'the maintenance of social or order'.

To begin with, a description of the feasts. The first banquet unfolded in a rustic country house outside of Palazzoverde, where the peace-making hosts, assisted by local friends, prepared a splended fish stew, followed by roast meat, vegetables, fruits and dessert, and accompanied by abundant wine. No women either attended this affair, or contributed cooked food -- this was the case as well on subsequent occasions. The central figure of the host group was Don Totò, a butcher who was nicknamed 'Vescovo' (Bishop) because in his youth he had wanted to be a priest, and now lived unmarried with a spinster sister, as priests often do. Vescovo (names and nicknames are fictitious in this account) was closely connected to the diocese of Palazzoverde, and was reputed to control several hundred votes -- enough to be a king-maker for Christian Democratic politicians in the area. He was joined by his cousin, Mimo, an accountant for an exporting firm in Palazzoverde, and Pippo G., reputed to be of gentry background and a 'man about town' who was not regularly employed.

Vescovo, Mimo and Pippo sat at the middle of a long table, immediately surrounded by other close friends and relatives from Palazzoverde. At one end of the table sat the meat wholesaler, his

son, and a distinguished elder statesman mafioso from a settlement
near their home town of Solera. Facing them at the other end of the
long banquet table were three butchers of Villamaura and their
friends. The merchant from Montebello and his support group (consisting of a cheese merchant, two animal traders, and a building
contractor) shared the middle of the table with the peace-makers
from Palazzoverde. Vescovo was master of ceremonies, frequently
standing to propose toasts -- to the elder statesman present, to the
value of friends, to the greater importance of friendship than
money, and to the meal as an occasion for friends to get together.

Towards the end of the dinner, he, Mimo and Pippo disappeared
into a small store room for a few minutes, to emerge ringing a bell,
and draped in tablecloths and other paraphernalia as priestly vestments. With Pippo holding a beach umbrella over his head, and
Vescovo assisting, Mimo, the accountant, sang a mass. This liturgy
had the rhythm and tone of an official Latin service, but was sung
in dialect, and was a ribald commentary on the people who were
present, the food and wine they had consumed, and the behavior of
their wives and daughters. Instead of 'amen' at the end of each
verse, the congregation was led to chant 'minghia' (prick). This
transformation broke the tension that had been building during the
verse, and left members of the congregation doubled over in laughter.
The mass was then followed by singing and dancing, in which some of
the bon vivants from Palazzoverde performed erotic parodies of women
doing a strip tease.

At each subsequent feast, both meal and mass (now nicknamed the
'*messa minghiata*') became more elaborate. On the second occasion, the
butchers of Villamaura prepared octopus, goat stew, and roast lamb,
which they served at a rustic restaurant in the countryside near
town. At Montebello, three weeks later, the banquet took place in
the summer house of an employee of the public utility company, a
friend of the interim meat merchant. There was an even greater
abundance of food at this event, and wine flowed through two tubes
with spigots attached, that were suspended over the table from
barrels on the second floor. Just as the last chorus of the mass was
fading out, everyone was startled by a great burst of fireworks from
outside the villa.

By the Montebello banquet, which was number three, the roster of
guests had grown to over 50, as the principal participants began to
invite other friends. A few of the additions were of lower status
than the men in the original four groups -- for example, a drummer
whom Pippo knew, and three soccor players from Palermo invited by
the wholesaler's son. Others were of equal or higher status, being
notables or professionals of the town involved. In fact, the mayor,
vice-mayor, veterinarian and two priests from Villamaura so enjoyed
themselves at the second and third banquets that they joined in

hosting a fourth one, held in the same country restaurant as the second. Inspired by events at Montebello, the Villamaura butchers also commissioned a fireworks display as a finale to the mass at this banquet. Unfortunately the fireworks specialist, jeopardizing his future career as a pyrotechnician at religious festivals in south-western Sicily, failed to show.

He redeemed himself, however, with a brilliant display at the last banquet, which the Solera wholesaler and his friends hosted at a large resort area restaurant on the southern coast. Nearly a hundred people attended this occasion, including the fire chief and veterinarian of the port city in whose territory the restaurant was located. As someone quipped, only the police were missing. All present welcomed the opportunity to mingle in an atmosphere that by its congeniality encouraged the consolidation of agreements and deals. Here, moreover, the 'entertainment committee' -- still Pippo, Mimo and Vescovo -- outdid itself, Pippo having brought along pink silk women's underwear with lace trim, a pink satin nightgown and a hooded black satin cape. Creating an illusion of breasts with plump Sicilian oranges, he spent the latter part of the evening cavorting about in drag.

Several aspects of the banquets evoke Christian imagery, or its opposite. First, they partook of an ancient feasting tradition which the Reader's Guide to New (Cambridge) Bible traces to the belief that "a common meal creates a close bond". From this the word, company, whose Latin root, co-panis, means to break bread together. Vescovo and others consistently referred to the assembled guests as 'la compania'. The best known feast of the New Testament is of course the Last Supper, where Jesus explicitly chose food and drink to be the symbols of the body and blood that he would sacrifice for the redemption of humanity. Perhaps Vescovo had this meal in mind when on the occasion of the first banquet, he placed himself at the center of a long narrow table, from which position he delivered speech after speech on friendship. More than familiar with the Last Supper's ritual representation in the Catholic mass, where table is altar, he knew the message that "by means of a meal, two or more persons unite their lives as they share human sustenance". The mass creates the "family of the Christian Church", explains the *New Catholic Encyclopedia.* "No Christian who understands what takes place in this sacred assembly of God and people can withdraw into an isolated world of individualism".

But the banqueters also understood another message inherent in Last Supper symbolism: that among the participants there may be a potential traitor, a person who, after enjoying the pleasures of eating and drinking in company, is nevertheless capable of committing a hostile act. Most no doubt knew the myth of the classic mafia-style murder, recorded by Alongi in 1886. The killer, or his agent, attracts his victim, already condemned for vendetta, to a clamorous *tavoliddu* for the purpose of feigning a reconciliation sealed by food, drink, toasts to the health of adversaries, a hug and a kiss. This kiss, wrote Alongi, is a Judas kiss of coming death when the friendliness of the banquet, warmly remembered by witnesses, will serve to convince a judge of the killer's innocence (1886:151).

In fact, the tension of the butchers' quarrel with the wholesaler, which had occasioned the banquets in the first place, never dissolved except when laughter obliterated every other emotion. The wholesaler's son invited three friends, semi-professional soccer players from Palermo, to the banquet at Montebello. As they were also friends of Vescovo, and without sensing that they were only marginally part of the company, they began to tease him and mock his more or less serious attempts at preaching. Provoked by their rudeness, another person who was close to both Vescovo and the butchers of Villamaura, became angry and heatedly rose to denounce them. The soccer players were offended and stormed out of the house, closely followed by the wholesaler's son shouting, "you have insulted my friends!" It took another peace initiative on the part of a lawyer from Villamaura together with the mayor from that town, to bring the four young men back into the room, and Vescovo's defender did not appear at the subsequent gatherings.

If the banquets called to mind a great deal of Christian symbolism concerning food and social relations, they also mocked the Church, emphasizing transgressions that in theory it abhorred. For example, in contrast to the supposed asceticism of monks and clergy, the tables were laden with tempting foods, meat playing a central role. Indeed, two or more courses of mutton, sausage, goat, ragu of beef or innards, supplemented a fish course at every meal, and were in every case the sort of red flesh that threatens piety. Even more provocative was the titilating mass, built around obscenities and the blurring of male and female. Banquet entertainment, in short, consisted in those rituals of reversal that, with carnival burlesque, have enlivened Christianity for hundreds of years.

How do social scientists interpret such rituals and what kinds of interpretation best illuminate the reasons for, and characteristics of, the sacreligious pattern of banquet revelry described here? For many historians, folklorists and early anthropologists, inversions and reversals constitute magical rites of pagan past whose contemporary presence is not all that problematic. Consistent with Tylor's understanding of all survivals, such rites are said to persist, however diluted in form, because "force of habit" carries them forward from an "older condition of culture" into new conditions that evolve (1873:16). A more complex perspective on survivals points to an historical process through which the official religion tolerated pagan practice, because the costs of totally eradicating it were prohibitive, or because tolerance was politically savvy. By letting the people 'play the fool and make merry', the forces of order

channelled resentment into catharsis and recreation, thus avoiding
-- with occasional exception -- an open rebellion against established
norms. Natalie Davis summarizes this position among historians of
European folk culture as follows: rituals of reversal offer relief
when a structure has become too authoritarian, but although they
"can renew the system ... they cannot change it... A world turned
upside down can only be righted, not changed" (1975:97, 131).

Even as it draws attention to a long trajectory, with roots in a
'pre-religious' past, this mode of interpreting rites of reversal is
curiously similar to the functionalist perspective in modern anthropology. In common are assumptions regarding the existence of an
'established order', or established norms, that are reflected in,
and bolstered by, religious institutions, and the idea that farcical,
mocking rituals in the long run reinforce that order. Whereas the
historian/evolutionist locates the conservative mechanism in the
recreational and diversionary aspects of ritual, however, the modern
functionalist sees it also in symbolic content. Thus Victor Turner,
in a general commentary on ritual process, argues that rites of
inversion "make visible in their symbolic and behavioral patterns
social categories and forms of grouping that are considered to be
axiomatic and unchanging...". While emotionally, nothing satisfies
as much as extravagant or temporarily permitted illicit behavior,
"it is also the case that cognitively, nothing underlines regularity
so well as absurdity or paradox" (1969:176). By turning men into
women, the mass into farce, abstinence into gluttony, upside-down
rituals dramatize the parameters of their opposite: an ordered social
world.

It should not surprise us that there are continuities between the
evolutionism that is implicit in a long historical trajectory, and
the idea, so pivotal to Turner's thinking, that ritual must be
understood in terms of what it does for society. At the core of
Durkheim's social science are the interwoven concepts of, on the one
hand, vastly different orders each held together by mechanical or
organic forms of solidarity, and, on the other hand, a quite straightforward process of increased differentiation and division of labor
as the means for moving from one of these orders to the other. Nor
does organic solidarity replace its mechanical forerunner in Durkheimian thought. The latter persists at the level of family and
community from whence, in ritual form, it bursts through the organi-
cally integrated structures of estate and class to temporarily
reassert its fundamentally egalitarian and undifferentiated ethos.
In Turner's view, the principle of group unity keeps the principle
of hierarchy in some sort of balance or proportion. Exemplary are
rituals in which the low mimic and degrade the high, laymen their
priests, serfs their lords. At one and the same time such rituals
foster the experience of community solidarity and "underline the

reasonableness of everyday culturally predictable behavior between
the various estates of society" (ibid.:175-176).

Turner, in discussing the connection between rituals of reversal
and the reinforcement of a hierarchically organized social order,
suggests that the message is strengthened by structural regularity.
Thus such rites tend to be calendrical: associated with fixed or
moveable, annually recurring festivities such as, in the Christian
calendar, Carnival, Hallowe'en, Christmas mumming (ibid.:177).
Already we have a problem with our mafioso banquets where an obscene
and topsy-turvy mass developed with apparent spontaneity as a unique
event. Most participants, upon being asked if they had witnessed
such goings-on before, said no, although a few had and most knew
stories about other, similar occasions. A return visit to Sicily in
1977, eleven years after the cycle, provided the information that
there had been no elaborate ritual *tavoliddi* involving the meat
trades in the interim.

Apart from their non-calendric aspect, the mafia banquets and
their associated rituals pose another problem related to the kinds
of people who attended. An evolutionary functionalist understanding
of mocking rituals leads us to anticipate their appearance in the
periphery, on the margins of society, in the most 'primitive' groups.
By implication such arenas lie closer to a remote and pagan past, an
egalitarian and undifferentiated baseline, an experience with
mystical (as distinct from social) power -- perhaps even to a social
form in which human instincts are relatively unrepressed. Frequently
this expectation has a geography. Thus LeRoy Ladurie observes that
in the South of France, the devil resided where people were
"entrenched in their crannies", isolated by the rugged Pyrenees from
the Catholic mass. Here, in these magical mountains, mythical thought
regularly turned the world upside down (1969:169).

Our case suggests a different pattern for, although the meat
dealers and butchers, the cheese merchants and elder-statesmen
mafiosi, had social and genealogical antecedents in the semi-pastoral
groups that once dominated the mountainous Sicilian interior (see Schneider
and Schneider, 1976), they were also entrepreneurs in a commercially
developed country. Like the contractors, businessmen, and public
officials whom they invited to join the 'company', they were 'middle
class'. In other words, the *messa minghiata* of the mafioso banquets
was neither a calendric ritual nor the folk practice of backward
peasants magically bringing down their overlords. Hardly a regular
event of the isolated, it was an isolated event among much engaged
men. Rather than deal with it as an exception to a general rule,
however, we have looked for parallels elsewhere.

An interesting example is suggested by a brief and incomplete
description of events at Bohemian Grove, in contemporary North
America (Anderson 1981). There, each year, the exclusive San

Francisco Bohemian Club organizes a two-week encampment in the
California redwoods for such national leaders as Ronald Reagan,
George Bush, Caspar Weinberger, Richard Nixon, David Rockefeller,
William French Smith, William F. Buckley, Gerald Ford and others
(some 2,000 in all). Far away from public scrutiny and in all-male
company, the participants eat, drink, carouse and revel at "the
world's most elegant stag party". Rituals highlight their good times.
In one, a torch of fellowship ignites a symbolic representation of
'Dull Care' in a cremation ceremony that is intended to abolish
every nagging reminder of worldlyresponsibilities. In another, "a
feminine touch is provided ... by club members who dress as women
and put on burlesque shows" (Anderson 1981:16). No more than at the
mafioso banquets in Sicily do these rituals constitute a sentiment-
laden attack on structure, paradoxically supportive of hierarchy in
the end. For at elite and fraternal gatherings, burlesque means
something else. What follows is an historical reconstruction of some
aspects of fraternity and hilarity in Europe intended to project two
quite different functions of ritual reversal. It helps order social
relations among men involved in commercial and related activities in
which mutual trust and the predictability of rules are at issue, and
it lends to such men a measure of autonomy from religious institutions and ideas. Autonomy, and an alternate moral order, rather than
emotive opposition to structure, are, we propose, key social processes underlying various examples of profanity and burlesque among
emergent bourgeois cliques.

Before proceeding, let us briefly examine the concept 'bourgeois',
in many ways so nuanced by its association with industrial capitalism as to no longer convey its simple (and original) meaning --
namely citizen or freeman who is neither lord nor peasant, and who
lives in a more or less urbanized settlement. Defined as such, the
word is convenient shorthand for the heterogeneous nexus of shopkeepers and artisans, traders and professionals who in the past
articulated local populations with a mercantile network of long
distance trade. 'Bourgeois' in this sense did not refer to the great
merchant-financiers who controlled the purchase and sale of imported
luxuries, who capitalized indigenous cloth industries through the
putting out of raw materials, and who were close to, or wanted to
become, nobles. It did, however, identify a social stratum that
arose because, over centuries, the expansion of foreign exchange,
and of manufacturing within Europe, drew even remote populations
into a money economy in which some, though never all, goods were
produced for local and extra-local exchange. Nascent bourgeois were
the specialists -- often the semi-specialists -- who managed the
more local and regional aspects of this circulation process, and
whose workshops and small factories produced imitations and
substitutions of luxury wares for local consumption. Such direct

producers and small-scale traders influenced the surrounding rural
populations in which they were embedded without, however, seriously
disrupting them. We would recognize their descendants today in what
we call 'local business communities', the middle class elites of
neighborhoods and small towns. Because in the interim the word
bourgeois has become a synonym for manufacturers who, in the wake
of the industrial revolution, invest in capital-intensive technology
and mobilize wage labor, we now qualify its application to local
businessmen calling them 'petit bourgeois'.

A recent book by Michael Tigar, assisted by Madeleine Levy, *Law
and the Rise of Capitalism* (1977), provides us with a useful entrée
into the problems of a fledgling and internally fragmented medieval
'bourgeoisie', attempting to forge its own institutions in a sea of
customary or feudal, and ecclesiastical or Canon, law. Neither legal
system was sympathetic to activities that took place outside the
jurisdiction of feudal lords, of whom the Church was the greatest,
for although both lords and Church encouraged trade and craft
manufacture from which they stood to benefit, they did so only to
the extent that they could control these enterprises themselves.

The development of relations between Church and merchants is
especially instructive. Canon law incorporated enough of Roman law,
as codified by Justinian, to enable ecclesiastical courts to invite
cases having to do with the enforcement of contracts, and limited
liability in corporate groups. Moreover, as Tigar and Levy point out,
the Church "could not ignore the great wealth that trade accumulated,
for only by tapping that wealth could ecclesiastical rulers build
cathedrals and universities and live in the style to which they had
become accustomed" (ibid.:41). And so we find the Church supporting
merchants "against monarchs or feudal lords" and attempting to
"bring commerce within its universal system of theology, morals and
law" (ibid.:41-42). Yet an insurmountable trap ensued from the fact
that merchants could not know where they stood in relation to Canon
Law. In some times and places it was policy to permit, in others to
suppress, such practices as taking interest on loans, monopoly
pricing and the expropriation of debtors (ibid.:106). Even where
the Church helped businessmen to evade its strictures (since it
"stood to gain when they succeeded in business"), it persisted in
the message that had been a cornerstone of its ideology from the
days of Jesus and the apostles -- that an overly rapid accumulation
of wealth was anti-social and jeopardized a merchant's soul. Of
course, a soul in jeopardy could be saved through substantial contributions to the Church, but this stood squarely in the way of
wealth accumulation in private hands. Only long-distance traders,
located in commercially and financially precocious core regions
such as northern Italy, escaped this dilemma; here, in fact, merchant
families were bankers to, and creditors of, the papacy, and even gave

rise to popes (ibid.:102-110).

The ambivalent position of small-scale merchant and artisan groups in relation to the Church's moral and legal order was the source of a great deal of autonomous institution-building on their part. Such were the groups which, from the Middle Ages, formed associations, fraternities and guilds whose corporate status and commitment to a formal equality among members resembled, and yet opposed, the monastic cell. These associations made their own laws -- a kind of 'third law' as some call it -- and set up their own tribunals. Their associates co-swore mutual aid in the name of brotherhood and friendship, under oaths that took precedence over testimony in other courts. Tigar and Levy show that the most developed form of bourgeois association in the medieval period was the 'commune', a collective of "several dozen to several hundred artisans, lords' officials, minor clerics, peasants, runaway serfs and others" who pledged not only internal equality and mutual aid, but commitment to a life of struggle for the removal of "all manufacturing and trading functions ... from the body of feudal life". According to these authors, the "oath to struggle for such a severance of feudal bonds was called 'communal', and the term 'commune' variously described the oath, the oath-swearers, and the area" in which the right to make laws, administer justice, regulate artisans, protect escaped serfs, hold daily markets and periodic fairs, was claimed (ibid.:83-87). Although communards had an active religious life, "they paid little attention to the Church hierarchy and had little patience with tithes" (ibid.:88).

Through a series of strikingly similar charters, feudal and ecclesiastical lords -- also a few monarchs and princes -- granted legal status to communes in cities and towns along routes of trade. It is a reasonable hypothesis that ritual innovation helped form the resulting 'communities', both internally and in relation to other domains. Such, at least, is a conclusion implicit in the work of Natalie Davis, an historian of culture in urban France of the fourteenth through seventeenth centuries. Her account of Misrule Abbeys will illustrate this point. A Misrule Abbey was a group of men who constituted themselves as a court with jurisdiction over a small settlement or neighborhood in a town or city. These courts punished certain vices or faults, intervened in domestic crises, suppressed dissent, patched up quarrels, and generally promoted peace and amity. But they did so through means quite alien to the rival ecclesiastical courts, city councils and rudimentary judicial arms of parliaments or kings. Their principal means of law enforce- ment was the performance of outlandish and hilarious rites, aimed at humiliating wrongdoers en encouraging rivals to suppress their enmity in frolic. In Davis's words, the Abbeys had a 'carnival licence' to conduct charivaris and impose fines. They were not

unlike other forms of popular recreation, fools' societies, play
acting groups, that developed in similar places and at similar times
(1975:97-124).

Two things strike us as significant about the Misrule Abbeys:
their social composition and their mockery of the Church. Regarding
the former, Davis notes that in the earliest centuries of their
existence, and in the most rural settings, the abbeys were often
joined by young, unmarried men, not yet regularly employed. But
later, and in more urban contexts, craftsmen, merchants and lawyers
formed the courts. The merchants were of the small and medium type,
as distinct from great merchant-financiers, and the lawyers were
also 'petit', although they were literate (ibid.:111-115). These
were precisely the sorts of emergent bourgeois for whom Canon law
was such an obstacle and it is interesting how much anti-clerical
burlesque was involved in the idea of 'misrule'. For example, words
like Pleasure, Folly, Sexuality and Improvidence were part of the
Abbey names and in a mocking commentary on the presumed sobriety of
real monastic life, 'judges' in the misrule courts regularly masked,
mummed and dressed as women. Davis reviews the various interpreta-
tions of transvestite imagery that anthropologists and historians
have put forth, including its capacity to communicate a blurring of
social boundaries and overturning of power relations -- its capacity
also to serve as a symbol of fertility. Her conclusion is that from
a very early time, the most powerful message of transvestitism was
"its carnavalesque derision of the celibate priestly hierarchy"
(ibid.:138). Priests and bishops, cenobetics and mendicants, were
the targets of a ridiculing attack.

The idea that nascent bourgeois sought to establish a moral order
autonomous of ecclesiastical institutions, and that they did so
through a rich associational and cultural life, is substantiated by
the Church's tendency to alternately suppress, regulate and coopt
fraternities, guilds and carnival-type rituals. Above all in the
wake of the Reformation, at the Council of Trent, bourgeois associations were looked upon as, in John Bossy's words, "something like
an alternative model of the Church ..." (1970:58). In the name of
papal authority the Council not only designed a system of parochial
conformity to be spread through education, confession and the
obligatory partaking of communion; it also took away the independence
of fraternities by bringing them "under a rigorous regime of episcopal authorization and supervision" (ibid.:57-60). From this effort
there developed centralized fraternity-federations or arch-
confraternities, attached to papally sponsored devotions like the
Sacred Heart of Jesus and the Eucharist. The diocese of Agrigento
in Sicily legitimized local branches of four such confraternities
for Villamaura between 1536 and 1631 (Giacone 1932). As in other
cases, legitimacy was predicated upon the dedication of fraternity

brothers not to a rigid asceticism -- that was reserved for monks and clergy -- but to sobriety, zeal and charitable good deeds. A growing presence of miracle-working Jesuits in the sixteenth and seventeenth centuries, plus the promise of free and automatic indulgences to brothers of the new associations, encouraged the ascendence of restraint over the fraternal rowdiness of the past.

In a way one must see the post-Reformation Church competing for souls not only with Protestants, but with the bourgeoisie of all those regions of Europe that emerged from the Religious Wars still in the Catholic camp. This meant curtailing the ability of merchant and artisan guilds to adopt as patron saints personalities who had not been canonized by Rome. Nor was it encouraged for guilds and fraternities to turn their saints into foci of popular devotion, such that followers would begin to offer sums of money and property to bourgeois associations rather than the various wealth-accumulating bodies of the Church. Where confraternities staged processions and festivals in honor of a saint, they could take up a collection to meet expenses, but episcopal authorities siphoned off accumulations that moved, as surplus, into fraternal mutual aid funds -- as indeed bishops and priests still do today.

In Villamaura, for example, there is right now a contest between the archpriest, an outsider appointed by the bishop, and the confraternity of artisans and wealthy peasants that manages the town's patron saint. The contest is over who shall control all the *lire,* dollars, and jewelry that this lady collects in the course of her annual celebration, with the archpriest staking a claim to everything laid at the statue's feet while it is still in the church, before the processional, and leaving to the confraternity everything else. The dispute has high stakes because this particular saint, the Madonna of Udienza, is a famous fund-raiser. In the early 1900s, when the confraternity failed to get a papal grant that would have bestowed on her and her baby two gold crowns paid for from a Vatican fund, the people of Villamaura brought coins and jewelry to the town's central piazza where a little burner was set up to melt them down. The resulting bullion weighed 6.432 kilograms and was valued at 10,000 lire. It was sent to Palermo to be made up into the desired symbols of regalia, independently of the Pope (Di Ruberto 1904:130-136).

It is surely symptomatic of Church hegemony over the confraternities that many of them contribute substantially to the renovation and upkeep of religious buildings. Also symptomatic is the prominence that Holy Week, and especially the Good Friday processional, now has in the religious calendar. For, during the period of the Counter-Reformation a special effort was made to elevate this observance over all other Saints' celebrations. The penitential tone and death symbolism so characteristic of the rite gained reinforcement from various sources, for example the Reformed Franciscans who constructed catacombs, even in rather remote places like Villamaura (Giacone 1932). Popes and bishops, meanwhile, tried to confine carnival burlesque to a single day, the Sunday before Lent. Their purpose, according to the *Encyclopaedia of Religion and Ethics* (the New Catholic Encyclopaedia has no entry for 'carnival') was to "render popular festivities innocuous by associating them with Christian ideas [and] by a rigid arrangement of the Christian year" that took away "all opportunity for their celebration" (pp. 225-229). Thus carnival coalesced as a relatively unthreatening feast of revelry, folly and license that said farewell (vale) to meat (carne) on the eve of Lent. Its link to bourgeois culture seems nonetheless clear, both from the extent to which famous carnivals are associated with great cities and in the cart (carro) - ship (navale) symbolism of this day of pleasure.

Despite a well-organized effort, neither papal authority, episcopal regulation, nor the expanded powers of the parish priest, nor even the teachings of the Jesuits, could canalize the ritual energies of merchants, artisans and their lawyer friends into the festivities of a single day. Thus, when the seventeenth century bishop of Cefalù, on Sicily's northern coast, attempted to mobilize the fraternities of his diocese to stage Good Friday processions in conformity with the new devotional spirit of the Counter-Reformation, he found himself totally bogged down in correcting abuses: the fraternity members wore masks to carry the Virgin and with rough and vulgar chants they went about inciting laughter instead of piety (Giarrizzo 1978:65-67). More to the point was the tendency, during the eighteenth and nineteenth centuries, for new fraternal associations, uncontaminated by episcopal cooptation, to form not only among merchant, artisan and professional men in towns and cities, but also among an important new category: bourgeois or gentry landowners whose emergence as a class owed everything to the liberal state's expropriation of Church lands. These new fraternities, of which the Freemasons were the most well-known, also proliferated in Protestant countries where bourgeois interests confronted a religious establishment committed to Puritanical values if not to celibacy. It is beyond the scope of the present paper to explore Masonic ritual, except to emphasize how important the gourmet and libertine pleasures of eating and drinking in the company of others were to the men involved.

Now, over the centuries, the Catholic Church became enmeshed in a great many struggles besides those that it waged with the fraternal associations of merchant, artisan and professional groups. Most serious were the challenges posed by the many so-called heresies that sought a return to apostolic poverty and the reform of a clerical hierarchy too corrupted by worldly things to do the will of God.

Serious also was the challenge to follow Christian adventurers and
kings as they expanded the domain under their control far beyond the
boundaries of Europe. To keep up on these two fronts, one internal
and one external, the Church could not fall behind in the interrelated tasks of developing new orders of itinerant friars; alloca-
ting funds to dioceses and parishes; building, purchasing and
restoring real estate; and acquiring productive resources to consolidate gains. It was the need to expand, and the compulsion to
retain hegemony over souls when 'heretics' threatened to mobilize
them, that led to increased demands and restrictions on still-
Catholic bourgeois. We suggest that burlesque rituals of reversal
helped the latter counteract these impositions. Aimed neither at
eliminating religious authority, nor at reinforcing it, such rituals
ordered relations among these bourgeois, at the same time erecting
some semblance of a boundary between them and the Church. In other
words, through ritual, bourgeois groups created their own set of
rules, independent enough of the clerical establishment that they
could benefit from a growth environment, too.

This interpretation differs from the evolutionary functionalist
understanding of topsy-turvy, where the emphasis is on "changeless
oscillation between hierarchy and non-hierarchy", estate-ordered
society and undifferentiated, emotionally bound communitas. As
Richard Werbner has suggested in his introduction to a collection of
essays on African religious cults (1977:xxxiii), this "all-too
familiar pendulum model is inadequate to understand changing interdependence" -- in our case between two overlapping modes of resource
mobilization, one based on a religiously-sanctioned feudalism, and
the other on small manufacturing and mercantile exchange. These
modes did not differ significantly with respect to order. That is,
there is little to be gained in portraying one -- the feudal-
religious one -- as 'the' social order, when both modes consisted of
many distinct and competing parts that, as they expanded and contracted over time, evidenced moments of order, moments of chaos, moments
of structural consolidation and structural demise.

Nor did the two modes differ with respect to the presence or
absence of community, this being a concept of significance to both,
but for different reasons. In Christian theology, community meant
communion; that is, the formation of a fellowship in Christ through
sharing a ritual meal. The mass, however, was never just a spontaneous
outpouring of sentiment in which all are equal. Following policy set
down at Trent, bishops and priests made this ceremony an obligatory
sacrament, and organized confraternities whose mission it was to
further eucharistic devotion. Meanwhile, among bourgeois, community
meant 'commune' -- an institution whose commitment to formal equality
had more to do with creating a favorable climate for various contrac-
tual relationships than with furthering solidarity of the whole.

If rituals of reversal served to consolidate bourgeois communities so that they could expand on a par with the Church, they seem to have done so most explicitly and intensely where these two institutional matrixes evolved in relative isolation from a third force, the state. As Tigar and Levy stress (1977:42-49), bourgeois groups eventually discovered monarchs to be the best endowed and most constant protectors of their interests, preferable by far to lords and Church not only for the increasing efficiency with which they constructed roads and bridges (later canals and railroads), and eliminated internal barriers to trade, but because their judiciary and police apparatus provided a more reliable structure than other courts and customs for the social protection of 'freely moving goods'. As forming states separated lords from the judicial, police and military prerogatives once attached to feudal domain, their alliance with bourgeois interests took on an ever more concrete form. Royal courts enforced legislation that facilitated the expansion of business and protected it from foreign competition, while merchants and craftsmen repaid the state through taxes, duties and financing for foreign wars. The alliance was neither harmonious nor everywhere possible. Significantly, where it was most effective, bourgeois groups also embraced Protestantism; that is, they precipitated a revolt against the Church that went far beyond rebellious rituals to actually bring about a drastic contraction of religious ceremonial and ecclesiastical domain. Contraction on this scale paved the way for a true counter-hegemony, leading to new relations of production based on wage labor.

To find the contexts in which rituals of reversal were and are most significant, we must look to the centuries that preceded the consolidation of modern states in Europe, and to those domains where the institutions of these states, bolstered by industrial capitalism, were slow to penetrate. We are reminded in this search of Gerald Sider's interesting (1976) interpretation of Christmas mumming in nineteenth century Newfoundland, in which he shows that roving clusters of men and women, dressed as their opposites or as animals, extended and underlined relationships of significance to independent producers who sold processed codfish to trans-Atlantic shippers. According to Sider, the culture of mumming had an especially salient role to play in the ordering and reproducing of social relations among these small-scale entrepreneurs because, in their articulation with great mercantile companies, they had no institutions beyond family and community to organize them.

Sicilian mafiosi are in a similar structural position, although not because the Italian state is absent from their world. In their case a relative separation from processes of state formation is the consequence of mafia cliques having challenged the police and judiciary. One can therefore ask about their rituals, as Sider asked about mumming, in what specific ways they helped create a moral order?

First of all, the banquets were good for business. In the hour or
so before each dinner was served, men gathered in pairs and small
clusters to explore the possibility of various deals and contracts.
Many of those present also took the opportunity to enlarge social
networks, joking and talking with others who had theretofore been
strangers but who, because of the feasts, became 'recommended'
friends. Younger participants may even be said to have experienced
the banquets as an initiation ceremony, in which they learned the
most fundamental rule of all commercial activity: that it cannot
advance in the absence of trust among friends. Toasts and convivi-
ality called attention to this maxim, and made it an ideology.

This did not mean, however, that friends must be equal, except in
the formal sense that all are equally obliged to make good on their
word. On the contrary, status differences played an important role
in the proceedings. Elder-statesmen mafiosi sat in special seats and
did the honors of cutting the cake. These statesmen, the notables
present, and all of the participants from Palazzoverde, wore white
shirts, ties and suit jackets, whereas most of the others were
dressed in flannel shirts or casual sweaters. From time to time
Vescovo, the master of ceremonies, commented to a few of the central
participants on the defects of guests whom he felt did not measure
up. Such commentary, also woven into the mass, fostered an atmosphere
of inclusion and exclusion that made the included feel privileged.

According to Arthur Koestler (1964), a good joke is constructed
by gradually bringing together two contradictory planes of thought
so as to create a tension that must then be resolved. The intersection of priestly authority and the solemnity of the mass with a
chorus of *minghias* and a feminized clergy is, for Catholics, potentially a riotous joke. Yet someone might take offense, and the
banqueters knew this. Conversations with the Villamaura butchers
after the first banquet indicated that they were nervous with regard
to the capacity of the Montebello men to understand the sophisticated
antics of Mimo and Pippo. Perhaps they would mistake the transvestite
clowning for homosexuality instead of urbane theater; perhaps they
would even walk out of the next banquet in disgust. As it turned out,
however, the entertainers enjoyed prestige by virtue of their urban
provenience and no one wanted to appear stuffy and provincial in
their presence. Men who were reluctant, at first, quickly convinced
themselves to relax and have a good time. Thus the Montebello
contingent not only laughed heartily at the vulgar mass, but with
considerable delight arranged the surprise burst of fireworks when
it was their turn to host the festivities.

What happened to the Montebello participants was representative
of a general process: the more outrageous the entertainment became,
the more the 'company' felt supportive of the entertainers. How many
other people would have had the guts to stage so daring a performance?

Significantly, among the funniest clowns were the very mediators who
had brought the butchers and the wholesaler together and negotiated
their reconciliation. It would be misleading to argue that the topsy-
turvy mass took place just to help Vescovo paper over a serious
quarrel. But, if anything could reduce a conflict so potentially
disruptive of commercial relations, then one that played on risqué
humor, and the prestige of inclusion in the culturally sophisticated
circles that embellished it, stood a good chance. At the very least,
risqué humor neutralized the tensions that had necessitated the
banquets so that barbed remarks and unpleasant exchanges could not
easily surface to undo the peace.

And so we see that the mafia banquets provided a context for
dispute settlement, and a forum for articulating an ideology of
friendship and trust. As such they reinforced not 'the' social order,
but a kind of moral order among participants. It should be noted that
this order had little to do with participants' responsibilities to a
wider world of clients, constituents, customers, employees, and so
on -- responsibilities that in theory, at least, are a concern of
religion or 'Dull Care'. This is consistent with our argument that
bourgeois culture necessitated autonomy from the hegemony of the
Church, both because the Church was also in the 'business' of mobil-
izing people and resources, and because at its core were ideas about
the danger of usury, indebtedness and foreclosures to its very life
blood -- the souls of the common people.

The argument about autonomy is speculative and difficult to prove,
yet it seems to us worth pursuing because it accounts as no other
explanation can for the *content* of the banquets' major ritual -- an
obscene and vulgar mass performed by men in women's clothes in
mockery of the priesthood, also in mockery of women for their blind
allegiance to the Church.

Given this Church's continued capacity to mobilize people and
resources, acquire property and expand in the world, given also its
continued potential to convincingly stigmatize profit-making as an
immoral and anti-social activity, it is perhaps significant that the
'company' took special pleasure in having two clerics (also a
communist mayor) witness their burlesque goings-on.

NOTE

* This article has previously been published in *Sociologisch Tijd-
  schrift* 9(3):408-433, 1982.

BIBLIOGRAPHY

Alongi, G.
  1886   *La Maffia nei suoi fattori e nelle sue manifestazioni;*
          studio sulle classi pericolose della Sicilia. Roma:
          Fratelli Bocca.
Anderson, J.
  1981   Is Trouble Brewing for the Paradise of the Rich? *Parade,*
          February 22.
Bossy, J.
  1970   The Counter-Reformation and the People of Catholic Europe.
          Past and Present 47:51-70.
Davis, N.Z.
  1975   *Society and Culture in Early Modern France; Eight Essays.*
          Stanford, Cal.: Stanford University Press.
Di Ruberto, S.
  1904   *Sambuca-Zabut e la Madonna dell' Udienze, Patrona di detto*
          comune. Napoli: Stabilimento Tipografico Michele d'Auria.
Giacone, G.
  1932   *Zabut: Notizie storiche del Castello di Zabut e suo*
          contiguo casale oggi Comune di Sambuca di Sicilia.
          Sciacca: Tipografia Editore B. Guadagna.
Giarrizzo, G.
  1978   La Sicilia dal Viceregno al Regno. In: *Storia della*
          Sicilia, Volume VII. Società editrice Storia di Napoli e
          della Sicilia, pp. 1-183.
Koestler, A.
  1964   *The Act of Creation.* New York: Macmillan.
LeRoy Ladurie, E.
  1969   Les paysans de Languedoc. In: E. William Monter (ed.),
          European Witchcraft. New York: Wiley, pp. 164-177.
Schneider, J. & P. Schneider
  1976   *Culture and Political Economy in Western Sicily.* New York:
          Academic Press.
Sider, G.
  1976   Christmas Mumming and the New Year in Outport Newfoundland.
          Past and Present 71:102-126.
Tigar, M.E. & M.R. Levy
  1977   *Law and the Rise of Capitalism.* New York & London: Monthly
          Review Press.
Turner, V.
  1969   *The Ritual Process: Structure and Anti-Structure.* Chicago:
          Aldine.
Tylor, E.B.
  1873   *Primitive Culture. Researches into the Development of*
          Mythology, Philosophy, Religion, Language, Art and Custom.

London: J. Murray (6th edition).
Werbner, R.P.
    1977   Introduction. In: R.P. Werbner (ed.), *Regional Cults*.
            A.S.A. Monograph No. 15. New York: Academic Press,
            pp. ix-xxxvi.

'Civil Religion' or 'Civil War'? Religion in Israel

Daniel Meijers, Free University, Amsterdam

INTRODUCTION

Mrs. de G. had been visiting her daughter in New York and was now waiting for her flight to leave Kennedy airport for Europe. "I saw there", she said, "a man in a long black coat, a black hat on his head, and long curls behind his ears. He had tied a black belt around his middle and was holding on to it with both hands. And what I simply could not understand, was that he was standing there nodding to the wall. What on earth did he want with that wall?"

Mrs. de G. soon understood that she was seeing an orthodox Jew. She did not grasp, however, that this Hasidic Jew, a follower of a devotional movement within orthodox Judaism, was not simply nodding to the wall, but was praying. It was also not clear to her that he was merely moving his body as part of the accepted ritual. Mrs. de G. is not Jewish, and those Jews she was acquainted with, would not have been able to enlighten her very much on the subject. For many Jews from less orthodox backgrounds, the behavior of this man would also have been a riddle. Nevertheless, his behavior had a simple explanation. He was praying there so as not to miss the fixed hour for doing so. He was standing in the typical position of someone who is trying to concentrate on prayer in a place where this is very difficult. He had placed himself in front of a high wall in order to feel small, as is prescribed.[1] Mrs. de G. might have been even more amazed, had she known that within Jewish orthodoxy itself, there are enormous differences, that one group hardly resembles the next. The meat slaughtered by the ritual slaughterer of the one, may be rejected by members of the other, and conflicts are sometimes so heated that members of one group take the precaution of avoiding the neighborhood of the other. All this

notwithstanding, and this Mrs. de G. would have found even more
incomprehensible, members of these different groups would not
hesitate to take part in the religious service of another group,
because ... well, there are vast differences between religious
cultures.

The above incident serves as an introduction to this paper,
which wishes to comment on an article written by Aronoff, in which
the concept of 'civil religion' is applied to the situation in
Israel. Aronoff argues that we can typify the Israeli situation
with the term 'civil religion', in the sense of a rather general
ideological frame of reference. I wonder, however, to what extent
this concept is applicable to the Israeli situation, and to what
extent the emphasis on the concept of civil religion smoothes over
ideological conflicts. I have in mind in particular the issue of
the occupied territories. The population is sharply divided as to
whether land should be returned or not. This division is not merely
one between orthodoxy and non-orthodoxy. Furthermore, the different
opinions on both sides are based on different grounds.

CIVIL RELIGION IN ISRAEL[2]

In the many young states which gained their independence since the
Second World War, power struggles are playing an ever increasingly
important role. It would appear that this statement holds true for
a considerable part of the Third World. Various ideologies, whether
political -- referring to a secular social concept -- or religious
-- referring to a reality other than the empirical -- form the
guiding principle for collective behavior. In a great many cases
there has been a mixing of these two kinds of ideologies, so that
national symbols, myths and rites have been invested with certain
religious overtones.

Aronoff's article 'Civil religion in Israel', as published in
the *Royal Anthropological Institute News*, should be viewed in this
sense. He defines civil religion as "a special type of dominant
ideological superstructure which is rooted in religion and which
incorporates significant elements of religious symbol, myth, and
ritual that are used selectively and transformed through their
incorporation into the civil religion" (1981b:2). He shows how
several originally religious elements received a new and nationalistic
image, which are supported by virtually all groups[3]. This is relevant
to the most important Israeli political groups, with the exception of
a few Christian and Moslem minorities. At any event, the majority of
the Jews and part of the Druze population, practise this civil
religion (Aronoff 1981b:2). The importance of this notion is that it
gives us an entirely different view of the otherwise so divided Israeli

society. Ideological opinions and currents are all too often
distinguished from each other only in terms of conflict while the
points of agreement and the shared values are often overlooked. His
article is worthy of admiration for two reasons. In the first place,
because he has clarified our understanding of Israeli society by
showing that a great many symbols, rites and myths are accepted by
an important part of the population. In the second place, because
of his theoretical refinement of the concept of civil religion. In
a more elaborate article than that which appeared in *RAIN* and which
was presented at the IUAES-Intercongress in 1981, he places civil
religion between the "immutable transcendent religion on the one
hand, and rationalized secular ideology on the other" (Aronoff
1981a:11). In this way his civil religion has a bridging function
and is more dynamic than religion in the traditional sense, but
more static than the secular ideology[4]. A large portion of the
central values of Israeli society are represented within this civil
religion. In my opinion, each politician would do well to bear this
in mind when making his proposals and decisions.

The above notwithstanding, I have some reservations concerning
the term civil religion as applied to the situation in Israel. Are
those symbols, rites and myths mentioned by Aronoff indeed the most
important, or are they merely the most obvious, and are there others
which carry more weight? Another question would be whether a concept
like civil religion will always offer insight into a given situation.
After all, the Israeli situation has not remained unchanged since
the birth of the State in 1948. Furthermore, the various groups
which can clearly be placed under the banner of civil religion may
at some point become engaged in such conflict as to render the
applicability of a concept such as civil religion questionable.
Although the strength of the concept of civil religion is precisely
that it presumes strong differences within society, it is still
valid to question the limit of such a rift. One condition seems to
me, at any event, that the central values must always be viewed as
such and that they must not be allowed to lose their importance as
a dominant frame of reference for any reason.

What exactly does Aronoff mean by civil religion in Israel? He
presents those myths, rites and symbols which according to him occupy
a special place in the Israeli national consciousness, and which,
at the same time, possess religio-historical roots. They owe their
present form to Zionist ideals. They are found in Aronoff as follows (1981b:4):

MYTH/LEGEND	SYMBOL/SHRINE	RITE/RITUAL
Exile and Redemption	Israel	Aliyah (Immigration)
Jewish History (condensed)	Western Wall (Jerusalem)	Pilgrimage, Prayer and Tourism
Holocaust Legends	Yad Vashem (and secondary shrines)	Martyrs and Heroes Remembrance Day
Masada Legends	Masada	Army ceremonials and Tourism
Zahal Legends	Zahal/military cemeteries Yad Lebanim memorials	Memorial Day and other memorial rites
Biblical Legends and Myths	Mount Zion and Tomb of the Patriarchs	Pilgrimages and Tourism
Biblical and Archeological	Museum of the Book (Dead Sea Scrolls)	Educational and Tourism
Diaspora History and Legends	Diaspora Museum	Educational and Tourism
Religious Myth and Legend	Various (specific to each holiday)	Religious Holiday Rituals
National Legends	Flag, State Seal, Leaders, Offices, Army	National Holiday Ceremony

As to the content, it is possible to summarise this series of rites, myths and symbols as follows: *Israel is our historical inheritance which we have earned in waves of exile and redemption, through martyrdom and heroism.* These myths, rites and symbols serve no other purpose but to confirm this idea which clearly refers to a deep historical consciousness. Following the biblical story, if we date the birth of the Jewish people as such to the period of the Egyptian exodus then the same theme plays a central role there, too. The Jewish people are released from exile and at the same time are ordered to take possession of the land of Israel. In this context it is important to note that the terms used by Aronoff for immigration and emigration (*alyah* and *yeridah*), also have a symbolic meaning, namely, to ascend and to descend, while they are also the terms used in the Old Testament to signify the entering into or exiting from Israel. Judaism stands or falls by the following: continuous *exile*, with the hope for *redemption* through sacrifice and with a never-ceasing reference to '*the homeland*'[5].

Since the diaspora these themes have always played a role. Jewish communities all over the world and in all times have lived in *exile*. The many Messianic movements are an indication of the importance of the theme of *redemption*. The importance of the concept of a *'homeland'* becomes clear from the commentary of the medieval scholar Rashi (1040-1105) on the book of Genesis. His first commentary does not address itself to the creation or the Divine origin of the Torah, but expounds the right of the Jewish people to *their own land of Israel*. It should be noted that Rashi's commentary has remained one of the few which are commonly found printed next to the text of virtually every Hebrew edition of the Pentateuch. *Judaism, without the fundamental values of exile, the hope for redemption and the right to a homeland can therefore not be considered Judaism in any historical sense.* What we are dealing with are values which came into existence at the birth of the Jewish people, in a struggle of several tribes, all trying to achieve the same goal, after having collectively experienced exile and liberation. All other values must be examined in the light and limits defined by these. Land *is* a fundamental value. That is to say, a value not open to discussion, it is a value which has been brought forth by history itself.

Aronoff's enumeration of the myths, rites and symbols has been compressed by me into several fundamental values, culminating in *'the homeland'*. It is, however, not only important to determine which of those values are fundamental, but also how and in what way ideological disagreement may cause change in these. I am thinking of a very specific cause of disagreement, namely, what could be called the 'institutionalised sources of conflict' within traditional Jewish thought. Each complicated theology knows its own dilemmas and grey areas open to more than one interpretation. These are used by one current in order to move in a particular direction, whereas by another within that same religion and on nearly the same grounds in order to move in another direction. These dilemmas, which make different choices possible, can be traced by the comparison of different, yet simultaneous currents and by checking why the one preferred the one direction, and the other the other direction. Not only socio-economic conditions determine the direction taken, but within the doctrine there must exist the opportunity to legitimize such a choice as well.

DILEMMAS IN TRADITIONAL JEWISH THINKING

The present-day leader of the so-called Lubavitcher Ḥasidim, Rabbi M.M. Schneerson of Lubavitch, points to one such dilemma in one of his commentaries. He calls this the dilemma between spirit and matter, which he apparently considers as very ancient and historic,

and which according to him arose during the period after the exodus.
According to Rabbi Schneerson the choice between spirit and matter
was at the root of the disagreement among the twelve spies sent out
by Moses. According to the biblical account, these spies were given
the task to visit the land in order to see how it might best be
conquered. After meeting the mighty inhabitants of this land, ten of
the twelve spies returned with the message that it would be better
to remain in the desert, for "we were as grasshoppers in our eyes,
and so we appeared in theirs" (Numbers 13:33). The two remaining
spies, however, were of the opinion that the land could be conquered.
Rabbi Schneerson explains this difference of opinion among the spies
by their completely opposite views of man's destiny. The ten spies
who advised against the invasion had the underlying intention to
keep the Jewish people in the desert. According to the tradition,
the entire people occupied itself solely with the study of the Torah
and, in order to make this possible, they were being sustained by
supernatural means throughout their forty-year sojourn in the desert.
Should they, however, conquer the land, they would be forced to
support themselves in a more natural way. The two remaining spies
were, however, of the opinion that an inner-worldly way of life,
which forces man to occupy himself with material matters as well, is
more in keeping with the aims of creation than an outer-worldly isolation in the desert, no matter how elevated (Schneerson 1962:320-
325 and 1964:1041 ff.).
    The above-mentioned commentator Rashi implies such a dilemma when
he relates that the two tribes of Zevulun and Issachar divided their
tasks. Zevulun dealt in trade and seamanship, while Issachar studied
the Torah and in exchange for this was supported by Zevulun[6]. Both
cases -- the interpretation of the conflict among the spies and the
division of labor between the two tribes -- allow for the different
possibilities which flow from the dilemma between spirit and matter.
In the first case there arises a practically insoluble conflict, in
the second a complementary contrast. This latter solution now forms
the traditional pattern, which can be found all through the history
of Judaism throughout the world. Religious virtuoso were enabled
by others who worked in profane occupations to dedicate themselves
to continuous study 'day and night'. Whether this solution was satisfactory depended upon many different factors. A good illustration
of a period in which this was not the case can be found in the era
immediately prior to the rise of Hasidism, a devotional and mystical
popular movement in eighteenth-century Eastern Europe. The failing
of the Zevulun-Issachar pattern, fashionable until then, has had its
effect on the religious situation of orthodox Judaism until this
very day.

HASIDISM AND THE DILEMMA BETWEEN SPIRIT AND MATTER

Hasidism came into being during the first half of the eighteenth century, at the time of an extremely tense socio-economic situation[7]. During the period immediately prior to this, a large part of Eastern European Jewry had fallen victim to wars and progroms, and finally to mass impoverishment[8]. The Jewish community of Eastern Europe was in those days divided into two status groups, an elite of scholars and a much larger group of illiterates (Bosk 1974:141). The scholars showed little respect for the illiterates because they were unable to fulfil the most important religious ideal, namely that of con- tinuous study (Rabinovich 1950:125). Until that time, this probably occurred on a larger scale[9]. In order to realise such an ideal, a long and expensive education was absolutely necessary. In time of continuous persecution, such as was the case around 1650, there was neither the money nor the opportunity. It was simply impossible to withdraw boys from the work force for an extended period of time by sending them to the *Ḥeder*, the religious elementary school. A further education, traditionally often continued until after marriage, was even more out of the question[10]. The result was, however, that the Jewish population of Eastern Europe became impoverished in terms of knowledge on a large scale and this was hardly compensated for by the relatively small group of scholars (cf. Rubin 1964:140). These latter formed a status group all by themselves, which did not cease to make others aware of the fact that they were hardly living up to the religious ideals, and even that hell and damnation would await them (cf. Dubnow 1931:63 ff.). No doubt the life of the common man of those days lacked even the most elementary religious meaning. They did not meet official religious standards at all. There was no realistic possibility to prove themselves religiously, although they were far from secularised. Bosk rightly says: "Political repression, economic exploitation, and progroms raised for Judaism problems of meaning" (Bosk 1974:142).

It is in this light that the rise of the Hasidic movement under the leadership of its founder, Rabbi Israel Baal Shem Tov (1698- 1760), should be viewed. He and his successors emphasised time and again that also the unlettered could realise the religious ideals by dealing with the world in the right way. This is to say, that one should observe the religious precepts, covering all aspects of daily living, carefully. Study and the gathering of knowledge were no longer considered the sole road to salvation; 'G-d wants the heart'[11] became the slogan of the Hasidic movement[12]. Nevertheless, Talmudic study remained a desired and highly valued occupation.

This new view rested on an extremely intricate interpretation of a Cabbalistic theme which led to the conclusion that man can reach his destiny by dealing not only with spirit but with matter as well[13].

The result was that the Ḥasidic movement grew at a rapid pace. In the nineteenth century the East European Jewish community was largely composed of Ḥasidim (Dubnow 1931:22). Therefore, it should suprise no one, that even today Ḥasidic groups still grow in number. The conditions set for admission are less tied to education or to inborn qualities such as intellect which are a *sine qua non* for membership in a non-Hasidic group[14]. The groups under examination by us are mainly orthodox communities of European background. Among that part of the population which is considered more or less orthodox, being a quarter to a third of the total Israeli population (Aronoff 1981a: 2), there are of course many oriental Jews, but their general influence is clearly less felt. The orthodoxy of European origin can be roughly divided into Ḥasidim and non-Ḥasidim. The Ḥasidim form, with exception of some sub-groups, essentially one unified group. They live in their own neighborhoods and sometimes even their own villages. As in the past, they are important because of their numbers. They are also influential because most sub-groups are headed by well-known 'Rebbes' and particularly the larger groups among them are characterised by a good organisational apparatus. Within this dichotomy of Ḥasidim and non-Ḥasidim there is a wide range of political orientations which sometimes give rise to sharply differing opinions as to the necessity to keep or to return acquired territories[15].

ORTHODOX JUDAISM IN ISRAEL: LAND, SPIRIT AND MATTER

This double theme, the homeland as a fundamental value and the dilemma between spirit and matter, is important in order to grasp the standpoints held within the different currents, the most important of which will be dealt with here briefly.

The *Neturei Karta* ('Guardians of the City'), comprises the most important anti-Zionist, strongly fundamentalist, orthodox stream. As is the case with several other orthodox groups, they are of the opinion that Israel should never have been conquered by force but that one should have waited for the coming of the Messiah. The Neturei Karta bases this opinion on Talmudic texts[16]. According to this movement, the Zionist state can do no good whatsoever and certainly cannot contain any acceptable religious dimension. The supporters of this movement are indifferent as to whether Israel occupies, keeps or returns the land. 'Land' is valued so much from this negative outlook that most of the Neturei Karta's actions are directed towards bringing its viewpoint to the attention of the world opinion. Thus, for example, they demonstratively apply for a 'stateless' passport and some of them refuse to speak Ivrit (modern Hebrew) or to pay with Israeli currency[17]. The Neturei Karta receive financial support from some Ḥasidic and some non-Ḥasidic communities. An important Ḥasidic group which supports them is the New York based Satmar community. The latter is an independent group which has separated itself further and further from mainstream Ḥasidism since the establishment of the State of Israel. The political influence wielded by the Neturei Karta is fairly insignificant, partly because of their very limited support within Israel itself.

A variant of this particular current is the *Agudah* (lit. bond), which originally formed a single organisation together with the Neturei Karta but which broke away in 1937. The most outstanding difference between the two factions is that the Agudah has accepted the State *de facto*. The Agudah holds seats in parliament, while the Neturei Karta do not even vote. The Agudah recognises several sub-currents, varying from anti-Zionist to what amounts to very orthodox Zionism. The main difference between these latter and the generally accepted orthodox Zionists is that the left faction of the Agudah, which is closest to the orthodox Zionists, is much more fundamental in its outlook.

Until recently, Ḥasidim and non-Ḥasidim alike were unified under the banner of the Agudah. The theme of 'land', however, led to conflicts, which caused the split within this very orthodox party. In this fashion two camps sprung up. The leader of the one is Rabbi Schach, head of the Ponnevitch Talmud Academy, one of the largest and most influential Talmudic academies. At the head of the other group stands the Lubavitcher Rebbe, a scholar of no lesser fame and the most respected of Ḥasidic Rebbes. Both components, 'land' and the dilemma between 'spirit and matter', play a role in this conflict[18]. At first sight this does not appear to be the case. Rabbi Schach advises the return of the West Bank -- Judea and Samaria -- and the Golan Heights. His reasoning is that, according to the precepts of the Torah, except for certain special cases, the Jewish law has to yield in case of mortal danger. To keep these territories might lead to a life-threatening situation for the population of Israel, and it is for this reason that he deems the return of these areas necessary[19].

The Lubavitcher Rebbe is, first of all, of the opinion -- and he bases this on the previously mentioned Rashi commentary on Genesis -- that the land of Israel is a divine gift to the Jewish people. For this reason, no piece of land which had originally been part of the Jewish territories can be given away[20]. Secondly, he bases his argument on a law which prescribes what has to be done in the case of a Jewish settlement being threatened with attack. In such a case it is even permissible on the Sabbath, the day of rest, to initiate an attack in order to defend the territory. This decision holds true for any Jewish area, be it part of Israel or outside its borders. *The underlying thought in both ways of reasoning, that of Rabbi*

*Schach as well as that of the Lubavitcher Rebbe, is that the proper
application of the Jewish Law, as a code of divine origin, is the
only guarantee for the well-being and continued existence of the
Jewish people.* Only by closely observing these precepts and laws
can a deadly threat be avoided.

According to the Lubavitcher Rebbe's reasoning, Jewish territory
is what is under consideration. And since there are carefully prescribed rules as to what should be done in every case, these rules
and laws should be followed, and no others. Beyond this, the Rebbe
reasons that in case of a serious illness, the opinion of medical
specialists should be taken seriously. Here the military strategists
are the accepted specialists and many among them believe that a
return to the borders of pre-1967 would put the State in real danger.
For this reason, also the West Bank and the Golan Heights should be
retained.

Rabbi Schach, as well as the Lubavitcher Rebbe, argues his case
from a *Halakhic*, Jewish legal point of view. Their arguments are
not based on eschatological ideas, such as is the case with many
orthodox Zionists who regard the State of Israel as the first sign
of the Messianic redemption[21]. Rabbi Schach and the Lubavitcher
Rebbe both maintain the basic point of view that the land of Israel,
on religious grounds, belongs to the Jewish people as part of its
inheritance. This outlook, however, is detached from any Messianic
belief. However, in their final opinion, the dilemma between spirit
and matter plays an important role. The world of Rabbi Schach is a
world of scholars. Whoever does not belong to his kind of orthodoxy
falls under a different category of being. This is also apparent in
the policies of the Agudah party, of which he is one of the most
important leaders. The policies of this party are directed mainly at
safeguarding religious practice. This party appears to be engaged in
an ongoing struggle with the non-orthodox segment of the population,
and the Agudah does not consider this part of the population as a
partner in any way. The group around Rabbi Schach is not merely non-
Ḥasidic but even anti-Ḥasidic. In their view, spirit is not only the
opposite of matter but is also superior to it. This view leads to a
qualitative distinction between those who occupy themselves with
'spirit' and those working in the profane professions, who are
identified with 'matter'.

The Lubavitcher Rebbe takes a different attitude. This not only
because the Lubavitcher movement distances itself formally from the
political world. There is no such thing as a Lubavitcher party. Nor
can the Lubavitcher Rebbe be identified with Agudah policies, or with
those of any other party, in the same way as many other religious
dignitaries are. In the Lubavitch way of thinking, a doctrine concerning the brotherhood of the Jewish people is paramount. These

ideas are not mere theory but have practical consequences. The
Lubavitcher movement maintains many connections with the non-
orthodoxy, and many of its activities are aimed directly at this
section of the population[22]. A distinction between orthodox and non-
orthodox is not made, an attitude which Liebman rightly deems as
having "tremendous social and political consequences" (1965:81).

All this in contrast to Rabbi Schach's way of thinking. To him,
the question of keeping or returning the occupied territories is not
one worth the cost of lives. The issue does not touch the essence of
his group. He has no need to retain the West Bank for purely
Zionistic ideological considerations, because he does not share this
ideology. The group of people directly involved -- because, for
example, they moved into settlements established in these regions --
are not his followers. On the contrary, the colonists who have
settled in these areas do not study the Torah as their occupation.
They mostly practise the profane professions. They have not chosen
for 'spirit' and therefore occupy only a position of secondary
importance.

According to the Lubavitcher ideology, which in itself advocates
a thoroughly systematic version of general Ḥasidism, the profane
professions are not considered less worthy than the religious ones.
Beyond this, Ḥasidism is based on ideas which have as their cornerstone the unity of the Jewish people. Furthermore, Ḥasidim do not
consider matter less G-dly than spirit. This holds even more for the
'matter' from which the Holy Land is wrought. The question of keeping
or returning of territories is viewed on a different level by the
Lubavitcher Rebbe. For him this is a much more fundamental question
than for Rabbi Schach. The essential concepts of 'land' and 'matter'
are raised in a completely different order of importance and are
therefore totally different issues than they are for Rabbi Schach
and his followers. Their main question is whether or not spirit
triumphs, which is merely an extension of the old controversy between
Ḥasidim and their opponents about which way leads to salvation: the
way of the spirit only, or the one which emphasises both spirit and
matter. This triumph of the spirit is translated in daily practice
into the extent of benificent influence that political decisions
have on the well-being of a religious elite. All other problems are
subordinate to this and should preferably be avoided[23]. The conflict
between these two religious leaders is not one which is limited to
small religious groups. The two leaders are considered as outstanding
and command a large following among Jews, in Israel as well as
abroad. Both are sought out for guidance by political leaders. Their
influence reaches considerably further than their immediate following.

A different religious movement which is important in this context
is the *Gush Emunim*, the Block of the Faithful. They have sprung up
mainly from the ranks of orthodox Zionism, but are not identical to

this group. Part of their focus centers around the epigones of the
first Chief Rabbi of Israel, Rabbi Cook[24]. He was an orthodox Zionist
whose teaching bore a mystical character. He also emphasised the
importance of 'matter'. In his philosophy the concept of the 'Jewish
Land' occupied a predominant place.

The standpoint of the Gush Emunim is not determined solely by
these ideas. The views expressed by the Lubavitcher Rebbe, based
entirely on different grounds, greatly strengthen this movement. For
their main aims are further colonisation and retention of the occupied territories. It is therefore not surprising that Lubavitcher
ideas are greeted with much sympathy by many supporters of this
group. That the Rebbe is friendly towards Gush Emunim appears from
his gift to them of *Beth Schneersohn*, a house in Hebron which had
belonged to the Lubavitcher community[25].

In short, there are at least four different currents visible,
namely[26]:

1) the anti-State *Neturei Karta*. All their other views are
subordinated to this objective;

2) *Rabbi Schach's group*, which prefers 'spirit' and as a consequence sees no need to keep the occupied territories;

3) the formation around the *Lubavitcher Rebbe*, who emphasises the
importance of 'matter' and of keeping the occupied territories;

4) a part of the orthodox Zionists, who are motivated by political
and religious reasons, advocate keeping the occupied territories.
The most obvious representative of this group is the *Block of the
Faithful* (Gush Emunim).

We can at this point ask ourselves to what extent this more
detailed picture of Israeli orthodoxy fits in with Aronoff's concept
of civil religion.

CIVIL RELIGION ONCE AGAIN

According to Aronoff's criteria, at least three of the above-
mentioned currents fall under civil religion. It is quite clear that
in this way the extreme differences, especially between the second
and the third currents recede to the background. The same is true of
the differences which exist between the orthodox and non-orthodox
Zionists, et cetera. The former, such as the Gush Emunim, are largely
in favor of the retention of all territories, but many of the non-
orthodox Zionists are sharply opposed to this. Especially now, at a
time when the issue of keeping or returning of land is a crucial one,
the use of a concept like civil religion appears to smooth over
essential conflicts. This is perhaps not necessary, since civil
religion, as stated earlier, presupposes the existence of certain
tensions within a state. Nevertheless, the temptation is strong to

present a situation fraught with tension as a harmonious one, or at
least as a single whole. This is only possible as long as civil
religion dominates as an ideological superstructure. However, civil
religion unites in itself different dimensions. On the one hand,
there is a reference to religion, whereas on the other hand, to the
political system. When the contrasts between these two components
become irreconcilable, civil religion as a dominant superstructure
ceases to exist. We can check this for the Israeli situation by
distinguishing different kinds of ideologies. Some ideologies refer
to the supernatural and are basically 'real' religions. Others refer
to society and are basically political ideologies. Not only do they
differ in orientation, but also in goals.

Weber has rightly concluded that religions strive towards salvation, by which, in my opinion, he meant individual salvation[27]. The
different political ideologies in Israeli society also strive towards
salvation, but a collective salvation for the society as a whole. It
is assumed that the achievement of this collective salvation will
also be to the benefit of the individual. The kibbutz movement is an
illustration of this. There the ideal was a new society with better
human relations, which in turn would bring happiness to the individual as well (cf. Selier 1976:58).

The different Israeli ideologies can be distinguished on the
basis of these criteria. Some have as their point of orientation a
concept of society which is almost of a metaphysical nature, and
their primary aim is to establish a more perfect society. I call
these *political ideologies*, because their starting point is a
'natural' orientation and their aims are first and foremost social
in character. All forms of non-religious Zionism fall into this
category. They can further be subdivided according to their different
aims, which vary from an ideal socialist state to the establishment
of a state as a haven for the persecuted Jewish people. In this
sense, here too, a distinction could be made between a more spirit-
ualistic aim and a more materialistic one.

Other ideologies refer to the supernatural. Their primary aim is
the perfection of the individual, and thereby the perfection of
society. I call these *religious ideologies*. Both the group around
the Lubavitcher Rebbe as well as the one around Rabbi Schach fall
into this category. Both ideologies can be distinguished from each
other on the basis of differences in outlook as to how individual
salvation should be achieved, whether through spirit or through
matter.

The application of these criteria makes two more combinations
possible, namely, one of orientation towards society (or nature)
with an individual aim, and one of supernatural orientation with a
social aim. To the first category, which is of less political and
religious importance, belong the more personal *'Lebensanschauungen'*

of individuals and currents. In the second and more important category there is a reference to the supernatural while the goal aimed for is first and foremost social, rather than individual. I call these kinds of ideologies *political religions*. Religious Zionism, as a movement, falls under this category, as does the Neturei Karta, which strives towards the perfection of society and tries to realise this by opposing the State of Israel and its institutions. The Neturei Karta holds that collective perfection is impossible, as long as the State, as such, prevents the coming of the Messiah[28]. The above can be presented schematically as follows:

IDEOLOGIES

Aiming for the perfection of:	Referring to: the supernatural	society (or nature)
individual	RELIGIOUS IDEOLOGY	PERSONAL IDEOLOGY
society	POLITICAL RELIGION	POLITICAL IDEOLOGY

Civil religion does not fit into this typology because it is a generalising concept, whereas here we are dealing with categories which are specified according to their defining and distinguishing characteristics. The different points of view taken concerning a central value such as 'land' could render impossible the fruitful application of a concept such as civil religion. This would be the case as soon as such a central value arouses the kind of discussion which is closer to '*civil war*' than to '*civil religion*'[29]. Obviously, the ideological superstructure would then have lost its dominance. The distinctive character of a political or a religious ideology, or of a political religion, each with its different orientation and special goal, comes more to the fore than certain shared values. *At this point, a dominant superstructure no longer exists.*

The integrative picture which civil religion pretends to present is based on Durkheimian thought, which, on the one hand, easily leads to neglect of the individual and, on the other hand, tends towards, or may even be viewed as the product of, collectivistic and nationalistic ideas (cf. Schoffeleers 1978). In this context that is not without importance. The differences between political and religious ideologies do not exist solely in their orientation. There are also different goals and aims which are primarily of a collec-tivistic or an individualistic character. Civil religion has no room for profound conflicts concerning the achievement of salvation for the individual. Such conflicts cannot have a central function in civil religion, despite the fact that they can play a decisive role in determining how best to deal with central values, and even whether a given value should indeed be considered as central or not.

At least two different tendencies are here under consideration.
On the one hand, there is a blurring of values which runs through
all layers and sectors of society. On the other hand, different
points of view become hardened with respect to the central value of
'land'. Not only in religious circles is there disagreement about
which values should be central, but this phenomenon is also to be
found among non-religious Zionists[30]. The disagreement about keeping
or returning of land has split the population of Israel into two
camps. At a higher level within the religious segment of the population there is a division of opinion, which also has its influence
at other levels. The statements made at this higher level are authoritative. They are important as a possible legitimation for other
groupings which on completely other grounds arrive at the same conclusion. This also holds for the non-orthodox groupings. Religious
legitimation has far-reaching consequences because religious sentiment does not restrict itself numerically to formal orthodoxy[31].
The result is a deep rift within the entire population. Some are
prepared to give up their lives to retain land, whereas others
believe that only giving up land can serve peace. The clash between
the two camps might turn out to be much more serious than at any
time in the recent past.

In the historical past this was, however, different. Together
with an individual striving for salvation 'the eye was directed
towards Zion'. There were no real conflicts over the central value
of 'land', because Zion was in Turkish or in other foreign hands.
As a collective goal from a distance, Zion had a unifying influence,
whereas the issue of land now gives rise to conflicts which could
better be described as dividing. These conflicts already arose at
the time of the establishment of the State in 1948. But they lost
their importance in the light of the enormous confrontations with
the Arabs, which resulted in war. The danger to which the whole of
Israeli society was exposed at the time, especially after the
experiences of the Second World War, made civil religion not only
acceptable, but even necessary. A dominant ideological superstructure
was also necessary to unify the various ethnic groups. These problems,
typical of any pluralistic society, are regarded by some as the roots
of civil religion (cf. Markoff & Regan 1982:343). In the meantime,
the situation has greatly changed. Now Israel has a second and third
generation with entirely different experiences.

I am of the opinion that until long after the Six-Day-War in 1967
one could indeed speak of a civil religion. In this war the West Bank
and Jerusalem were conquered. The land became more easily defendable
than before. Until then, the distance between the Mediterranean and
the Eastern border was less than 20 kilometers in some places. As a
result of the conquest of the Golan Heights security in the North
was also increased. Some of the ever-felt tension in the country

lessened. Israel's military superiority could no longer be doubted by anyone. During this period, on the one hand, the pressure on the population, which had been conducive to unity, decreased, while, on the other hand, the conflicting opinions concerning 'land' remained in effect latent, since the returning of the occupied territories was not yet a real issue. Only after 1973, after the Yom Kippur War, did this situation change. This was the first war which Israel almost lost. In the years that followed, in particular after Camp David, the issue of keeping or returning the occupied territories has become more and more urgent under American pressure.

My conclusion is, that Aronoff's analysis is applicable to the situation such as it was up to the Yom Kippur War. Civil religion had a unifying effect. But since then the conflicts concerning land, both political and religious, have increased to the extent where it has become meaningless to speak of civil religion. A sign of the seriousness of the situation is that during the transference of the Sinai to Egypt in 1982, a number of opponents threatened to commit suicide and had to be restrained by their religious leaders. No doubt, this action was meant as a reference to the collective suicide committed by the defenders of Massada, a fortress which was besieged by the Roman army and which is also mentioned by Aronoff in his list of national symbols. The opponents of the transference of the Sinai to Egypt appear to have identified themselves with the fighters against the Roman oppressors and considered the returning of land to Egypt, land which originally had been within Israel's borders, as treason. Can it possibly still be permissible under such circumstances to speak of civil religion[32]?

'Land' as such does not comprise an independent, isolated value within Judaism but is part of a total complex which is found in different contexts. In the present-day situation, the problem of land can be defined as a classical Jewish theme with some new, specific components. The prototype for this theme is formed by the story of the exodus from Egypt, namely, a history of exile and redemption, with different roads to salvation. The already quoted commentary on the conflict between the spies testifies to this latter fact and is also symbolic of a fairly general historic dilemma. The Jewish community always found itself in a threatened and dependent position, in a continuous struggle for survival. The only hope in this situation of continuous exile was the hope for redemption as represented by the 'Promised Land'. Meanwhile, the land one lived on, was at stake. 'Land' as such meant far more than a mere place of residence. 'Land' had an existential meaning.

At the same time the question of 'spirit' or 'matter' played a role. In the final analysis more than physical survival was at stake, spiritual survival was an issue as well. One could only protect one's identity effectively by supporting and maintaining a spiritual elite consisting of the work-exempt. This elite occupied itself with the study of the Torah 'day and night', as this was the only part of the cultural heritage upon which the surroundings had no influence. Both categories -- those solely occupied with 'spirit' and those who supported them -- were necessary and even mutually dependent. During the founding-period of the Ḥasidic movement, both groups had grown apart. The present situation seems similar in many ways. Once again a spiritual elite isolates itself during a period which, just as then, is preceded by persecution and war. The difference lies in the fact that now in Israel a greater part of the population is secularized and the community as a whole is independent. This, however, increases the pressure of existential issues, since the responsibilities are greater. Different charismatic personalities, the Lubavitcher Rebbe and Rabbi Schach on the religious front and Menachem Begin on the political front, have their own answers to these kinds of questions. The fact that Rabbi Schach is representative of a scholarly elite and not of the man in the street, determines and restricts his influence[33]. The Rebbe's choice, however, appeals more to the majority of the religious population occupied in the profane professions, as is evident from the interest shown in the Lubavitcher ideas within the camp of the Block of the Faithful. That this group is identifiable as a political religion is also important here. The Lubavitcher movement is not formally involved in politics, but because of politically active groups such as this one its influence should not be underestimated.

It seems to me that in principle Begin refers to the Rebbe's choice of matter and land, thereby emphasising values shared by a large segment of the population. The support for him found among the population may be larger than is suspected. It is in this light that Israeli politics will also have to be viewed[34].

NOTES

1. Kitsur Shulḥan Arukh, volume I(18):8.
2. I wish to thank several critical readers of this article for their very helpful comments, in particular Professor Matthew Schoffeleers. Special thanks to Drs. Derek Rubin for his excellent translation of this article into English.
3. A possible difference between Aronoff and Beliah is that the latter tends to place less emphasis on nationalism, as appears from the following: "I think it should be clear from the text that I conceive of the central tradition of the American civil religion not as a form of national self-worship but as the subordination of the nation to ethical principles that transcend it and in terms of which it should be judged. I am convinced that

every nation and every people come to some form of religious
self-understanding whether the critics like it or not" (Bellah
1970:168).
4. This view of civil religion as a bridge between traditional
religion and secular ideology entails a refinement and further
specification of the concept. It is possible that Aronoff moves
here in a slightly different direction from that taken by Bellah,
since the latter's civil religion is more overarching than con-
necting.
5. Both self-sacrifice and the offering of sacrifices can be considered an essential part of Judaism. During the time of the
Temple in Jerusalem, animals were sacrificed. It is a widespread
notion that since that time man should sacrifice 'the animal
within himself'. Death through martyrdom, as a result of persecution, is an extension of this way of thinking. In exile, the
three daily prayers take the place of the different daily
sacrifices once made in the Temple. Only in the Messianic era
will these sacrifices be restored.
6. Cf. Rashi's commentary on Deuteronomy 33:18.
Rashi's commentary on the Pentateuch is of more than ordinary
significance. It is accepted by the entire orthodoxy, without
exception, and is considered the standard exegesis. It is also
the first commentary learned by all children attending religious
schools.
7. For a more extensive description of the rise of the Hasidic
movement see Meijers (1979a:8-30). For a treatment of the cosmo-
logical setting of 'spirit' and 'matter' see Meijers & Tennekes
1982.
8. Bosk cites Dubnow in order to show that in some areas of Eastern
Europe a mere ten per cent of the Jewish population survived the
progroms (Bosk 1974:134). There are estimates which say that some
300 Jewish communities were completely wiped out (Dubnow 1931:46)
and that more than 250,000 people died in the progroms (Schochet
1961:31-33). At any event, the result was enormous poverty
(Rabinovitch 1950:125).
9. For example, during the Middle Ages a division into scholarly
elite and illiterate masses could not be made, "for every
Israelite studied the law" (Abrahams 1973:357). This is not to
say that people were not employed otherwise, but it does mean
that Talmudic knowledge was widespread.
10. Tradition demanded, and still does, that the orthodox education
of a male child begin at the age of three. Learning as religious
ideal and precept applies only to the men. This notwithstanding,
Jewish history also tells of learned women, although they formed
a minority (Abrahams 1973:342). Learning does not further women
in the attainment of religious perfection. The woman's way to

salvation is achieved through direct devotion, which according
to Ḥasidism includes several forms of asceticism. Nevertheless,
there were true scholars among Ḥasidic women, some of whom even
had an extensive knowledge of Jewish mysticism (cf. Metzger
1973).

11. In accordance with orthodox Jewish usage, I do not write the
word G-d in full.

12. Not without reason did the term Ḥasidism find acceptance;
Ḥasid = 'pious one'; plural Ḥasidim.

13. This relates to the interpretation of the concept of *Tsimtsum*,
which means 'contraction' or 'concentration'. The question which
forms the basis of this concept is: How can the world exist if
G-d is infinite? According to Jewish mysticism, the Cabbalah,
G-d contracted Himself in order to, as it were, make space for
the creation. This contraction, *Tsimtsum*, was explained in different ways. According to one explanation, G-d had withdrawn
Himself in Essence, so that, in a certain sense, matter became
less G-dly than spirit. The only real relationship with G-d
could be established through the study of the Torah, in which
He had revealed Himself. According to Ḥasidic teachings, however,
Tsimtsum referred exclusively to a *concealment of a Divine
manifestation*, and not to a *withdrawal of G-d Himself*, Who before
and after the act of Creation remained unchanged. From this it
followed that G-d's Essence was in fact present in matter as
well, because His infinity had not been affected.

According to these teachings, G-d is neither spirit nor matter
-- because both of these are part of creation -- but He can be
found in both of them (cf. Meijers 1979a:17-18 and Meijers &
Tennekes 1982, for further elaboration on this theme). By studying Torah, a relationship with G-d is established through spirit.
By observing all the other precepts, a relationship through
matter is brought about. Ḥasidism denies neither possibilities,
but emphasises that not everybody must necessarily reach his
destination through spirit only. Ḥasidism also expounded other
teachings which emphasise the same idea.

These concepts finally led to a new form of 'inner-worldly
asceticism', the goal of which was to act in such a way that the
person performing the act would not have any enjoyment from it.
This form of asceticism was practised in all daily actions, such
as eating and working. With eating, for example, essential was
not to eat for the taste, but only in order to be better able
to serve G-d. With work, it was demanded of one to strictly
observe the Jewish legal precepts (such as the honest use of
weights), to say Psalms during work, and to use one's earnings
for charity and not for unnecessary luxuries. The most important
aspect of this form of asceticism is that it is not dependent

upon a high level of learning. It can be practised without much previous education.

14. This does not mean that the study of the Torah as an occupation is not found among the Ḥasidim. The Zevulun-Issachar pattern still exists. Worthy intellectuals are supported by the community. The average Ḥasid chooses, however, a profane profession despite the fact that he has received an extensive religious education. This in contrast to some non-Ḥasidic communities, where, to this time, there is a clear preference for the study of the Torah as a profession. Sometimes this is even considered the only legitimate occupation (cf. Meijers 1979b).

15. Several of the currents dealt with here are examined in greater detail by Friedman 1975.

16. See Babylonian Talmud: Ketuboth 11A.

17. Another example of such an action is the request of Neturei Karta's then current leader to President Nixon, during his visit to the State of Israel in 1974, to make Israel one of America's states. Nixon did not reply in the positive.

18. Both leaders are regarded by their respective following as the most important Jewish religious leaders. Their followers decorate their homes and schools with pictures of them. They are greatly honored and their word is law. The Lubavitchers regard their Rebbe as a holy man. The followers of Rabbi Schach see him as the greatest scholar of his generation (*Gedol Ha-Dor*). Both can be considered charismatic personalities. Politicians and Jewish leaders from Israel and abroad seek their advice. On Begin's first appearance on American television, during his first visit to the United States in his capacity of Prime Minister of Israel, he was shown visiting the Lubavitcher Rebbe. In this he followed the example of the late President Shazar, who had visited the Rebbe as well.

19. To Menachem Begin's statement that the Jewish people have managed to exist for 3700 years without a strategic accord with the United States and could do so for another 3700 years, Rabbi Schach answered that the Jewish people have existed without the Golan Heights for 2000 years and could do so for another 2000 (*Nieuw Israëlitisch Weekblad*, 15 January 1982).

20. We are talking about territory that is already in Jewish hands. The Rebbe's opinion is not an incitement to further conquest.

21. Messianic ideas do not by definition imply that one is in favor of keeping the occupied territories. Recently, among orthodox Zionists, a movement has also sprung up which favors, for reasons of peace, the return of territory. This despite their conviction that Israel is the beginning of the fulfilment of biblical prophecy (*The Jerusalem Post*, International Edition, December 12-18, 1982, p. 8).

22. Lubavitcher activities are appreciated widely in Israeli circles.
    Typical of this are requests by the army to Lubavitcher insti-
    tutions to set up religious programs for divers occasions, as I
    personally observed while doing fieldwork in Israel in Kfar
    Habad in 1978.
23. The group around Rabbi Schach belongs to the anti-Hasidic camp.
    The original leader of the *Mitnagdim*, the opponents of Hasidism,
    was Rabbi Eliah, the *Gaon* of Vilna (1720-1797). According to
    Rabbi Eliah the proper task of the orthodox Jew is continuous
    study of the Torah. However, he deemed it permissible to earn
    one's living in a profane manner, since not everyone would be
    capable of studying the Torah without ulterior motives (and not
    in order to become famous, et cetera). By working in a profane
    occupation, this category of people would also be guarded from
    committing wrong (Ben-Sasson 1966:83-86, VIII). From this also
    it is evident that matter, according to this view, can never be
    more than a means to an end, and never an end in itself. A
    person who occupies himself with matter would automatically
    belong to another category than a scholar, who is the only one
    truly able to realise the religious ideals.
       Such teachings may lead those harboring other opinions or
    behaving differently to be considered as inferior or as actual
    opponents. That Hasidism has managed to maintain itself may be
    due precisely to the fact that the Baal Shem Tov himself was a
    scholar who surrounded himself with a group of learned disciples
    right from the start. For this reason, it was not easy for the
    opposition to fight his movement effectively (cf. Schochet 1974:
    185-193).
24. Rabbi Cook (1865-1935) should not really be designated the
    first Chief Rabbi of Israel, since he functioned as such before
    the establishment of the State. He should, however, be con-
    sidered one of the founders of orthodox Zionism.
25. This is at least what was related to me by a Lubavitcher inform-
    ant.
26. There are more currents than these within orthodox Judaism.
    Those mentioned here, however, are the most important regarding
    religio-political issues.
27. As appears from several passages, such as "Salvation may be
    viewed as the distinctive gift of active ethical behavior per-
    formed in the awareness that G-d directs this behavior, i.e.
    that the actor is an instrument of G-d" (Weber 1965:164). See
    also Weber 1965:184 ff.
28. Generally speaking, many millenarian movements can be placed,
    also outside of this particular context, under the heading of
    political religion, because almost invariably they have as their
    main aim a new order. In a certain sense the Neturei Karta could

be seen as a variation of this.
29. The use of the term 'civil war' is Abba Eban's, according to
    The Jerusalem Post (International Edition, February 20-26, 1983,
    p. 2), and not mine: "... Eban added that both political camps
    were afraid of violence but that talk of the country being on
    the brink of civil war was grossly exaggerated and was scaring
    people unnecessarily".
30. There is much discontent among Zionists over the blurring of
    essential values, as appears from an article in *The Jerusalem
    Post* (International Edition, December 12-18, 1982, p. 22): "The
    Zionist dream was to build a country which would mirror the best
    in Jewish history. It envisioned a reality that would be
    representative of the Jewish People. The dream was borne by a
    movement whose task was not only to realize it, but also to
    reflect the values inherent in it. The dream -- as is the way
    with dreams -- has been only partially realized. The state
    exists; the values it mirrors need much amelioration. But the
    movement which bore it stands in need of even greater repair. It
    has become a sapless shell, held erect not by a vision, but by
    distributions of privilege, echoing not with values, but empty
    rhetoric".
31. According to a survey held among pupils of Israeli high schools
    approximately 21 per cent identified themselves with the term
    'religious', approximately 35 per cent with the term 'traditional',
    and 44 per cent with the term 'non-religious' (cf. Zuckerman-
    Bareli 1975:54). Although those questioned were not representative
    of Israeli society as a whole -- this survey covered only high
    schools in Tel Aviv and students of 17 years of age -- the
    results, at any event, show that religious influences go far
    beyond formal orthodoxy (see also note 22). According to an
    orthodox source (*Hamachane Hachareadi*, March 24, 1983), this
    year 80 per cent of the population observed the main precepts
    of the Passover by not eating leavened bread during the week of
    the festival and by participating in the ritual of the first
    night.
32. It is not without significance that shortly after this the re-
    interment of the Bar Kochba warriors took place. These were the
    fighters against the Romans, whose remains had already been
    found in 1960. The funeral took place on the initiative of the
    Chief Rabbi of Israel, Rabbi Goren. It was carried out with full
    military honors in the presence of President Navon and Prime
    Minister Begin (*Nieuw Israëlitisch Weekblad*, 21 May 1982, p. 1).
    This sudden show of honor to these historic freedom fighters may
    have been intended to placate part of the population: president,
    prime minister, army and religion will not give up the land. It
    seems, however, that this sort of symbolic action, as can be

seen from the many protests, no longer has the desired effect.
I wonder whether the discussion concerning civil religion in
Israel did not arise at a time when supporters of the dominant
superstructure in Israel began to seriously ask themselves just
how dominant their ideology still is. Bellah also published his
article in a period during which national American values, due
to Korea and Vietnam, became less self-evident than before and
the need for official legitimation became perhaps more urgent.
33. The conflicts between the Lubavitcher Rebbe and Rabbi Schach
have, in the meantime, intensified. Several other Ḥasidic
Rebbes, among them the very prominent Gerer and Klausenberger
Rebbes, have taken the side of Lubavitch in these conflicts.
Others have also become involved. One of the most noticeable
new points of disagreement is that of the definition of a Jew.
The Lubavitcher Rebbe is of the opinion that the Israeli law
should state that only those to whom the *Halakhic* definition is
applicable should be recognized as Jewish. Although Rabbi Schach
subscribes without reservations to this definition he does not
support the Lubavitcher Rebbe's proposal. This is undoubtedly
because he does not view as his that part of the population
which in practice would have to do with this law. Among his
followers there would not be instances of doubt concerning the
religious and national identity of a person. His opposition
implies a different frame of reference from that of the rest of
the population.
34. Part of the information used was gathered during fieldwork in
Israel in 1978. This was made possible thanks to the financial
support of the Netherlands Organization for the Advancement of
Pure Research. Other data were gathered in 1981 in New York,
where the headquarters of the Lubavitcher movement are situated.
This was made possible thanks to the support of the Free
University.

BIBLIOGRAPHY

Abraham, I.
    1973   *Jewish Life in the Middle Ages*. New York: Atheneum.
Aronoff, M.J.
    1981a Civil Religion in Israel. Paper presented at the IUAES-
           Intercongress, Amsterdam.
    1981b Civil Religion in Israel. *RAIN* 44:2-6.
Bellah, R.N.
    1970   Civil Religion in America. In: R.N. Bellah (ed.), *Beyond
           Belief. Essays on Religion in a Post-Traditional World*.
           New York: Harper & Row, pp. 168-189.

Ben-Sasson, C.H.
1966   Personality of the Gaon and his Historical Influence. *Zion* 31(3-4):39-86 and 197-216.
Bosk, C.
1974   Cybernetic Hasidism: An Essay on Social and Religious Change. *Sociological Inquiry* 44(2):131-144.
Dubnow, S.
1931   *Geschichte des Chassidismus*. Band I. Berlin: Jüdischer Verlag.
Friedman, M.
1975   Religious Zealotry in Israeli Society. In: S. Poll & E. Krausz (eds.), *On Ethnic and Religious Diversity in Israel*. Ramat-Gan: Bar-Ilan University, pp. 91-111.
Liebman, C.S.
1965   Orthodoxy in American Jewish Life. *American Jewish Year Book* 66:21-97.
Markoff, J. & D. Regan
1982   The Rise and Fall of Civil Religion: Comparative Perspectives. *Sociological Analysis* 42(4):333-352.
Meijers, L.D.
1979a   *Chassidisme in Israël: De Reb Arrelech van Jeruzalem*. Assen: Van Gorcum.
1979b   Religious Collectivities in Orthodox Judaism. Paper for the Conference on Religion and Religious Movements in the Mediterranean Area, Amsterdam.
Meijers, L.D. & J. Tennekes
1982   Spirit and Matter in the Cosmology of Chassidic Judaism. In: P.E. Josselin de Jong & E. Schwimmer (eds.), *Symbolic Anthropology in the Netherlands*. Verhandelingen van het Koninklijk Instituut voor Taal-, Land- en Volkenkunde 95. The Hague: Martinus Nijhoff, pp. 200-221.
Metzger, A.B.Z.
1973   Kaitz: The Time of Messianic Redemption. A Letter attributed to Fraide, the Baal Hatanya's daughter. *Tradition* 13(4) and 14(1):180-185.
Rabinovich, W.
1950   Karlin Hasidism. *Yivo Annual of Jewish Social Science* 5: 123-151.
Rubin. I.
1964   Chassidic Community Behavior. *Anthropological Quarterly* 37:138-149.
Schneerson, Rabbi M.M.
1962   *Likutei Sichois*. Volume II. Brooklyn, N.Y.: Kehot Publication Society.
1964   *Likutei Sichois*. Volume IV. Brooklyn, N.Y.: Kehot Publication Society.

Schochet, J.I.
    1961   *Rabbi Israel Baal Shem Tov.* Toronto: Lieberman's Publish-
            ing House.
    1974   *The Great Maggid.* Brooklyn, N.Y.: Kehot Publication
            Society.
Schoffeleers, M.
    1978   Clan Religion and Civil Religion. In: M. Schoffeleers &
            D. Meijers (eds.), *Religion, Nationalism and Economic
            Action: Critical Questions on Durkheim and Weber.* Assen:
            Van Gorcum, pp. 11-52.
Selier, F.J.M.
    1976   *Kiboets, gezin en gelijkheidsideaal.* Assen: Van Gorcum.
Weber, M.
    1965   *The Sociology of Religion.* London: Methuen & Co.
Zuckerman-Bareli, C.
    1975   The Religious Factor in Opinion Formation Among Israeli
            Youth. In: S. Poll & E. Krausz (eds.), *On Ethnic and
            Religious Diversity in Israel.* Ramat-Gan: Bar-Ilan
            University, pp. 53-90.

Ritual Escalation in Malta

Jeremy Boissevain, University of Amsterdam

In 1976 I was confronted with a puzzle when I returned to Malta to
film the Holy Week celebrations in Naxxar.[1] The Good Friday
celebration had expanded greatly since I had last seen it in 1961.
I learned that this expansion was general, and that the annual
festas celebrating parish saints had also grown. In 1965 I had
predicted that such celebrations would decline. I saw this decline
as the result of long-term secularising developments reflecting
general European trends (cf. Bras 1955:480-481 and Stacey 1960:72-
73).
　　In the early 1960s there were sound reasons to suppose that
processions and *festas* would decline and that parochial rivalry
would abate (Boissevain 1965:78-79). Heavy emigration was sapping
the manpower needed to staff brass bands, manufacture fireworks,
erect *festa* decorations and take part in processions. Relaxation
of boy/girl segregation and growing interest in football were
drawing young men out of the band clubs and firework factories. The
intense conflict between the Church and the Malta Labour Party
seriously affected the ability of villagers to organise celebrations.
Finally, I thought liturgical reforms would reduce religious
pageantry, especially Good Friday celebrations and annual *festas*.
The second Vatican Oecumenical Council had propagated a more Christo-
centric worship. The liturgical accent was to fall more clearly on
events which celebrated Christ's salvation. These were to be given
preference over feasts of saints, many of whom were downgraded if
not eliminated (Knox 1966:122 ff.). In short, there were strong
arguments to support the prediction that religious pageantry in
Malta would decrease, as it had elsewhere in Europe.
　　I was wrong. Although celebrations held simultaneously in all
parishes (such as St. Joseph the Worker, the Holy Rosary, Corpus
Christi and the Sacred Heart of Jesus) had indeed declined, *festas*
and Good Friday processions, which are purely parochial, have grown.
Why then should the scale of such parochial events increase?

Informants attributed the growth of the Good Friday celebrations
to innovations by Dun Karm, Naxxar's new Holy Week coordinator.
This, of course, did not explain the increase in other parishes.
Friends in Kirkop, for example, attributed the increase in the
scale of *festas* to the removal in 1975 of restrictions on the
celebration of secondary feasts. This supposedly took the lid off
competition between village factions celebrating rival saints. But
this did not explain satisfactorily the gradual increase in *festas*
apparant before 1975, or their growth in villages not divided by
this type of *festa* rivalry.[2]
A recent sociological study of Malta advanced another explanation:

> ... the at times forceful opposition by conservative elites in
> the different parishes, and the demand to exploit the past as a
> commodity with which to lure tourists, combined to preserve the
> traditional *festa*. But even this festivity, and such other pre-
> viously purely religious activities as the Good Friday pro-
> cessions ... became regarded less as coherent elements in
> everyday activity, less as essential features of the community's
> symbolic universe, and more as isolated, saleable artefacts of
> culture, to be produced and performed 'to order' for outsiders
> for whom they bore no intrinsic meanings but only qualities of
> spectacle ... What was once sacred, jealously guarded, and good-
> in-itself, had become another item to be put into the balance of
> payments as a credit-earning product (Vassallo 1979:207).

Vassallo's views were given local prominence when his book was
reviewed in Malta's *Sunday Times*, which is widely read by the
middle-classes, bureaucrats and political leaders. The review
reflects the opinion of many of the paper's readers:

> The 'mass servant ethos' engendered by tourism has artificially
> prolonged the life of much of our religious pageantry but it has
> also secularised it by transforming it into something picturesque
> merely to be exploited and sold. Most notably, our Good Friday
> processions have become gaudier, more vulgarly elaborate, mainly
> a spectacle for the amused or patronising tourist and largely
> divorced from the solemnities that originally gave them birth
> (Xuereb 1979).

The view that tourism leads to a commoditisation of culture has
also been expressed by some anthropologists (cf. Greenwood 1977:
136-137). Does the massive increase of tourism in Malta provide the
answer to the puzzle? Before coming back to this it is important
to have an overview of other developments in Malta and a clearer
idea of Good Friday and *festa* celebrations.

RECENT DEVELOPMENTS IN MALTA

Malta is located half-way between Gibraltar and Lebanon, midway between North Africa and Europe. It has been firmly a part of the European culture area since Roger the Norman threw out the Arabs in 1060. The Maltese islands, comprising Malta, Gozo and Comino, covering 120 square miles, have a population of 315,000. The country is 20 per cent smaller than the Isle of Wight and has more than three times the population density of Holland. There are more than fifty villages and towns which range in size from just under 1,000 to over 15,000 inhabitants. The islands' isolation, small scale and dense population have important social repercussions and contribute to the striking cultural homogeneity.

Each village is a parish. There are no hereditary or elected headman, mayors or other leaders besides the parish priest. Traditionally he has represented the interests of his parishioners. This has given him prestige and power. He now has to share his power as a patron with the elected members of parliament representing the constituency in which his parish is located.

The Maltese are intensely devout Roman Catholics. They also have the highest priest-people ratio in the world (Vatican 1970 in Vassallo 1979:88). As one turn-of-the-century ex-patriate remarked, "Malta would have been a delightful place if every priest were a tree ..." (Wignacourt 1914:129 in Vassallo 1979:88). Not surprisingly, religious practice is also intense, though decreasing slightly (Vassallo 1979:76). Nonetheless, mass attendance is high.

Since Malta became independent in 1964, the economy has expanded considerably. Tourism has played an important role in this economic expansion. Between 1960 and 1980 tourist arrivals increased from 20,000 to over 700,000. Wages have also expanded by more than 300 per cent since the early 1960s. Compared to the early 1960s people are now more smartly dressed, own their own transport and live in new or modernised houses equipped with many of the latest gadgets. Maltese kitchens and bathrooms have become show pieces in the on-going competition of keeping up with the Mifsuds.

Political developments have also been rapid and radical. Malta's recent political history can be divided neatly in two. From Independence in 1964 until 1971 the country was run by the Nationalist Party. Since then the Malta Labour Party has controlled the Government. The Nationalist Government was characterised by a *laissez-faire* economic policy and a, traditional, pro-European (and pro-NATO) cultural and political orientation. In 1971, peppery Dom Mintoff became Prime Minister and set rapidly about implementing the Labour Manifesto. This set out a programme of administrative discipline, a renegotiated defence treaty, a 40-hour work week, more help to underprivileged social categories, the take-over of

the giant ex-naval dockyard, and income tax reform.
   Malta's foreign policy also shifted radically. The new government sought to make Malta a bridge between North Africa and Europe.
It broke relations with NATO and sought accommodation with the Arab
world, finding Libya's Gaddafi particularly receptive. After nine
hundred years of being linked to Europe, Malta began to look
southward. The Moslem, a traditional enemy still remembered in
folk lore for savage pirate attacks, was redefined by Mintoff as a
blood brother. Libyan investment funds began to flow. Libyan male
tourists increasingly came in search of Maltese wine and women.
Arabic became a compulsory secondary school subject.
   By 1976 government controlled the banks, telecommunications,
broadcasting, air and sea transportation and the dockyard. Following the 1976 elections, the Labour government took on the university, the doctors and the Church. It merged the old university
with the polytechnic and downgraded or eliminated all arts subjects.
It introduced a National Health scheme. It also introduced legislation forbidding the clergy to interfere with elections, established
civil marriage, taxed religious bodies, abolished many customary
feast days and obliged chaplains to hold traditional services after
school hours.
   To sum up, changes since independence have been far-reaching
and rapid, especially following 1971. They have not been painless,
for the Labour government has had a heavy hand. Many civil servants
resigned and many intellectuals, including nearly 100 consultants
and junior doctors, emigrated (cf. *The Sunday Times* (London) 11
January 1981:11). In short, Malta is a small, reasonably prosperous
industrialised country which has experienced twenty years of rapid,
sometimes dizzying, social change. It is now riven with political
tension. What has remained constant, however, is the on-going
importance of parish-centred ritual more reminiscent of pre-
industrial society than twentieth century Europe.

RITUAL ESCALATION[3]

National and parochial feasts and processions, besides being major
religious occasions, are eagerly looked forward to as recreational
events. Though secular spectacles, such as political rallies, carnival, Independence Day and Republic Day, football and the cinema,
are becoming increasingly important, the principal amusements of
the Maltese still have connections with their religious ceremonies.
This was noted 140 years ago by a French consul in Malta, and his
observations are still applicable:

   Le Maltais a de la religion au fond de l'âme, cette religion
   dont il remplit les devoirs sans ostentation, il l'aime autant

plus qu'elle prend sa source, non seulement dans une foi sin-
cère, mais encore dans cette habitude, contractée dès l'enfance,
de chercher au sein des cérémonies religieuses un délassement,
que les autres peuples trouvent dans les spectacles et les
réjouissances publiques   (Miège 1840:168).

Let us now look at some of the religious spectacles in Naxxar,
a village of 5,000 odd where I have lived for several extended
periods during the past twenty-five years. Each year there are
approximately fourteen major religious celebrations which involve
processions. The greatest concentration is around Easter, though
the most joyous and crowded is the annual September *festa* of the
Nativity of Our Lady (*Marija Bambina*), the parish's patron.[4]
In 1976 Naxxar Good Friday celebration began, as always, with
visits to the Holy Sacrament which had been deposited the previous
evening in the altar of repose. This had been constructed in one
of the side chapels, and surrounded by a mountain of flowers. Each
group of visitors passed before the nine huge tableaux-statues
depicting scenes from Christ's passion. Each stopped to pray
before the sacrament. Every parish association and club, including
the Labour Club, visited the altar of repose. Many passed five
times before it. Numerous families also made pilgrimages to the
other twelve parishes which displayed tableaux. At each they prayed
and examined the flowers, the statues and funereal hangings before
proceeding to the next village. At the same time, visitors streamed
into Naxxar to see the church, to pray at the altar of repose and
to inspect the decorations.

The Good Friday procession was a superbly directed religious
drama with a cast of hundreds. In 1976 the procession lasted from
five o'clock in the afternoon until 9.30 that night. Some 550
persons took part. They were watched by the rest of the village and
hundreds of visitors from all over the island. There were also
sixty foreign tourists, brought by two travel agencies and seated
on chairs rented from the Peace Band Club. A subdued commentary
broadcast via speakers in the square explained in both Maltese and
English the details and meaning of Christ's passion. White robed
men carried the heavy tableaux. The largest, Christ's monumental
gilded mausoleum, was carried by ten men, accompanied by four
attendants and guarded by four Roman soldiers and two Renaissance
knights. In addition, there were 79 costumed men representing Old
and New Testament personages. Twenty masked penitents dragged heavy
chains tied to their ankles. Others crawled part of the way on
their knees. They were followed by a dozen black clad, veiled
women reciting the rosary. It was a most solemn and impressive
spectacle which had taken the vice parish priest, Dun Karm Catania
and his band of fifteen helpers many weeks to prepare.

Late that evening, the sacristan began to remove the black damask
that covered the walls and pictures.[5] On Saturday the helpers
dismantled and transported the tableaux to the parish warehouse,
where they would remain, carefully wrapped, for another year.

Although most of the Holy Week celebrations were much as they
had been in 1961, the Good Friday procession had grown more complex
and larger. To begin with, the 79 biblical costumes were new. They
were personal property and each had cost its owner an average of
£M70 (in 1976 £M1 = £1.30), roughly the equivalent of a month's
wages for an unskilled labourer. Those who took part in the procession worked with their hands. The cost was for material only,
for Salvu Pirotta, a retired tailor, made up most of the costumes
free of charge. The statue of Judas was new. Christ's mausoleum had
been regilded in 1974. The brass bands were larger and a second
band had been hired to assist Naxxar's own Peace Band.[6] Ten more
penitents dragged chains. The loudspeaker commentary was new.
Altogether the procession had grown by 130 persons, and expenses to
stage it had increased from £M90 to £M292. Moreover, it lasted an
hour and a half longer. Spectators, both Maltese and foreign, were
more numerous.

Such changes were not restricted to Naxxar. They were paralleled
in the twelve other Maltese villages which celebrated Holy Week
with some form of pageantry. In fact, this growth forms part of
the steady expansion that has taken place since the confraternity
of St. Joseph attached to the church of the Franciscan Minors in
Rabat first organised such a procession in the sixteenth century
(Cassar Pullicino 1976:30).

Though the details of Holy Week pageantry in each parish are
unique, they bear a family resemblance to those of Naxxar. So do
their developments over time (Cassar Pullicino 1965 and, especially,
1976:28-35).

The expansion of the solemn Good Friday processions has been
paralleled by that of the more exuberant annual celebration of
patron saints. In 1980 I was able to attend the annual *festi* in
Naxxar and Kirkop.[7] The Naxxar festivities celebrating the
Nativity of Our Lady, the parish's patron, lasted two weeks, culminating in the principal celebration on Sunday, September 14.[8]
It was a heady mixture of sacred and profane elements, a time of
prayer and celebration, of ceremony and amusement. The *festa*, like
that of all villages, consists of religious ceremonies which take
place principally within the church, and celebrations outside the
church. The Maltese make a distinction between these two elements
in the *festa*. These often take place simultaneously. Thus the
prayers, songs and sacred music of the internal celebrations compete with the crash of exploding fireworks and brass bands, and
the smell of incense with that of gunpowder.

The celebration of the feast required months of preparation, primarily to raise funds for the brass bands and decorations (see Table 1). The streets were decorated and festooned and the church finery moved into place by the band of helpers who regularly assist Dun Karm Catania prepare for major celebrations. Dun Karm was also treasurer of the small parish *festa* committee.[9] The 1980 *festa* cost £M1979. This had been collected over a period of nine months via a variety of lotteries, fairs and door-to-door collections.

The *festa* began on Wednesday, September 3, when the statue of the Nativity of Our Lady was taken out of her niche and placed on a pedestal in the main door of the church. This was followed by a torchlight procession from the chapel of the Immaculate Conception to the main square, where an open air mass was held. During the following week, the week of the Novena, religious exercises were conducted by a variety of visiting clerics. The parish clergy also held open air masses in several newly constructed neighbourhoods to integrate residents there into the parish. On Monday, 8 September, the actual liturgical feast day of the patron, the facade of the church was illuminated and Naxxar's Peace Band marched through the neighbourhood behind the church. The band was led by about twenty wildly dancing and cheering youths. On Thursday, 11 September, there was another march by the Peace Band, this time along the recently constructed 21st of September Avenue. This march, much staider than the Monday march, was followed by a concert in the main square. On Friday, 12 September, besides the usual evening *festa* mass there was also a special mass for bed-ridden parishioners, who were transported to the church. At 8 p.m. the traditional wild demonstration march began from the little chapel of St. John and headed for the parish church. This was one of the high points of the *festa*. More than fifty young men proceeded slowly up St. Lucy Street, jumping, shouting and dancing with others on their shoulders to demonstrate their loyalty to the saint. From time to time spectators showered them with confetti and fired hand-held coloured rockets (*stoppetti*). Most wore T-shirts and jeans and several had *Viva Marija Bambina* crayoned on shirts that proclaimed that they had been donated by a local snack bar. Other sported the BVM logo of the Blessed Virgin. Yet others wore odd hats or carried stunted umbrellas. The arch-priest, Dun Karm, the elders of the band club and a cordon of seven policemen served as a buffer between the bandsmen and the slowly moving, frantically careering mass of demonstrators. To slow the march down and so to prolong the homage to their patron, the demonstrators periodically lay down in an exhausted heap in the middle of the street. They succeeded and were more than an hour late arriving at the square.

This wild demonstration on the eve of the *festa* is traditionally a village affair. No outsiders were present. The few scuffles were quickly broken up by the bored, patient and remarkably good humoured police contingent. There were no serious incidents, such as had occurred in a neighbouring village the previous year, where demonstrators had smashed the windows of an impatient car.

On Saturday, the eve of the feast, there was a high mass and a Te Deum to mark the end of the Novena. In the late afternoon visitors began to arrive to watch the Translation. This is a ceremony during which a relic of the patron is escorted in procession around the square. After Vespers, the two guest bands, accompanied by relatives and celebrating parishioners, moved slowly through the village on separate routes, stopping at the various clubs for drinks. They arrived around ten o'clock in the main square, where they continued to play from bandstands. The square was packed with spectators waiting for the display of coloured rockets and stationery fireworks. This began just before eleven p.m.

On the morning of the *festa* there were a series of masses and an extended panegyric to the saint by a guest speaker. Late in the afternoon three guest bands began playing. At about half past six, following Vespers, the procession emerged from the church. Then the patron herself appeared amidst a barrage of petards (*il-kaxxa infernal*) and firecrackers. The patron's procession, comprising 70 costumed men and boys, priests as well as laymen (but no women), accompanied by a guest band, slowly wound through the village. When the saint arrived at the church's entrance at ten p.m. she was turned to watch the final barrage of coloured rockets. She then re-entered the church for another year. The packed square quickly emptied as the thousands of visitors streamed homeward in scores of buses and hundreds of cars. Several groups of Naxxarin went on the noisy traditional *xalata* (picnic excursion) the day after the *festa*.

Informants agreed that the 1980 *festa* had been the most crowded ever held. It had also been the most peaceful, for there had been few of the incidents provoked by tipsy celebrants that had been common in the past. Compared to the 1960 and 1961 *festas*, there had been a considerable increase in the scale of the celebrations. The most notable change was the remarkable increase in the number of spectators, many of whom were foreign tourists, including quite a few Naxxarin who had returned from abroad for the *festa*. The *festa* committee, gambling on good weather, had celebrated the feast late in the season so that there would be no rival *festas*. Their gamble paid off and there had been large contingents from the rival parishes of Senglea, Mellieha and Xaghra, which also celebrated the feast of the Nativity of Our Lady, but had done so the week before. A striking difference with 1960 was the size and frenzy of the

Friday night demonstration. This now resembled similar manifestations in villages which, like Kirkop, are divided by two *partiti* celebrating rival *festi*.

The size of the procession had also increased, from forty to seventy. Though the number of bands taking part remained the same, there had been changes (see Table 2). Thus from the exuberant peak in 1952 that followed the resumption of outdoor celebrations cancelled during the war, the Peace Band Club participation had declined from four to two performances by 1970. But by 1980 it was again giving three performances, although they were now held during the run up so that local musicians could attend the final *festa* celebration as spectators. The open air mass at the beginning of the Novena was also new. Though introduced as part of the 1980 International Marian Year celebrations, there was strong sentiment that this mass should be continued, as should the masses in the newly built areas.

Minor changes had also taken place. These included the use of crushed polystyrene plastic as confetti, several huge flares on the Band Club roof, many new street decorations and a notice on the church door asking spectators to enter only if decently dressed. There were also fewer aerial fireworks, particularly the noisy petards (*murtali*), though the number of hand-held *stoppetti* had greatly increased. Last but not least, four times as much money had been spent on the *festa* (see Table 1).

The growth of *festa* activities was also obvious in other villages. Everywhere there were more fireworks, especially in villages which, unlike Naxxar, still had their own firework factories. The Naxxar factory, which had exploded several times during the 1920s and 1930s, was not rebuilt after the war. Consequently, Naxxar's firework tradition is slowly dying. This is the exception rather than the rule. The increase in fireworks is illustrated by the escalation of accidents related to the manufacture of fireworks.

During the 1970s, the use of coloured fireworks increased dramatically. Unfortunately, so did the dangers inherent in making fireworks. The chemicals used for coloured fireworks are more unstable than those used for the traditional petards. Petards, popular among villagers, are abhorred by most influential middle class town dwellers, bureaucrats and foreign residents. The pressure of elite public opinion to replace noisy fireworks by coloured fireworks had tragic consequences. Between 1953 and 1969 sixteen Maltese firework factories exploded injuring 23 people, of whom seventeen died. But between 1970 and 1974 no less than ten explosions claimed thirty victims, of whom 21 died.[10] The annual accident rate during the 1970s rose from one explosion and one fatality to two explosions and four fatalities.

The little village of Kirkop rival feasts, celebrating two saints,

St. Leonard and St. Joseph, have also grown substantially during
the past twenty years. Each is better attended, noisier and more
colourful than it was in the early 1960s. Their respective partisans
have also bought each saint a new carved pedestal. In addition to
the blue and red scarves introduced in the late 1950s, demonstrators
now carry coloured umbrellas and cardboard lions.
    The greatest innovation, however, has been the introduction of
an exuberant noon band march on the day of the feast. This leaves
the saint's partisans so limp that they can hardly greet him when
he emerges from the church in the evening.
    In 1966 St. Leonard's partisans opened their own firework
factory. Unfortunately, the long established St. Joseph factory
exploded in 1976, but without injuring anyone. Both *partiti* have
renewed and increased their street decorations. Moreover, their
brass bands, dormant for years following the heavy emigration of
the 1950s, have come to life again. This little village of 1200
now has two active bands. For the first time these include a number
of girls. Contrary to my prediction rivalry between the supporters
of St. Leonard and St. Joseph has increased considerably (Boissevain
1965:78-79). In 1978 there were street skirmishes during St. Joseph's
centenary and the police had to intervene. In 1979, St. Joseph's
partisans refused to allow St. Leonard out of the church until their
rivals removed offending portions of their habits. Although in 1980
there were no open skirmishes during St. Leonard's feast, there was
considerable tension in the village. But in neighbouring Zurrieq,
however, there were open clashes between the rival supporters of
St. Catherine and Our Lady of Mount Carmel. This increased *festa*
rivalry was replicated in all villages divided over the celebration
of saints.
    The growth of parochial rivalry and *festa* activity during the
past two decades is part of a long term development (Cassar Pullicino
1976:35ff). It stretches back at least to the sixteenth century. The
increase, however, has primarily concerned rituals that take place
outside the church building. Although processions are extensions
of activities that take place inside the church, from which they
cannot be separated liturgically, the very fact that they do take
place in the public domain gives them a different character. The
rituals which take place inside the church change much more slowly.
Apart from the steady increase in decorations, I noticed no
appreciable changes inside the church.[11] The number of people
attending devotional services *appear* to have changed not at all over
the past twenty years. On the other hand, I did not count those
present in 1960 and 1980.
    So much for the ethnography. Why has the scale of Maltese re-
ligious spectacles increased over the past twenty years?

WHY ESCALATION?

The answer to this question is complex. I think it is possible to isolate three sets of reasons. The first is related to a number of structural constraints; the second, to certain political-economic developments; and the third, to the changing social and cultural environment. The first of the structural factors is the continuing importance of religion in Malta. This provides the necessary condition for continuing religious pageantry. The Maltese are extremely devout and have been so since their history has been recorded. I am not arguing that the increase in pageantry is a result of an increase in religiosity. It may be, but I have little evidence that it is. On the contrary, the increase in scale is taking place despite the slight drop in religiosity as measured by mass attendance and the performance of other religious obligations (Vassallo 1979). Most Maltese go to mass regularly and nine out of ten who work with their hands do so.

Given continuing religious observance, parochialism or *pika* (rivalry, competition) may be seen as a prime mover of the increase in scale. The continuing one-upmanship, the desire to be equal to or better than neighbouring parishes generates innovation. Like decorations to the church, innovations are added to existing ritual. They become part of the village's claim to excellence and may be imitated by other parishes. Why then is there continuing parochialism? This in turn is related to the continuing importance of the parish in Maltese community life. The village as such has no leader, no property, no territory, no ritual, no recurring activity. But the village as a parish, has a leader in the parish priest, property in the parish church, a common history represented by the accumulated wealth within the church, a clearly demarcated territory, a unifying symbol in the patron saint, and an elaborate series of recurring rituals that bind parishioners together via communal activities. As a parish, the village is a corporate community. The ceremonies of the parish then are the ceremonies of a community of neighbours. They provide ritual activity through which villagers express their sense of belonging to a unity greater than the family. While the mobility between villages is increasing, most residents in Maltese villages have been born there or married into them. Few outsiders without roots live there. The intensity of this parochialism is partly a function, in the mathematical sense, of the identification with the community in which one resides and worships. It is also a function of the islands' smallness. With one or two exceptions, no villager is more than a few minutes by public or private transport from the central square of the neighbouring village. There is thus a very clear sense of identity with a residential community composed of kinsmen, neighbours, fellow association members and co-participants in a series of events focussed on the community's chief symbols, its patron saint and parish church.

Organisers of functions such as Good Friday and *festas* are selected for their village patriotism and organisational abilities. Dun Karm Catania was appointed coordinator of the Naxxar Good Friday procession in 1972. The year after his appointment he invited the actors in a passion play in neighbouring Birkirkara, to accompany the Naxxar Good Friday procession in their biblical costumes. It was a big success. He then suggested that Naxxarin should take part the following year in their own costumes. The idea was enthusiastically received. As noted, Naxxarin attribute the sudden growth of Good Friday to the vision and energy of Dun Karm. The idea of biblical costumes, however, had been gradually spreading since the 1950s from Qormi, a wealthy village of 15,000 and a centre of ritual innovation. So in time they would most likely have spread to Naxxar. On the other hand, the developments would not have assumed the form they did had it not been for Dun Karm. In 1960 and 1970 and again in 1980 he visited the Oberammergau passion play. Consequently the Naxxar costumes are closely patterned on those used there. These are described in a book (Theimig 1960) on the production belonging to the parish's 'artistic adviser'.

Dun Karm's predecessor, the late Wigi Spiteri, a schoolteacher, coordinated the procession from 1940 to 1972. He, in his turn, especially during his early years as coordinator, had also increased its scale and intricacy. He collected and spent about three thousand pounds on various embellishments: 16 new standards, the black damask for the church, a new statue, a new pedestal, and costumes for the approximately 120 extra men and boys who took part in the procession. The procession has been growing slowly since it was established in 1833. Each generation leaves its mark, beautifying and enlarging and rarely, if ever, discarding. The head of the procession now re-enters the church before the tail has left, creating traffic problems. The four and a half hour manifestation has become tedious to some spectators and exhausting for the participants. It seems likely that a certain consolidation will take place to improve its theatrical qualities and to avoid audience fatigue.

Among the political-economic developments that help explain the increase in village spectacles, the most important is perhaps rising income. Though much of the extra income has been spent on housing and, especially, on such consumer durables as glittering bathrooms and ceramic encrusted kitchens, a good deal is also being spent on ritual. The rate of increase of expenditure on ritual has paralleled the increase in wages (see Figure 1).

The fact that most unmarried women are employed is also important. This has provided them with an independent source of funds to contribute (cf. Boissevain 1973). They have done so generously, although they still do not take part in the religious processions as formal participants. Increasing emancipation of women has also provided new resources for the bands, which during the 1960s and early 1970s had slowly been declining. Most can not only maintain their strength by enlisting the support of bandswomen.

Another important development has been the growing number of returned migrants. Many contribute funds and labour to parochial activities. Those still abroad plan holiday visits to Malta so that they can attend their village *festas* (King 1978 and King and Strachan 1980). In 1980 there were nearly 30 Australian and North American Naxxarin who had timed their holidays to coincide with the *festa*.

Tourism also has had an impact on religious spectacles. But not in the way which Vassallo and Xuereb suggested. Those who supervise and participate in such spectacles do not sell themselves. On the contrary. In 1976 Naxxarin earned little or nothing from their Good Friday procession. All food and wine shops were closed. In fact it cost Naxxarin £M261 to stage the procession. This money was collected laboriously by the clergy and others organising the procession. Much was contributed by those taking part in the procession. In short, the people of Naxxar organised, participated in, and contributed in- dividually to finance a pageant that was offered free to local and foreign tourists alike. It is also totally without fundation to suggest that all tourists are 'amused' or 'patronising'. Many in fact were deeply moved by the devotion displayed by those who took part in the rituals.

Foreign tourists, through their interest in what are basically traditional working class village events, have helped to make them more acceptable to the middle class, city dwelling elite. Many par- ochial pageants were denigrated by the Maltese white collar classes. As was usual in colonies, this class identified with the culture of its foreign masters rather than with its own heritage. Recitals by British Council musicians and Shakespearean plays were legitimate cultural events. Village Good Friday processions and *festas* were not. Yet these events formed part of the indigenous cultural legacy. This heritage became particularly important to a new nation searching for its cultural identity after imitating the literature and art of its foreign masters for more than 450 years. Thus religious pageantry is beginning to play a new role. It is being accepted by government, many young intellectuals and, somewhat more grudgingly, by some members of the urban middle class as an important national asset. This, in turn, has provided new meaning to those who organise and participate in such pageants. It has made them more enthusiastic. Tourism thus has played a part in the increase of pageantry. But not in the materialistic way that has been suggested.

Increased transportation and the extension and improvement of the road network has also contributed to the growth of pageantry. More buses and private cars now travel to all villages. This has enlarged the audience and, therefore, the enthusiasm of participants.

Another political-economic development has also contributed considerably to the escalation of *festas*. In 1975 the police ended their enforcement of church limitations on the scale of secondary *festa* celebrations. This had a long history. In 1935, alarmed at the extremes to which the devotion of saints was carried in certain villages, the church had taken steps to control the competition (Boissevain 1965: 75-76). It had promulgated regulations designed to reduce secondary feast celebrations. These, among other things, permitted only one band on the eve and one on the day of the feast. The church authorities thus sought to ensure that secondary feasts would not eclipse their titular rivals. The police had faithfully enforced these regulations by refusing licences for decorations, illumination and band marches that exceeded those permitted by the church. In 1975 the police were suddenly instructed to cease discriminating against the secondary feast of Our Lady of Lourdes in Qrendi. This was the village of the important Labour minister, Dr. Joseph Cassar, Honorary President of the Our Lady of Lourdes Band Club. At the time of this directive he was acting prime minister. The move was overtly political, for band clubs celebrating secondary saints usually have more Labour supporters than those celebrating titular saints (Boissevain 1965:107-111, 128-130). The Labour government thus effectively removed limits to the competition between *festa partiti* in the villages divided by this type of rivalry. By ending many of the 1935 restrictions, it also implemented a concession for which the Association of Secondary Feasts had been petitioning the archbishop for forty years (cf. Boissevain 1965:140). The consequences were predictable: the heightened rivalry between *festa partiti* escalated *festa* celebrations. This increase then spread to villages without *festa* factionalism, such as Naxxar.

Finally, a third set of factors which have influenced the growth of religious spectacles must be mentioned. The first of these is the rising voice of the worker since the advent of the Labour government in 1971. The participants in and most active supporters of Good Friday processions and *festas* are by and large manual workers. The introduction during the past decade of a 40-hour work week, increased wages, free Saturdays, and sick leave are important resources for the working man interested in participating in parish pageants. The increasing self-confidence of the working class, the coverage of their cultural events by the Labour controlled radio and television and the removal by their government of church restrictions on their feasts have contributed substantially. Other examples of this growth include the growing popularity of the traditional *ghana*, the improvised folk songs long popular among the poorer urban and rural classes. These are now often heard on cable radio and television. Twenty years ago they were heard only on Sunday mornings on 'The Farmers' Half-Hour'.

Secondly, cooperative participation in parish spectacles has contributed to security and mental peace. To some it has meant a release from the political tension that is rife in Malta today. By working together to bring honour to the village, people who don't see eye to eye politically can cooperate as members of the same community. This acts to neutralise the political divisions that in these small densely-populated islands often assume corrosive proportions. Immersion in the round of activities required to produce a good parish spectacle also provides shelter from the disorienting vortex of social change which has swept the Maltese along for fifteen years.

Friends explained the escalation of *festas* this way: Following independence in 1964, they had been swept along on a modernistic band-wagon. They had been urged to abandon traditional views, to look to European values, new literary forms, night-clubs and radical political change. After the transfer of government in 1971, even more rapid changes occurred. This was also a period of threats, of a heavy-handed government increasingly impinging on people's lives. Hence they "felt the need to return to the bosom of tradition as a shelter from the incumbent menace: at least in tradition one does not experience the threat inherent in novelty".

In the face of increased bureaucracy, harsh penalties for opposing the State, propaganda against Europe and unknown menacing Arab neighbours, "we simply go back to our origins; we cultivate them again and complicate them".

Traditional spectacles that celebrate the community, provide a familiar cooperative activity and a release from tension and uncertainty. At the same time such rituals provide an explicit sense of identity. After nearly a thousand years of identifying with Europe, and viewing North Africa as sinful, heathen, evil and dangerous, Maltese were told by the socialist government to turn their backs on Europe, to look to North Africa, to study Arabic, and to embrace their 'blood-brothers' in Libya. Yet in September 1980, angered by Libyan threats to Maltese off-shore oil operations, Mintoff broke with Qaddafi and sent Libyan diplomats, military advisors, students and tourists packing. Overnight the new blood-brother became public enemy number one. These rapid changes have made many people insecure, uncertain of who they are and where they are going. Clear-cut parish membership, participation with one's neighbours in century-old rituals and loyalty to community provide an unambiguous sense of belonging. The search for identity then, in a changing uncertain world, must also be regarded as one of the factors contributing to increased community ritual.

CONCLUSION

Emphatically increased pageantry is not 'cultural commoditisation' to lure tourists because of a 'mass servant ethos', and an interest in the balance of payments. Nor do I find any evidence that those who participate in such spectacles have been 'divorced from the solemnities that gave them birth'; nor that they are 'produced and performed to order for outsiders for whom they have no intrinsic meaning'. Such explanations, in fact, reflect the prejudices of many middle-class Maltese. They are statements about the social distance of these critics from the people for whom such events are important.

The persistence and growth of public local rituals are evidence that religion is very much alive in Malta. They are also evidence that popular religion is on the increase. The growth of *festa* and Good Friday celebrations contradicts much of the teaching of Vatican II which favoured a Christ-centred worship and sought to emphasise Easter rather than Good Friday. The costumes that offend middle-class critics reflect the taste of the working-class participants who have paid for them. Rising wages, influential patrons in power and tourists who have legitimised their rituals, have provided leverage to expand popular culture.

In spite of contradictions to Vatican II, the Maltese clergy generally have not opposed the expansion of religious pageantry. Where they have done so, there has been a backlash of protest which has alienated people from the church (cf. Boissevain 1969a), and fed the ever present anti-clerical current in the Islands. As one priest remarked, commenting on Good Friday, "It is practically the only public religious event which still can attract young men to make them participate actively.... From the religious point of view, it puts across the message of the Good Friday procession through 'attractive pageantry'".

Popular rituals have also increased elsewhere in Europe. Carnival societies in Holland, for example, have multiplied. They have not only increased among Catholics, for whom they were traditional, they have also spread to Protestant communities, where carnival was formerly anathema (Werdmölder 1979).[12] In London, the Notting Hill Carnival is also growing, becoming more overtly political, infusing a collective consciousness among West Indians and drawing public attention to their plight (Cohen 1980).[13] In the Roman suburb of Morlupo, an attempt was recently made to obtain religious patronage for the secular 'Festival of the Sausage', and regional minorities have begun celebrating their saints (Korovkin 1979). These developments bear a family resemblance to those in Malta. I suggest they too represent in part a search for identity and contact, a celebration of 'us' against 'them'. In a rapidly changing world becoming ever more complex and dominated by impersonal institutions, such celebrations provide in some measure a sense of belonging and an opportunity for communication. It is likely therefore that such rituals will continue to increase too.

NOTES

* Preliminary versions of this paper were presented to seminars at the universities of Amsterdam, Utrecht, Groningen, Gothenburg, Sussex, the London School of Economics, the School of Oriental and African Studies and to the conference on Religious Movements in the Mediterranean organised by the Department of European and Mediterranean Studies at the University of Amsterdam and the Department of Anthropology and Religion, Free University of Amsterdam, December 1979. I am grateful to the many participants at these meetings and to Peter Serracino Inglott, Ad Koster, David Boswell, Peter Xuereb, Lawrenz Cachia, Charles Delia, Edward Scicluna, Joe Friggieri, Anton Xiberras and, of course, Carmel Catania, for most helpful discussions and assistance in various ways. Hannie Hoekstra and Pat Lacey kindly typed various versions from tapes and drafts. The final draft was written while I was a Visiting Fellow at the Institute of Development Studies at the University of Sussex.

1. The film was used for the series 'Face Values', first broadcast on BBC1 during April and May 1978. Also see Sutherland (1978) which accompanied the series.
2. For a detailed examination of rivalry between *festa* factions see Boissevain 1965:55-96; 1974 and 1978.
3. My argument that public rituals are expanding is based on a fairly continuous general contact with Malta since the late 1950s and detailed familiarity with the parishes of Naxxar and Kirkop (Boissevain 1965, 1969a, 1969b, 1973, 1980). Observations and detailed conversations with informants in other villages made it clear that developments in these two villages are a fair reflection of those taking place in other parishes. See also Cassar Pullicino 1976:14ff.
4. Also called Our Lady of Victories in commemoration of the lifting of the Turkish siege shortly after the Feast of Our Lady in 1565.
5. Though the black damask was forbidden in the new liturgy, the people of Naxxar continued to use their expensive traditional wall coverings. When asked about it, Dun Karm, the procession's coordinator, replied with tongue in cheek, "I don't think the Pope knows about it".
6. The second band was from the village of Mellieha, which had once formed part of the parish of Naxxar and is dedicated to the

same patron saint.
7. This was made possible thanks to a travel grant from the University of Amsterdam.
8. Officially the Feast of the Nativity of Our Lady is on September 8th. Three years previously government decreed that thenceforth *festas* would be celebrated on weekends so as not to interfere with the working week. In fact few titular *festas* even then were celebrated according to the church liturgical calendar. Most had been shifted to the summer to take advantage of the good weather and to avoid rain and storm damage to costly street decorations.
9. The committee consisted of the archpriest, chairman, Dun Karm, treasurer, and a layman, secretary.
10. These details were kindly made available to me in 1974 by the Malta police.
11. Since 1976, for example, Naxxar parishioners have spent more than £M6000 on construction, sculpture, silver, painting and damask to beautify their parish church.
12. Werdmölder explains the growth of carnival in transactionalist terms: the organisers are the businessmen and café owners who profit from them. This argument may shed light on the organisers' motives, but it provides no insight into the enthusiasm of the participants.
13. The growth of Maltese religious pageantry lacks this overt political dimension. Though opposition to the anti-clericalism and heavy-handedness of the ruling Labour government may indeed motivate the participation of some, I found no evidence for this. To the contrary, many of the strongest Labour supporters were also among the most fervent Good Friday participants and *festa* celebrators.

BIBLIOGRAPHY

Boissevain, J.
1965   *Saints and Fireworks, Religion and Politics in Rural Malta.* London: The Athlone Press. (Second Edition 1969).
1969   1968 Postscript to Second Edition of Boissevain 1965.
1969   *Hal-Farrug: A Village in Malta.* New York: Holt, Rinehart & Winston. (Second Edition 1980).
1973   Some Notes on the Position of Women in Maltese Society. In: K. Weibust (ed.), *Kulturvariation i Sydeuropa.* Copenhagen: NEFA Forlag, pp. 125-143.
1974   Conflict and Change: Establishment and Opposition in Malta. In: J.Davis (ed.), *Choice and Change. Essays in Honour of Lucy Mair.* London: Athlone Press.

1978   Of Men and Marbles: Notes Towards a Reconsideration of
          Factionalism. In: M. Silverman & R.F. Salisbury (eds.),
          A House Divided: Anthropological Studies of Factionalism.
          St. John's: Memorial University of Newfoundland, pp. 99-
          110.
1980   1979 Epilogue to Second Edition of 1969.

Bras, G. le
1955   *Etudes de sociologie religieuse.* Paris: Presses universi-
          taires de France.

Cassar-Pullicino, J.
1956   La settimana santa a Malta. *Phoenix* 2:1-24.
1976   *Studies in Maltese Folklore.* Malta: The University of
          Malta.

Cohen, A.
1980   Drama and Politics in the Development of a London Car-
          nival. *Man* 15:65-87.

Greenwood, D.J.
1977   Culture by the Pound: An Anthropological Perspective
          on Tourism as Cultural Commoditization. In: V. Smith
          (ed.), *Hosts and Guests: The Anthropology of Tourism.*
          Pittsburgh: University of Pennsylvania Press, pp. 128-
          138.

King, R.
1978   Return Migration: Review of Some Case Studies from
          Southern Europe. *Mediterranean Studies* 1:3-30.

King, R. & A. Strachan
1980   The Effects of Return Migration on a Gozitan Village.
          Human Organization 39:175-179.

Knox, R.J. (ed.)
1966   Constitution on the Sacred Liturgy. *The Documents of
          Vatican II.* New Delhi: St. Paul Publications.

Korovkin, M.A.
1979   Old Modernity and New Tradition: Social Change in a
          Central Italian Community. Unpublished MA Thesis.
          Toronto: York University, Dept. of Social Anthropology.

Miège, M.
1840   *Histoire de Malte.* (Three volumes). Paris.

Stacey, M.
1960   *Tradition and Change: A Study of Banbury.* London:
          Oxford University Press.

Sutherland, A. (ed.)
1978   *Face Values: Some Anthropological Themes.* London: BBC.

Thiemig, K.
1960   *Das Passions Spiel.* München: Karel Thiemig KG.

Vassallo, M.
1979   *From Lordship to Stewardship: Religion and Social Change*

in Malta. The Hague: Mouton.

Vatican
1970   *The Clergy in the World*. Vatican: Congregation for the
        Clergy.
Werdmölder, H.
1979   Karnaval anders bezien. Een studie naar het organisa-
        torische aspekt van het karnaval te Venlo. *Volkskundig
        Bulletin* 5(1):1-20.
Wignacourt, J.
1914   *The Odd Man in Malta*. London: G. Bell & Son.
Xuereb, P.
1979   Review of Mario Vassallo, 'From Lordship to Stewardship:
        Religion and Social Change in Malta'. *Sunday Times*
        (Malta), September 16:10.

TABLE 1: NAXXAR *FESTA* EXPENSES: 1929-1980

	Total Expense (£M)	Bands	Lighting	Fireworks	Other	Total
			Per Cent Spent on:			
1929	122	34	12	23	31	100
1938	207	29	29	20	22	100
1961	550	41	31	19	9	100
1975	1276	29	21	30	20	100
1980	1979	33	27	21	19	100

Source: Documents made available by Reverend Carmel Catania.

TABLE 2: NUMBER OF BAND PERFORMANCES AT NAXXAR *FESTA*: 1909-1980

Year	Peace Bands	Hired Bands	Total
1909	2	1	3
1920	3	4	7
1930	3	4	7
1940	N O N E		
1950	4	5	9
1960	3	5	8
1971	2	5	7
1974	2	5	7
1980	3	5	8

Source: Documents made available by Reverend Anton Xiberras.

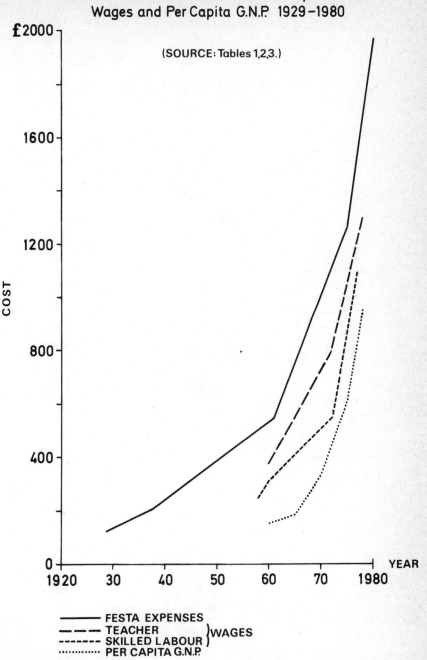

Fig.1

Cost of Naxxar External Festa Compared To Wages and Per Capita G.N.P. 1929-1980

(SOURCE: Tables 1,2,3.)

£2000

1600

1200

COST

800

400

0

YEAR

1920   30   40   50   60   70   1980

————— FESTA EXPENSES
— — — TEACHER   }WAGES
- - - - - SKILLED LABOUR
········· PER CAPITA G.N.P.

The Kappillani: The Changing Position of the Parish Priest in Malta

Adrianus Koster, Free University, Amsterdam

INTRODUCTION

"Have you heard the sad news?" Salvu Ellul, the local butcher, almost made the query part of his greeting: a direct follow-up to the warm words of welcome to one who had been away from Has-Sajjied[1] for three months. "Who died?" I reacted promptly. "Nobody, but the *kappillan* (pastor) will soon be leaving us."

During the nine months of my second stay in Has-Sajjied there was only one topic to which conversation never failed to come round: the promotion of Dun Alwig Debono to a larger parish and all this was to bring about: the protests filed by the parishioners with the archbishop, the appointment of a successor, the village outing when people said goodbye to Dun Alwig and at the same time welcomed his successor, the induction of Dun Alwig into his new parish and of his successor into Has-Sajjied.

It was not until the hectic general election-campaign of September 1976 that people turned their minds to other matters, and even in 1979, when I spent another two months in the village, many people were still judging the new incumbent by the standards of Dun Alwig.

Malta, one of the oldest nations in Europe, is a sovereign state made up of six islands, three of which are inhabited[2]. On account of its unique strategic position, Malta's fate until recently was for it to be ruled by a succession of foreign overlords. The sovereign and military Order of St. John, the ruler from 1530 to 1798, was succeeded by the French, but they held the islands for a short time only. The British took over in 1800 to remain in Malta until 1964, when independence was granted. Tradition has it that the islanders were converted to Christianity by St. Paul himself, and that Malta has been Catholic ever since. Among the inhabitants there are very few who have not been baptised according to the rites of the Roman Catholic Church. For this reason, the parish priest has always been one of the most influential members of Maltese society.

The pastor, the appointed representative of the bishop, is in charge of the parish. As the leader of a Christian community he is responsible for the spiritual welfare of all his parishioners. At the crucial moments in their lives he administers the rites of passage: baptism, first Holy Communion, marriage and the last sacraments. He is in charge of all the church services and ceremonies, including the celebration of major and minor feasts and the leading out of processions. He gives the Sunday-sermon in the parish church and no priest can say mass or preach there unless he invites them. The installation ceremony of a new parish priest is called '*Il-Pussess*', which means that he takes possession of his parish.

The story with which this paper opens gives the impression that parish priests, even in present-day Malta, still have the same considerable amount of influence they had in the not too distant past (Boissevain 1965, 1969). This is contrary to what could be expected when it is considered that since independence (1964) the state has increasingly interfered with every sphere of society, even overwhelmingly so since Dom Mintoff's Malta Labour Party (MLP) was returned to power in 1971. It is widely held that growing penetration by the state leads to a loss of functions, and consequently of power, for the people and their non-governmental institutions. Does Malta make the exception to this rule? The only way to find out is to undertake a systematic study of the interdependence of church and state, and how this has changed through periods of time. This is what the present paper attempts to do. The focus is on the change in the relations between the parish priest and his parishioners, on the one hand, and with his colleagues and with the bishops, on the other, a change which will be tentatively related to the changing relationship with the state.

After a brief survey of the pre-independence situation, an analysis is presented of the position of the parish priest. The incisive influence of the Second Vatican Council is the subject of the following section, which in the many references to latter-day politics anticipates the next item: the fundamental impact of the victorious socialists. The churchmen's reaction to the Labour onslaught is described then, together with an analysis of the new attitudes towards individual Laborites and the hierarchy adopted by the parish priests; in most cases it appears that compromise, itself inspired by the wind of change blowing from Rome, was the main feature. Next, the focus is on the bishops themselves and their relations with the government, the priests' newly gained freedom making them take a stance which is less than before characterised by unswerving loyalty. In conclusion, the author gives as his opinion that under increasing pressure from the government, the church may revert again to its overtly anti-Mintoff position, which postconcillar tendencies had led it to abandon.

COLONIAL CATHOLIC MALTA

Contrary to what one would expect, the position of the Catholic
church in Malta was much stronger under colonial British rule than
it is now that the islands are independent. The Protestant British
authorities, whose main concern with Malta was the fortress-island,
respected the position of the local hierarchy and clergy. It was
their general policy not to interfere in religious matters, as the
church might become a powerful opponent and even an advocate of
British withdrawal[3]. Only a few adjustments were made in order to
guarantee the smooth administration of the colony. The church was
allowed to continue its accumulation of wealth, be it that a Mort-
main Law, proclaimed in 1822, forced it to sell or dispose of newly
acquired immovable property. On the other hand, a few concessions
to the Catholic hierarchy could well persuade them to adopt a rather
benevolent attitude towards the colonial overlords and make them a
powerful ally in maintaining the *status quo*. So the British made the
archbishop of Malta second in rank, after the governor, in the Table
of Precedence of official occasions and gave him the right to the
military honours of a Brigadier. The Catholic ritual was preferred
for important state functions. Bishops could not be taken to a
government court (*privilegium fori*) and were exempt from taxes of
any kind. Other religions were tolerated, but proselytising among
Maltese Catholics was not encouraged and public religious ceremonies
held by non-Catholics could be banned whenever the government
expected a disturbance of the peace. In all schools, religious
instruction was given according to Catholic principles. Canon law
was indiscriminately applied to all Maltese with respect to marriage.
Consequently, civil marriage and legal divorce did not exist[4].
Maltese Catholic morals generally blended happily with those of their
Victorian British counterparts.

   With few exceptions, British policy proved effective throughout
the colonial period. While the church gave to Malta its own identity,
the local bishops, unlike their Cyprian colleagues, never challenged
the British colonial authority, and on the whole they were quite
satisfied with their privileged position in colonial Malta. This
does not mean, however, that the dominant position of the church and
its hierarchy was never challenged by local authorities and politicians. Lord Strickland, prime minister under a dyarchical system,
became engaged in a fierce struggle with almost the entire clergy
when he sought to curtail their influence in secular matters.
Finally he had to give in, as the use of ecclesiastical weapons
threatened to ruin his political career[5]. Many years later, when Dom
Mintoff was prime minister under an adapted system of dyarchy,
relations between the church and the Maltese government were hostile
again, the church obstructing Mintoff's plans for the integration of

Malta with the United Kingdom because the church authorities were not given the required assurances that their position would remain unchanged after the implementation of the plans. When in 1958 Mintoff dropped his project of integration and proposed independence instead, archbishop Gonzi's condemnation of the violent behaviour of Mintoff's supporters triggered off a bitter quarrel which was not yet settled when Malta became independent under Mintoff's arch-enemies, the more pro-clerical Nationalist Party. During this dispute the faithful considered it a mortal sin to vote Labour. Mintoff formulated pro-posals for church-state relations in Malta which envisaged separation of church and state, recognition of civil marriage (and possibly divorce), abolition of mandatory religious education, state-inspection of those private schools that were subsidised, dispensation of social services without favouritism, financial restrictions to be placed on the church, limitation of *privilegium fori*, the exclusion of church intervention in state censorship of books and films and, finally, an end to the religious meddling in politics. The Independence Constitu-tion, however, put the stamp of legality on the dominant position of the church. When the British left, Malta still had a triumphant, wealthy, almost medieval church[6].

THE TRADITIONAL PARISH PRIEST

At the time independence was granted, Malta was divided into 49 parishes[7]. Until recent changes were effected, every town or village formed a single parish. Only Valletta and Qormi were split into two parishes, while Sliema had three. Not more than 5 out of 49 parish priests were members of religious orders. Their parishes, with the exception of St. Dominic's (Valletta - 1571), were founded between 1913 and 1918. These priests are appointed by the bishop after nomination by the superior of the order, as a rule they are replaced after a couple of years. They work in close cooperation with their fellow religious and have only to care for the pastoral needs of the parish. The financial and organisational problems are dealt with by the prior. They do not enjoy the same prominence in their parish as diocesan priests do in theirs. In this paper we are primarily con-cerned with the diocesan priests.
    Prior to the Second Vatican Council, whenever a position fell vacant the competitors had to sit for an examination in moral theology and canon law. If an incumbent was among the applicants for a larger parish, he was automatically chosen; and if two parish priests both wanted to be promoted, the one who had held office for the longer period received the appointment. Once appointed, the new *kappillan* was relatively independent in parochial affairs. For example, when Dun Alwig wore his *muzzetta* for the first time after

his appointment, an elderly colleague said to him, "In this vestment you are a pope". Dun Gorg, who has for many years been the archpriest of one of the biggest parishes (and quite an imposing figure he is) gave this reply to my question as to why, contrary to custom, he never invited a bishop or monsignor to carry the relic of the patron saint in his annual procession: "In my parish I am the bishop, so I'll lead the procession myself".

A parish priest could not be removed: at best, he could be persuaded to accept a larger parish or, in old age, a canonship, carrying the title of Monsignor, in the Cathedral Chapter. The canons of the Cathedral Chapter used to be the main counsellors of the bishop. The traditional benefices and the right to wear a mitre were much envied amongst the clergy. Dun Gorg, however, confided to me, "Monsignor ... I never want that. Now I am Dun Gorg Farrugia, archpriest of Hal-... Everybody knows me, but once you are a monsignor, people wonder, 'Monsignor who?'. They will be forgetting your name". Eventually, however, Dun Gorg became Mgr. Farrugia and with his impressive bearing, his head crowned by a mitre, he can be sure that no one will overlook him.

The parish priest's income was raised by the parishioners; most of it was given to him as a stipend during his annual blessing of the houses.

It was the task of the *kappillan* to supervise the local clergy and assign various duties to them. One of them, the procurator, was in charge of the parish church and its possessions; conflicts between parish priests and procurators were not unusual.

The parish priest used to pay frequent visits to the government schools in his parish, saying mass and hearing confessions there. The *kappillan* appointed the officials of the local lay-organisations[8] and the men who helped him organise the village *festi*; he was also in charge of local charities. Consequently, he had the power to reward those who obeyed him. He also was the moral guardian of the parish. Whenever one of the previous archpriests[9] of Zejtun noticed a young couple kissing he 'confiscated' the girl's *ghonella* (traditional headdress) and told her that her mother could come and collect it at his office. People living 'in sin', or generally not at peace with the church would have their home ignored by the parish priest when he made his round for the annual blessing. This put a social stigma on them. The traditional way of checking whether one was still a practising Catholic was by the *bolletini* (tickets). During the blessing of a home each member of the family entitled to receive Holy Communion received a ticket from the *kappillan*. It had to be exchanged for another one by the parishioners as they came up to the altar-rails for Holy Communion during Easter tide[10]. New *bolletini* would be given out in exchange for the old ones again during the next blessing of the homes.

Traditionally, the *kappillan* has been the chief welfare officer
of the parish, a role which has hardly diminished in importance even
now. He took care of orphaned children, placing them in one of the
many Church homes; this also applied to children of broken families
or inadequate parents. When a wife was beaten up by her husband and
otherwise ill-treated she sought the aid of the parish priest, who
would speak to her husband or see to it that the wife was temporarily
taken care of by nuns. In the case of an illegitimate pregnancy the
girl would turn to the *kappillan* who found her a place in a convent
until after she had given birth to her child, for whom the Catholic
Adoption Society would then find adopters: often childless couples
who, through the parish priest, approached the Society. As a rule,
the *kappillan* would act with much discretion, never telling anybody
about the girl being an expectant mother, but just giving it out
that she had gone abroad to stay with relatives.

The traditional parish priest was the main adviser of his parishioners, not only in spiritual but also in secular matters, even
to the extent whether a woman should have a hysterectomy or not. He
often acted as the spokesman of his parishioners, on the basis of
his status and because of the absence of local government institutions. He was the natural representative of the parish and its
parishioners with the world outside. He used to act as a public
registrar, issuing birth, marriage and death certificates. In the
old days, he was one of the few literates in the village who gave
help to those that could not read and write, a task which gradually
diminished after the introduction of compulsory education in 1948.
Boissevain (1965:43) says that "he served his parishioners as lawyer,
banker and business adviser". Sometimes he acted as a matchmaker, or,
through his colleagues, provided parents with information about a
suitor coming from outside the parish. Often he occupied a prominent
place in the patronage circuits. Boissevain also mentions that because
of the numerous services a parish priest performed he also had the
power to withhold them, a sanction varying from "declining to write
a good conduct certificate to denying absolution in confession"
(ibid.:43). The latter punishment, however, is in the power of each
individual priest. He mentions people referring to the parish priest
as '*il-principal tar-rahal*' (the head of the village, ibid.:43).

An interesting example of the role of the parish priest in church-
state relations was provided by the traditional Candlemas ceremony.
Ever since the time of the Knights, on 2 February, the parish priests
presented the Grandmaster of the Order of St. John, and later the
archbishop and the governor, with a two-pound candle as a token of
respect for the highest authorities on the island. The ceremony
symbolised the close links between church and state. A more recent,
but significant development was for the governor to address the
parish priests on important state affairs, so that they, as the

traditional leaders of the villages and towns, could inform their parishioners.

In spite of his relative independence in parochial affairs, the parish priest was expected to scrupulously follow the directives of his bishop in matters of diocesan importance. The so-called 'politico-religious conflicts' (1927-1932 and 1958-1969) were examples of these matters. In those days, it was the responsibility of the parish priest to separate the 'true Catholics' in his parish from the supporters of a party 'alien to the church' (the Constitutional and Labour parties). The adherents of the latter parties could, in case of sudden death, be denied the right to a proper Catholic burial by the *kappillan* and this was a mighty weapon[11]. The College of Parish Priests, founded in 1943, was an outspoken ally of the Maltese bishops in their quarrel with the Labour Party. In those conflicts there were parishioners who challenged the authority of the parish priest. Actually, this has never been uncommon in Malta: especially in those parishes where *festa partiti*[12] existed, the decisions of the *kappillan* in favour of one party would antagonise the supporters of the other. The latter would appeal to the bishop, beat up the parish priest, or do both. "Occasionally a parish priest is threatened, frightened by a home-made bomb, or attacked; he then often requests, and generally receives, a transfer to another parish," says Boissevain (1965:86).

So we may conclude that the pre-independence parish priest fulfilled many functions both in the religious and secular fields and was even encouraged by the secular authorities to do so. Consequently, he wielded considerable influence and authority, although this authority never went completely unchallenged. If his position became untenable, he would ask for a transfer.

CONSEQUENCES OF VATICAN II

The many changes implemented by the decrees, and even more so by the spirit of the Second Vatican Council (1962-1965) and the *aggionornamento* it brought about in the various departments of the Roman Curia, have not left traditional Catholic Malta untouched. The liturgical renewal, heartily welcomed by the large majority of churchgoers, which introduced the use of Maltese in liturgy and in hymn singing and altars facing the people, brought the clergy, including the *kappellani*, closer to the people[13]. But some changes directly affected the position of the parish priest. The Council suppressed the examinations in which priests could compete for a vacant parish[14]. Now the bishop may lawfully remove or transfer a parish priest from his parish and all parish priests must submit their resignation to the bishop before their 76th birthday[15]. The Council also emphasised

the importance of the optimal size of parishes and encouraged the
bishops to achieve this by creating new parishes and merging existing ones[16].

Consequently, 15 new parishes have been erected since 1964,
making a total of 64 parishes. It is remarkable that 10 of them have
been given to religious orders, thus increasing the number of parishes
entrusted to an order from 5 to 15. As a result of the splitting of
their parishes, several parish priests lost a considerable part of
their flock and consequently of their income[17]. The pastor, however,
is now himself custodian of the parish church and its finances, as
the office of procurator has been abolished. Now he has to share
some of his responsibilities with the presbyterium consisting of all
resident priests in his parish. Although he is in the chair, he can
be outvoted.

It is important to note that, in the new spirit of the post-
Vatican II Roman Catholic church, the clergy was allowed more freedom
than before in ventilating opinions dissident from those held by
their bishops. In Malta, some of them, including parish priests, now
managed to establish excellent personal relations with the Vatican.
So, as a perhaps unintended consequence of the Council, the Maltese
parish priests individually and collectively became sought-after
coalition partners in intra-church disputes, this in spite of their
increased formal dependence on the bishop.

The importance attached by Vatican II to the laity led to the
introduction of parish councils in Malta. Another result of the
winds of change raised by the Council was that the Holy See no longer
backed the Maltese hierarchy in its conflict with the Labour Party,
but forced the bishops to come to terms with Mintoff. In 1969 a
'peace treaty' was signed which paved the way to Labour's return to
power in 1971.

It is interesting to find out how parish priests reacted to the
changing situation. Several cases-in-point are cited now. As I
mentioned before, the parish priests individually (and collectively
in the College of Parish Priests) gave strong support to the hierarchy
in this grave conflict with the MLP. But gradually some moderates
changed their minds and started a covert rebellion.

Dun Peter Falzon was a parish priest in a small village in a
Labour area. Some of his old friends from his native town were in the
Labour Party. He was not a MLP supporter himself, but he thought
Mintoff's ideas were broadminded and progressive. In his opinion the
attitude of the hierarchy and the clergy, indiscriminately condemning
every form of socialism, was wrong. Unfortunately, Mintoff and archbishop Gonzi personally disliked each other, and this made the conflict much worse than Dun Peter could visualise. He sympathised with
the conflicts of conscience of the Labourites in his parish, who were
also sincere believers. This gave him the feeling of being squeezed

between the archbishop and his own parishioners. Gradually, he took
the latters' side and put his own interpretation on the instructions
of the hierarchy regarding the blessing of the homes or the giving
of absolution in confession. Dun Peter and those of his colleagues
who felt and did like him would never have thought of doing so before
Vatican II.

However, most parish priests did not behave in this manner. In
those days there was a marriage-witness who came to the ceremony
sporting a Mintoff badge. The parish priest refused to solemnise the
marriage unless he took it off. After an hour's arguing, the witness
gave in and the ceremony began. Even a moderate-minded parish
priest did not like a Mintoff badge in church: "I once saw a man
with a Mintoff badge coming to Holy Communion; I hesitated, but gave
him the host. After mass I called him to the sacristy and told him
this badge should not be worn in church. He became nervous, told me
he had forgotten to take it off and apologised".

After independence several parish priests began to realise that
even a Nationalist government could not stop the progress of secular-
isation in Malta. Furthermore, not all the Nationalist leaders were
shining examples of Catholic virtue, and the generally prevalent
laissez faire policy of the Nationalist government was one which
many clergymen considered reprehensible. The College of Parish Priests
became very annoyed when they were not granted an interview with
prime minister Borg Olivier as when they wanted to testify to their
moral concern over the opening of a casino and other such matters.
This made them gradually change their minds in the conflict with the
MLP, and when it drew to a close, quite a few *kappillani* began to
reestablish relations with the MLP supporters in their parish, continuing to do so quite openly after the 'peace treaty' of 1969.

In the meantime, Dun Peter had been transferred to the parish of
his native town. There, his predecessor, an outspoken Nationalist,
had chased many Labourites out of the church. It took Dun Peter a
couple of years to get them to come back. He visited his old friend
to show the people he was not biased, and this did not fail to
produce effects. Dun Alwig, too, tried to do his utmost, first to
prevent a split in the parish along political lines, and later to
restore relations. In his homilies he spoke a lot about brotherly
love, emphasising mutual understanding. Dun Alwig behaved with such
genuine friendliness towards everybody that most Labourites who had
given up church attendance began to come again. Sometimes he asked
them, "Would you like to reintegrate yourself with the church? Yes?
Then try to behave as a good Catholic. Pray for both the archbishop
and Mintoff". He found out that several Labourites had not ceased to
come to church, but refrained from receiving Holy Communion. Through
a gradual approach, he tried to achieve a settlement, especially on
such occasions as weddings and funerals. By his gentle behaviour he

encouraged them to join their friends who had remained faithful to the church. When he left the parish, only three people were left who still came to church without receiving Holy Communion.

During the relatively quiet electoral campaign of 1971 most parish priests did not speak out openly against the Malta Labour Party and tried to keep the balance between Labour and Nationalists. One of them told me that on election day he was called by a Nationalist MP, who vented his anger at a Labour banner having been put up against a wall of the church. Instead of removing it, which would have caused a lot of friction, the *kappillan* asked the MP to put up a Nationalist banner alongside the Labour one. Within a couple of hours the two banners fluttered side by side. Our parish priest never talked politics with anyone in his parish and went out to vote at the very last minute of the poll.

We learn from the first case that now, albeit secretly, parish priests were not executing directives of the bishops. Not only were there changes in the relationships between parish priest and parishioners, as we have seen in some cases. The post-conciliar spirit gradually prepared the minds of all but a few diehards for a change in view: the acceptance that some parishioners were Labour supporters whose political opinions should not be interfered with. The above-mentioned *kappillan* did not want to risk breaking newly established links by removing the Labour banner and promoting the Nationalist cause, as he certainly would have done ten years previously. In 1971, many *kappillani* were prepared to give the elected Labour government a fair chance, but this rather benevolent attitude changed once they became aware what Mintoff had *in petto* for the church.

THE SOCIALISTS AND THE CHURCH

When independence came, the church's main protector, Britain, had left, though not without safeguarding the church's position by inserting entrenched clauses in the Independence Constitution. The Nationalist government (1964-1971) agreed and respected the status quo. But the Labour government (since 1971) despised the Constitution and wanted to see Mintoff's old proposals for church-state relations implemented. A return to power of Labour, leave alone the implementation of Mintoff's proposals, would have been unthinkable in pre-Council Malta[18].

The socialist government does not recognise the parish priest as the representative of the local community. The first time this became evident was in February 1972, when the parish priests found out that the traditional Candlemas-ceremony had been modified: the governor-general had been instructed not to speak on the occasion, and this caused much frustration among the *kappillani* and many others. After the proclamation of the republic, the ceremony was abolished altogether by the government a few days before it was due in February 1975, "as its original goal had ceased to apply". The archbishop and the parish priests expressed their regrets and from that date on they stage their own annual ceremony during a pontifical mass in St. John's Co-Cathedral.

Since Labour took office, new patronage circuits were built around a new elite, circuits in which there was no room for parish priests. This meant a serious loss of prestige for the *kappillani*.

In December 1974, the republic was proclaimed and in the amended constitution the term 'corrupt practices' was introduced with respect to elections. According to its definition, "any temporal or spiritual injury" constitutes a corrupt practice[19]. This means that an election result can be annulled if priests have, for example, refused absolution to the voters of a particular party. The amended constitution paved the way for the implementation of Mintoff's 'old' proposals for church-state relations in Malta. Now it was only a matter of months before the Labour government enacted legislation concerning the church. First, *Privilegium fori* was abolished. Then the Burials Ordinance was amended, so that every Maltese citizen became entitled to burial in the Addolorata cemetery (the main cemetery in Malta) and interment there could no longer be denied to persons who, according to canon law, have placed themselves outside the pale of the Christian church. This amendment was clearly meant to undo the power of parish priests in this respect. However, they can still refuse to perform the Catholic burial rites.

A Marriage Bill was passed which provided for the introduction of civil marriage. Now ecclesiastical marriages are valid only if all provisions of the act are observed; this means that canon law ceased to have effect as part of the Maltese marriage law and that new rules apply to banns and the registration of ecclesiastical marriages.

The exemption of bishops, parishes, churches and religious communities from income tax was abolished.

Where the socialist government interfered most drastically was in education, a stronghold of the church. The teachers'-training monopoly, until then held by the religious orders, was suddenly abrogated: such training from September onwards was to be given by the Department of Education. In 1974 the state strengthened its control over the university in which many priests held teaching assignments, even outside the faculty of theology. Religion was dropped from the matriculation as a compulsory subject. A new 'reform' in 1978 stripped the university of its science, medical and theology faculties. The church, with the approval of the Holy See, constituted its own faculty of theology at the Seminary. Now most of the clerical professors and staff-members have been forced to leave the university and so many effective networks, of which parish

priests also formed part, disintegrated. Government policy towards
the private schools in the island, all of them run by religious
orders, has been next to hostile. Finally, since 1978, parish priests
are no longer allowed to say mass and hear confessions in government
schools during school hours.

In another sphere the government was also active: in 1977 eight
public holidays were abrogated, following upon the substitution in
1975 of Republic Day for Epiphany. As a result, these feasts henceforth have to be celebrated on the Sunday following, so that on these
Sundays no local *festi* can be held. This leads to various feasts being
celebrated simultaneously on the same Sunday in different villages,
and people from outside the parishes concerned now have a more difficult choice than before as to which one they will visit. Statistically
this should lead to a decrease in attendance and enthusiasm for each
festa. The government also directly involved itself by restricting
the use of certain kinds of fireworks, which is bound to have grave
consequences for the degree of participation within the village. As a
big *festa* is still important for the prestige of the parish priest,
both measures could have the effect, perhaps unintended, but certainly
not unwelcome in the eyes of the MLP supporters, of diminishing the
prestige of the *kappillani*.

One aspect of the penetration of the socialist state into all
spheres of life particularly affected the *kappillani* and in its consequence can never have been so intended by the Labour government. This
was the ever-increasing bureaucracy which caused many people to seek
his assistance. Thus he found additional tasks helping them to complete
their application forms for a wide variety of documents such as pass-
ports, permits and income tax declarations[20]. Although the public
registry in Valletta has replaced the parish priest as the official
registrar, apparently it is not very efficient in its operations and
relies heavily on baptismal, marriage and death certificates still
issued by the *kappillani*. Consequently, nowadays there is what amounts
to a dual administration of civil affairs, the parish records presumably being the more accurate.

KAPPILLANI IN ACTION

Though the Second Vatican Council made the parish priests more
dependent on their bishops, they could make themselves heard more
easily than before and the Vatican was now more accessible to them.
After the Council, the hierarchy was forced to come to terms with the
Malta Labour Party which presently came to power and immediately
started meddling in what used to be the preserve of the church. As a
result, the parish priest lost some of his functions. He is no longer
recognizes as the representative of the local community and he does

not usually form part of the new patronage circuits. His hold on the
government schools, the university, the teachers"-training and the
Addolorata cemetery has been undermined. The possibility to add to
his prestige through the celebration of a big *festa* seems to have
decreased. He is no longer a public registrar, although he spends
much more time than before filling in forms for his semi-literate
parishioners. His financial position is now being controlled by the
state through taxation and the various permits required, while his
erstwhile ability to influence people's political choices has been
curtailed.

The Vatican Council and the socialist government are, of course,
not the only factors to influence the position of the parish priest.
The introduction of television (in Malta one can also receive broad-
casts from Italy) together with a sharp increase in the number of
incoming and outgoing tourists, widened the view of the parishioners;
the spread of the secular and anti-clerical propaganda of the MLP
media also helped to create a more laicised mentality in the islands.
The increased mobility resulting from the improvement of public
transport and the rapid spread of private car-ownership have made it
relatively much easier than before to escape both from the *kappillan*
and from social control and to hear mass and go to confession outside
one's own parish, even not at all.

And yet, Malta is still a very Catholic country with, proportion-
ally, the highest number of priests and nuns in the world and the
greatest supply of missionaries to the Universal Roman Catholic
Church. Religious observance is general and many, including the president of the republic and several cabinet ministers, regularly receive
the sacraments. In summer, it is almost impossible to spend more than
a few days in Malta without seeing a procession. In populated areas
there is always a church or a chapel just around the corner, and
priests, monks and nuns go about in the apparel traditionally befit-
ting their status. To legislate away the power of the church is one
thing, but to change the traditional Catholic mentality is quite
another. As I have shown elsewhere, there are many outward signs of
the survival, perhaps even revival, of a Catholic mentality[21].

In order to define the present position of the *kappillani* a
number of cases will now be analysed where changes occurred in the
relationship between the parish priest, on the one hand, and his
parishioners, the bishop and their colleagues, on the other.

Dun Alwig runs his parish in his own way. During his term of office
in Has-Sajjied he changed nearly everything: the plans for the
building of the church, the date of the feast and the route of the
procession. He did not subscribe to the general practice of insti-
tuting committees for the running of the church or the village *festa*.
These, he thought, engendered envy and strife in such a small parish.
He asked people each to do the job they felt qualified for and,

consequently, these tasks were performed with a relish. He did not make it obligatory upon people to attend mass, but, at the same time, he was not going to tolerate a situation where people were at liberty to choose between attendance at mass or at the parish recreation centre. Therefore the recreation centre was not allowed to open until after mass. Although he remained an individualist at heart, his decisions were never challenged and he was held in high esteem. In his new parish also he gradually managed to have his way without opposition.

Dun Salv Cutajar, his successor, at once began to change many things. He appointed a number of his parishioners to a parish council and told them what he wanted to have changed in the annual *festa* and in the church. He met with some opposition and many people began to grumble. Three years later half the membership of the parish council had resigned and most of the remainder were apathetic. Quite a few volunteers had become uncooperative, but Dun Salv still had his way in all parish affairs.

In a neighbouring village the *kappillan* was beaten up by some hotheads when he decided to stop ringing the bells because the belfry was in bad repair. But the parish priest remained adamant and never asked for a transfer.

In one of the villages where the *partiti* are still fiercely competitive, the *kappillan* refused to turn the statue of the secondary saint around in front of the church, before re-entering the building at the close of the annual procession: he held the opinion that "seeing the *kaxxa infernali*" (fireworks) was the exclusive privilege of the titular saint, and in this he was quite correct. The partisans of the secondary saint beat him up, but this did not make him change his mind and the statue was never turned round.

The archpriest of one of the 'Three Cities' (the Dockyard area) recently denied a woman "who was living in sin", the right to act as a godmother. Angry relatives beat him up, but he had his way. In this case almost everybody agreed with the *kappillan*, but all the same there were many people who told me that "he deserved it". As he is known to be outspokenly anti-Mintoff while most of his parishioners are Labour party diehards, they are not fond of him, to put it mildly. But even one of his fellow-priests explained to me that the arch-priest's behaviour, which he frankly dubbed 'tactless', was courting disaster, in this case a sound drubbing.

The above examples show that in parochial affairs hardly anything has changed. A clever parish priest will get his way without any opposition, while a blunt character or one who hurts the pride of the village or of a *partit*, even though he will be challenged, also carries the day. In areas where *partiti* flourish the *kappillan*'s decisions have always been challenged, and even when *partiti* were not involved, grumbling and gossip-mongering aimed at the parish priest are certainly not novel to Malta. Thrashing, according to my informers, is exceptional and does not occur more often than in the past: in general, there is a tendency towards greater frequency in Labour strongholds than in Nationalist ones. In spite of the recommendations of the Second Vatican Council, it happens that a parish council is not instituted when the *kappillan* does not feel like having one, and existing councils are completely dominated by him. Nothing really seems to have changed, but we must not forget that in these cases the parish priest was acting in spheres that have been left untouched by the government and in the event of a conflict the church authorities would certainly back him. The refusal to participate in parish activities in Has-Sajjied on the ground of Dun Salv's untactical behaviour is a sign of protest which shows that nowadays people are not as sensitive to the opinion of the *kappillan* and his social control as before.

At this stage, we shall review a few cases in which not only the *kappillan* and his parish, but also the archbishop play a part.

In Has-Sajjied a committee had been set up to supervise the enlargement of the old parish church. The members became very annoyed when the archbishop refused to contribute so much as a penny to their church, while at the same time he donated £M6000 for the construction of a new church dedicated to St. Sebastian in Qormi. The committee decided that by the time their church was to be inaugurated the ceremony would be led by their own parish priest. Thus, when a few years ago that day had arrived, Dun Alwig faced a problem. If he were to invite the archbishop for the ceremony he would be in trouble with his parishioners; if he did not invite him, he would offend the archbishop. So Dun Alwig found out on what days the archbishop already had other appointments and then he set the inauguration ceremony for one of those days, a Saturday. Next, he cordially invited the archbishop, who had to decline the invitation, and so Dun Alwig himself led the ceremony, a concelebrated mass. The next day, when the archbishop also had other obligations, the vicar general came and blessed the church. A week later the archbishop came to say Pontifical Mass and this concluded the celebrations.

Before Dun Alwig left Has-Sajjied he had already declined another 'promotion' to a bigger parish. He told the archbishop he would like to consider the proposal provided he could have insight in the financial affairs of the parish. This was denied to him and so he refused to accept. He did not wish to become entangled in a financial mess. Then he was offered the opportunity to become the spiritual leader of the parish, while his predecessor would remain in charge as the financial administrator. He refused. Twice the archbishop came to entice Dun Alwig, but he would not budge. His persistance

made it impossible for him to refuse the next offer, which was not
long in coming. His parishioners objected to his leaving them and
took a petition to the archbishop. One of them told me, "The archbishop ridiculed us and we feel offended. If he dares to come to
Has-Sajjied I will throw him into the sea with my own hands. And
many other people here will gladly do the same".

Many of his former parishioners went to Dun Alwiġ's '*Pussess*' in
his new parish. They liked the ceremony and recognised their former
parish priest's hand in the organisation. But the women wept and one
of them hit a local priest with her handbag when he had the evil
courage to joke at the transfer. One of the men, grumbling under his
breath, said something which was highly insulting to the archbishop.

These two cases show that the average Maltese parishioner is still
more committed to the well-being of his own parish than to that of
the diocese. The church-enlargement committee, which mainly consisted
of professional people, never asked for the motive behind the archbishop's donation to St. Sebastian's, nor did they ever want to know
why he did not support their church. Nobody ever even hinted that
the totally different position of either parish could have justified
the archbishop's decision. In the case of the transfer of Dun Alwiġ,
the people of Has-Sajjied were just being unreasonable and selfish.
Dun Alwiġ had proved himself an excellent pastor. His capacities
would have fully justified his promotion to a larger parish at least
four years before he was actually given one, and he would certainly
have been promoted earlier if only he had been more ambitious.

In the first case Dun Alwiġ had his way, as usual. He acted with
great shrewdness and went along with the wishes of his committee
without insulting the archbishop. Another *kappillan* would either
have invited the archbishop against the will of his parishioners or
just have left him out. In both instances he would have had the final
say, although there would have been some trouble with the parish in
the former case and with the archbishop in the latter. In the second
case, Dun Alwiġ manoeuvred himself into a position where he could
refuse a transfer to a parish which would have involved him in
difficulties; thus he used up his credit with the archbishop and
could not refuse a second offer of a transfer. The people of Has-
Sajjied blamed only the archbishop for making the offer and not Dun
Alwiġ for accepting it. Before Vatican II, Dun Alwiġ could have
bluntly refused both the first and the second transfers. Now he was
definitely more dependent upon the bishop in this respect because he
could simply be sacked as a parish priest if the bishop should not
accept his refusal, an event which would have absolutely infuriated
the parishioners of Has-Sajjied. Although it is beyond our scope
here to go further into historical detail, the hostile reaction of
parishioners towards the bishop in case of an unfavourable decision

has never been uncommon in Malta[22].

I have already maintained that the pastor has lost influence in secular matters. Let us consider a case which on the face of it has contradictory aspects.

A few days before the beginning of the new scholastic year, it was announced in the press that the government elementary school in Has-Sajjied would not be open again, because the Department of Education needed the building for a regional trade school. The pupils would be taken by bus to another village. At once Dun Alwig checked the statement and when it was confirmed by the department he wrote a letter on behalf of his village. He reminded the authorities that it was only a few years since this school had been built, a most welcome substitute for the ramshackle homes in which it was housed before. Should the village children now be deprived of their new school again to be sent to another village where it would be impossible for the local priest, who did not know the children, to discuss their progress at school and their background with the headmaster? Dun Alwig not only wrote a letter, he also took up the matter with 'the king', an influential Nationalist in the village, who used to be a very effective broker during the previous administration. As a matter of fact, 'the king' had secured the new schoolbuilding for the village. The golden days of 'the king' were over when Mintoff assumed power again, but he still had one asset: he was related to an influential MLP member and to some high-ranking civil servants with whom, though he never hid his political colour, he had always remained on speaking terms. 'The king', with great discretion, took the necessary steps and on the eve of the first schoolday the decision was rescinded. This was quite unusual, as it is not the habit of the Labour government so quickly to reconsider its decisions, however wrong they may be. Such procedure is thought to be harmful to its prestige. The fact that Dun Alwig had given no publicity to his letter and that 'the king', too, proceeded by stealth gave the department an excuse to recall 'a technical decision' without giving the impression that it yielded to pressure from a parish priest and a Nationalist.

At first sight it looks as if even in present-day Malta a shrewd *kappillan* may still be able to influence government decisions, even though he cannot act as overtly as before in 1971. But the very fact that he has to proceed with care is proof of his loss of power. The following case will also show that a parish priest has to manipulate people to please those of his parishioners who are MLP supporters.

Dun Gerald, a parish priest in his forties, recently became the archpriest of a large rural village. The local committee and members of the band club are pro-Labour; they are suspicious of the clergy. Every year on the eve of the feast they play the hymn of St. Peter, the titular saint of the parish, in accompaniment to a choir led by

a local priest. But there has always been discord between this priest
and the committee. Not very long before the feast the priest, who had
several times been asked by letter to form a choir, informed the band
club that he was not able to comply; most probably this was to say
that he was not willing to. The committee requested an urgent meeting,
but Dun Gerald persuaded them to discuss the matter with him first.
He asked them, "Who is the owner of the hymn?" They said, "The club,"
and the priest confirmed this. Then Dun Gerald told them, "Alright,
you play it and I'll find you another choir". And so he did, telling
the priest that the music, which was still in his possession, should
be made available to the choir of Dun Gerald. The performance was a
success and the committee was very grateful. Ever since, Dun Gerald
and St. Peter's band club have cooperated to everybody's satisfaction.

This case shows that within the parish a wise *kappillan* who does
not flaunt his political (read: Nationalist) opinion may, by tactful
manoeuvring, still gain the esteem of the Labour supporters. But in
the days when Labour was not in power a parish priest might not have
cared and felt inclined to take sides with his fellow priest in a
conflict like this.

BISHOPS UNDER FIRE

In the previous section, the results have been recorded of the
priest's increased formal dependence on the bishop, whereas in the
section on the consequences of Vatican II it was demonstrated how
some individual parish priests began to ignore the bishop's directives, though the challenge never was an overt one. I have also
maintained (p. 192) that the Maltese parish priests became sought-
after coalition partners in intra-church disputes. The next case
will illustrate this.

Archbishop-designate Emmanuel Gerada was the chief negotiator for
the church in the discussions with the Malta Labour Party. In the
eyes of many priests, who were and are staunch opponents of the
Malta Labour Party, it was Gerada's fault that the church-MLP dispute
was settled the way it was in 1969. They referred to the 'peace
treaty' as the unconditional surrender of the church, which paved
the way for Mintoff's return to power in 1971. In the meantime,
within the church, a few pastors took the initiative and, together
with other influential members of the clergy, formed a strong
pressure-group. Availing themselves of excellent contacts in the
Vatican, they sought and finally obtained a far-reaching reform of
the diocesan finances. One of the elements, however, was that the
salaries of all parish priests were henceforth paid by the bishop,
no revenues accruing from the annual blessing of the homes anymore.
In spite of the resulting improvement in the financial position of

many parish priests, a new link had been forged in the relationship
of dependence on the bishop. When Mgr. Gerada tried to interfere
with these reforms and the names leaked out of certain parish priests
he wanted to replace after his eventual elevation to the archbishop-
ric, his would-be victims closed the ranks and became his staunchest
opponents. This pressure-group acted swiftly when it became known
that Mgr. Gerada, who was entrusted with the financial administration
of the church, had made a stupendous blunder. They rallied behind
the ageing archbishop Gonzi, who was expected soon to be obliged to
step down in favour of Gerada, and in Rome saw to it that this
prelate was 'kicked upstairs' by being appointed Apostolic Nuncio
in Guatemala and El Salvador[23].

In the eyes of his opponents Mgr. Gerada was to blame for many
mistakes, and what at first was annoyance at his role in the 'peace
treaty' grew into anger when they began to experience what it meant
to have Mintoff back as prime minister without, as under the previous
Labour administration, enjoying the protection of the British.
Archbishop Gonzi eagerly accepted the pressure-group as his allies,
though he was presently to realize that they might be a tough lot
to handle.

When the Marriage Act was published, the Maltese Episcopal Conference, the College of Parish Priests and all other Catholic organisations and newspapers united in protest. For a while it looked as if
a third 'politico-religious' conflict was in the making, priests in
their sermons fulminated against the new law and, in a report sub-
mitted at the archbishop's request by a commission of canon law
experts, theologians and pastoral workers, the implications of the
law for the church were surveyed and it was recommended that the
public registrars should be kept out of the sacristy henceforth[24].
Somehow or other this report materialised on the desk of the prime
minister, who reacted with lightning speed: Dr. Farrugia, the
ambassador to the Holy See, was sent to Archbishop Gonzi with an
ultimatum to the effect that the recommendation must be withdrawn
the next day and that in case of non-compliance the government would
-- with immediate effect -- introduce civil marriage by registrars
for all Maltese, whether Catholic or not, and dismiss all government-
employed priests, monks and nuns from their posts. The bishops struck
up a compromise allowing the registrar to attend nuptial mass and
arranging for his being received afterwards in a room next to the
church, but not in the sacristy. The next day the parish priests
were informed. Most of them were as furious as the archbishop himself. There were some who counselled moderation, and in the absence
of clear-cut directives from the archbishop, there was nothing to
do but demur, and in the end the law prevailed.

While a few years earlier some parish priests had felt as if they
were being squeezed between the archbishop and their parishioners,

now the archbishop himself sat uncomfortably between the parish priests and the socialist government. The archbishop gave in to the government in order to protect the interests of the church in other spheres, but this made him more vulnerable, as he lost considerable goodwill with his parish priests. The majority of them would have liked to fight the government but felt they could not win without the support of the bishops. This case represents the first conflict between the archbishop and the College of Parish Priests. The college vis-à-vis the MLP continued its 'natural policy' of the 1960s, while the archbishop's policy had changed completely as a consequence of the Vatican Council. The same Council had made it possible for the College to disagree with the archbishop. It would not be long before the final confrontation ensued.

In the 1976 election there was much at stake for the Catholic establishment in Malta, of which the parish priests formed a prominent part. The main issue, Malta's foreign policy, did not concern them directly, although most of them certainly preferred Malta to become closely linked with Christian Europe (the policy of the Nationalist opposition) rather than with Islamic North Africa and Communist China (the *de facto* result of the 'neutral' policy of the Labour government). But the Nationalists' pledge in their electoral campaign to reintroduce the exemptions from income tax and to bring marriage for Catholics in accordance again with canon law was no small bait. Besides, after having experienced what it meant to be governed by Mintoff and his MLP, most priests had forgotten their irritation with the Nationalist government, and were looking forward to its restoration to power. Unfortunately, they grumbled, their hands were now tied, as they had to refrain carefully from doing anything which would make them liable to being accused of 'corrupt practices' by the outgoing government, which was running the election. As a neck-and-neck race was expected and many predicted a narrow Nationalist victory, the clergy were afraid that even the slightest insinuation of a currupt practice might give the government a pretext to have an unfavourable election result annulled. So they were cautious, although when asked for advice they certainly did not advocate a vote for the MLP. Most of them were deeply disappointed with the result of the turbulent election: the proclamation of the MLP as the winner, albeit by a narrow margin.

Unfortunately, the contest was not without violence; at first, towards the end of the campaign, spasmodic outbursts, mainly by Labour supporters, were directed against Nationalist clubs, but as soon as the Labour victory had been announced, almost all Nationalist clubs in the island were rampaged and most of them gutted by fire. The police did not interfere and the violence did not abate until Mintoff, after taking the oath of office, ordered the mobs to desist. Only a few of the culprits were brought to book and archbishop Gonzi came out in strong terms against what he called irreligious and amoral behaviour, concluding that "Malta is spiritually and morally sick"[25]. Small wonder, therefore, that when, on Wednesday 10 November, the archbishop issued a pastoral letter in which he asked for clemency for those who committed violence during the last elections, it hit like a bombshell. It became the object of blistering attacks from the Nationalist newspapers, the *Democrat* even demanding that the archbishop resign[26]. On Friday the College of Parish Priests met and refused to read the letter during Sunday mass, as they considered it unfair to those who had suffered from this "savage outburst of violence". Every parish priest now received a phone call from the Curia urgently requesting him to read the circular, but many remained adamant in their refusal. The next day, in Zejtun where the archbishop led the traditional translation of the relic of St. Catharine on the eve of the village *festa*, several parish priests assailed him, voicing their indignation at the pastoral. This confused the ageing (91) prelate, who exclaimed, "If you don't obey me any more, what can I do".

To the surprise of many, Mgr. Gonzi announced his resignation eight days later. He did so in the course of his traditional Christ-the-King address, delivered in St. John's Co-Cathedral to a congregation which included many prominent Nationalists and most of the pastors.

The parish priests, once archbishop Gonzi's most powerful allies against the MLP and against a succession by Mgr. Gerada, were now fed up. They had been aggrieved by his leniency towards the socialist government in the last five years, and his yielding to blackmail in the aforementioned civil marriage question had made them especially angry. Now they were convinced Mgr. Gonzi had been blackmailed again and they finally dropped him. They were also afraid that reading the pastoral in church would make them lose their credibility with their Nationalist parishioners and that consequently it was to lead to a serious loss of prestige. Archbishop Gonzi clearly understood that without the support of the *kappillani* it was impossible for him to continue. It is interesting to note that while Mgr. Gerada disappeared because of pressure exerted by a small group of priests, including *kappillani*, on the Vatican, Mgr. Gonzi himself gave in to pressure from the parish priests in his diocese.

It took the Holy See only a few days to replace Mgr. Gonzi by Mgr. Mercieca. This was too soon for any pressure-group of the Maltese clergy to influence the Vatican. Some say the government pulled some strings in Rome in order to secure a 'quiet' archbishop. It is a fact that the appointment of Mgr. Mercieca did not improve the situation for the parish priests. Most admit that he is a hard-working and saintly priest, but that he lacks the leadership qualities required to guide the church internally and deal with the ever-

penetrating and secularising government. Individually and collectively, they more than once urged him to be firm. His attitude
towards the celebration of the termination of Malta's defence
agreement with the United Kingdom on 31 March 1979 grieved them[27].
   It is assumed that Mintoff just could not stomach the fact that
it was not him but the Nationalist Dr. Borg Olivier who secured for
Malta its independence. Ever since he had been returned to power in
1971 he did everything to undo the 'mock-independence'. The proclamation of the republic he could claim as the fruit of his constitutional endeavours, but there were hardly any festivities in 1974
whereas people remembered the pomp and splendour of the independence
celebrations. So every effort was made to celebrate the termination
of the defence agreement with the United Kingdom with a lot of
splash, and presumably some pressure was brought to bear on the
hierarchy to make them play their part. Therefore archbishop Mercieca
staged a Pontifical Mass with a *Te Deum* in St. John's Co-Cathedral
and issued a pastoral which proved to be almost a verbatim copy of
the one his predecessor had written on the occasion of independence.
He ordered a mass to be said with special prayers for the nation.
All churches had to be illuminated on March 30 and 31 and the bells
rung at midnight between Saturday March 31, and Sunday April 1. As
all the Nationalists ignored the celebration of "Mister Mintoff's
All Fool's Day", most parish priests were very reluctant to comply,
quite a few of them lit only the lamps on the façade of the church
for just one hour and ordered the minimum of bell-pealing. I heard
of only one parish priest who carried out the instructions with
gusto, but he is from a Labour family and, although he never committed himself, he is supposed to be a Labourite[28].
   Archbishop Mercieca has been told time and again not to stand
aloof while what power and possessions remain are gradually taken
away from the church. When they talk to him like this, the
kappillani mirror the present Pope's firm attitude towards the
communists. The tone of Mgr. Mercieca's latest pastorals might be
an indication that he is finally accepting the challenge. If he does,
it will be another example of the increased collective influence of
the *kappillani* within the church.
   The above cases demonstrate that the relations of the Maltese
parish priests with their bishops have changed considerably and that
their collective influence has increased. At one time they were
expected to tow the line of hierarchy, especially in the conflict
with the MLP. After the Council, some were given greater freedom to
hold opinions of their own and some wanted more leeway in dealing
with their Labourite parishioners. They also established links with
the Holy See while the College of Parish Priests became an important
pressure-group, a powerful ally of the bishop which on various
occasions also acted as his rival. As soon as the socialist

government began to curtail the powers of the church, the parish priests resumed their previous anti-MLP attitude and put the archbishop under pressure. The latter, once he had been forced by the Vatican into an 'agreement' with Labour (and possibly due to his age) was not prepared to start another fight. The actions against Gerada and Gonzi would have been unthinkable fifteen years before. It should be noted that, while previously the parish priests only had to worry about their relations with their Labourite parishioners, recently the Nationalists became quite annoyed at the attitude of the church towards the government, and to the *kappillani* this is a pastoral problem of increasing importance.

CONCLUSIONS

We have seen how as a consequence of the Second Vatican Council the parish priests individually grew more dependent on the bishop, while collectively they became more independent and influential within the church. The bishop cannot function properly without their support. The hierarchy was forced to come to terms with Labour and so paved the way for Labour's return to power in 1971. Ever since, the powers of the church have been severely curtailed, especially on the diocesan level, and therefore the bishops are the biggest losers. The parish priests too, lost secular functions and consequently some of their power and prestige. They have to behave with more circumspection, though their position in parochial affairs has barely been affected. The laity has hardly any influence on their policy in these affairs.
  Some top members of the MLP are worried about the popularity still enjoyed by parish priests such as Dun Gerald and Dun Alwig. They do not like the growing enthusiasm for the *festi* on which their own supporters are often quite keen, in spite of the *kappillan's* leading role. It is significant to note here that the government's restrictions on the use of fireworks during *festi* are ignored by the people and not enforced by the police. Some Maltese see in the revival of the *festi* and of some other church celebrations a manifestation of tacit resistance against the regime. The socialists do not like to seek the permission of the parish priest when they want to use the parish hall. In their opinion these halls were built by the people and should be under the control of their representatives. The loyalty of the people should first and foremost be to the country, government and party instead of to church and family, only then is it possible to raise a socialist generation in a socialist state. This was one of the motives behind the promise in the 1976 electoral manifesto to set up neighbourhood committees. These might fill the gap created by the absence of local government, many of its functions having

been 'naturally' filled by the *Kappillani*. But one wonders about the feasibility of translating these intentions into law, no bills giving effect to the plans having yet been drafted. In the meantime, however, the government has for the last few months been exercising direct control over church collections, thus interfering with the financial powers of the parish priests.

NOTES

* I am grateful to the late Onno A.S. Gorissen, M.L., Fellow and Deputy Director of the Royal Tropical Institute in Amsterdam, and to Dun 'Alwig Debono', Dun 'Peter Falzon', Mario Buhagiar, M.A., Joseph Cassar Pullicino, Dr. Charles J.M.R. Gullick (University of Durham), Jos. Micallef Stafrace, B.A., Ll.D., Joe Spiteri-Gonzi, M.D., and Professor Jeremy F. Boissevain of the University of Amsterdam, and the other participants in the Conference for valuable suggestions. I would also like to thank Professor John F. Parr of the University of Maryland for correcting an earlier draft. To Dr. Mart M.G. Bax, of the Free University of Amsterdam, I owe a debt of gratitude for many incisive discussions which have been a great help in the analysis of the basic elements of the subject of the present paper. The research undertaken in 1975 and 1976, on which this paper is largely based, was made possible by the grant from the Netherlands Organization for the Advancement of Pure Research (Z.W.O.) and by the Free University of Amsterdam.

1. Has-Sajjied means 'the village of Sajjied'. The names both of the village and of individuals are fictitious.
2. These are Malta, Gozo and Comino. The name Malta denotes both the largest island and the entire archipelago. In 1978 the population of Malta was 311,421.
3. The authoritative historian Harrison Smith describes the situation in these terms: "The antiquity of the faith of the Maltese, the close proximity of the Papal Court at the Vatican City, and the position of the state-religion of the Crown in England all combined to make the English possession of Malta a unique experience in colonial development. Other than remote Quebec, the British had not -- perhaps never would -- encounter a church medieval, a church militant, and a church that had lived under a theocracy long after the era of the national state had modified the feudalism of Europe" (Harrison Smith 1953, Volume I:73).
4. An extensive treatment of the hand-in-glove relations between the Protestant British rulers and their local Catholic subjects, and the petty quarrels between them can be found in Koster (1979b).

5. For details, see Harrison Smith and Koster (in press).
6. The souvenir-folder of the Malta Independence Celebrations (Anonymous 1964) provides us with splendid illustrations of the dominant role of the church during the independence celebrations. Only four years before, the nineteenth centenary of St. Paul's shipwreck had been celebrated with much pomp (ibid. 1960).
7. The Maltese islands constitute a province of the Roman Catholic church. It consists of the archdiocese of Malta and the diocese of Gozo. The latter, with 15 parishes, is not discussed in this paper.
8. The *Ghaqdiet*, or lay-organisations, have many members. In each parish there are independent branches, usually divided by age and sex. A chaplain, responsible to the parish priest, gives spiritual guidance and acts as leader. They organise social activities and often take part in processions. The most import- ant *ghaqdiet* are: Catholic Action, Legion of Mary, Society for Christian Doctrine (MUSEUM) and Young Christian Workers.
9. Some parishes are called archparishes and their parish priest has the titel of archpriest, a somewhat undefined honour which imparts some prestige to the holder. There is no actual differ- ence any more between an archpriest and a parish oriest. Senior- ity is by appointment as parish priest/archpriest.
10. The so-called Easter Obligation is the minimal requirement for a practising Catholic, who has to receive Holy Communion at least once a year in the week before Easter. One cannot receive Holy Communion without being absolved in confession.
11. Dying people were ministered to by a priest when he was sent for. He would ask them: "Do you repent your sins?" without any specification and if they said yes they would be given the normal burial.
12. *Festa partiti* are divisions within a Maltese parish, embracing the supporters of the titular saint and the supporters of a secondary saint, who has assumed almost equal social importance (Boissevain 1965:75). Boissevain (1965:74-96; 1969:81-86) gives an admirable description of this fascinating phenomenon of Maltese social life, which is far from extinct.
13. See for details: *Pastoral Research Services* (1967).
14. "The change aims at enabling the bishop to provide more easily and effectively for pastorates. The bishop, however, must still take into account not only the priest's knowledge of doctrine, but also his piety, apostolic zeal and other gifts and qualities necessary for the proper exercise of the care of souls" (Bonnici 1975:42).
15. Cf. Flannery 1975:603.
16. Ibid.:603-604.

17. The reforms introduced in the vestments and insignia of canons and parish priests have, however, been successfully sabotaged by them, with the tacit approval of the bishops and the outspoken support of their parishioners. The average Maltese Catholic loves pomp.

18. It is interesting to note that in the 1971 electoral campaign Labour 'played safe' as far as the position of the church was concerned. The MLP electoral manifesto did not make any reference to the church. This was clever policy as Labour's majority was so small that any mention of the church would probably have resulted in another Nationalist majority. Before 1971 Labour several times vigorously remonstrated at being called socialists. After 1971, however, they gradually began to call themselves so. As Dom Mintoff dominates the government ("of course there is no government, there is only Mintoff", -- personal communication) and rules the country, parliament and party with a fist of iron there is in the islands and among Melitensists a tendency to use the words Mintoff and government as synonyms, the same applies to Mintoff and Malta Labour Party. The author notes that he himself finds it difficult not to do the same.

19. *Electoral Polling Ordinance*, Cap. 163.

20. I even know of an archpriest who kept a measuring-tape in his office in order to take the appropriate measurements for a passport-application right away.

21. Cf. Koster 1979a.

22. Cf. Boissevain 1965:67-68.

23. An elaborate account of the dispute and of Mgr. Gerada's rather unfortunate performance as Co-adjutor to archbishop Gonzi, is given in Koster 1981:239-245.

24. According to Section 17(3) of the new legislative measure (Malta Government 1975) "the act of marriage shall be completed and delivered for registration immediately after marriage".

25. *Times of Malta*, 4 October 1976.

26. *The Democrat*, 20 November 1976.

27. See Koster (1980) for a detailed contribution on the developments preceding the termination of the defence agreement between the governments of Malta and the United Kingdom.

28. This parish priest, Dun Jimmy Vella, has managed through his provocative behaviour in parish affairs to estrange most parishioners of both political parties. He lives in a Labour area and his helpmate in church affairs is the wife of a prominent Nationalist. This, and the case of the school in Has-Sajjied, demonstrates the importance of the cross-cutting ties in a small nation such as Malta (cf. Boissevain 1965:138-139).

BIBLIOGRAPHY

Anonymous
1960   *XIX Centenary Celebrations of St. Paul's Shipwreck. A
       Pictorial Record.* Valletta: Progress Press.
1964   *Souvenir Malta Independence Celebrations.* Valletta:
       Progress Press.
Boissevain, J.F.
1965   *Saints and Fireworks. Religion and Politics in Rural Malta.*
       London: Athlone Press.
1969   *Hal-Farrug: A Village in Malta.* New York: Holt, Rinehart
       & Winston.
Bonnici, Mgr. A.
1975   *History of the Church in Malta,* Volume III (1800-1975).
       Zabbar: Veritas Press.
Flannery, A.O.P. (ed.)
1975   *Vatican Council II. The Concilliar and Post Concilliar
       Documents.* Dublin: Dominican Publications.
Harrison Smith, D.
1953   *Britain in Malta* (2 volumes). Valletta: Progress Press.
Harrison Smith, D. & A. Koster
in   *Church and State Crisis 1927-1932.* Valletta: Midsea
press Publications.
Koster, A.
1979a Malta - Katholieke smeltkroes van beschavingen. *VU-
       magazine* 8(4):34-37.
1979b Malta: Kerk, taal, Mintoff. *Spiegel Historiael* 14:532-540.
1980   Mintoff's Malta op zoek naar een nieuwe koers?
       Internationale Spectator 34:231-238.
1981   *Prelates and Politicians in Malta: Changing Power-Balances
       Between Church and State in a Mediterranean Island Fortress
       (1530-1976).* Vijfhuizen (The Netherlands).
Malta Government
1976   Marriage Act. *Acts of Parliament* passed during 1975, Part
       I:284-291. Valletta: Department of Information.
1978   *Demographic Review of the Maltese Islands 1977.* Valletta:
       Department of Information.
Newspapers
1976   *The Democrat,* 20 November.
1976   *Times of Malta,* 4 October.
Pastoral Research Services
1967   *Reaction to Liturgical Renewal.* Mimeographed.

Christian-Democrat Ideology in the Cold War Period

Jeffrey Pratt, University of Sussex

The stimulus for this article came from some relatively trivial events of the Italian Christian-Democrat (D.C.) campaign for the regional and local elections of 1975. Why did the nationally produced D.C. propaganda material include a series of rather crude cartoons which depicted the Communists as cuckolds? Similarly, why at an election meeting in the square of a village in Tuscany was there so much banter and abuse to be heard amongst those on the fringes, abuse which insisted that communist women were pigs and whores? The publication[1] of a series of D.C. campaign posters of the cold-war period (Romano and Scabello 1975) and some detailed questioning on the development of political divisions in the Tuscan village for the same period makes it possible to answer these smaller questions, and show that the sexual abuse of 1975 was a recurring echo of a much more important and widespread ideological theme of the earlier period.

The scope of this article is to analyse some aspects of the political struggle between the Christian-Democrat and Communist parties in the critical period of 1947-1953. When those working at the macro-level write that the anathema pronounced by the Pope against those of the left was an important weapon in the defeat of the Popular Front, or that the hegemony of the Christian-Democrat party over the rural masses was decisive to their maintenance of power, a knowledge of how those events came about for people of a particular time and place also has its value. The article is written in the hope that an anthropological view from grass-roots level has something to contribute to our understanding.

Even with such a limited objective, the writing of the article has been complicated by two, related, problems. Firstly the anthropologist is obliged to draw on material which is studied by other disciplines (historians, political-scientists and theologians), while the knowledge of, and use made of that material is bound to be partial from the point of view of those who practise these other disciplines. The second problem relates directly to the subject matter of the article. Apart from some brief introductory remarks

about the historical context of these elections and their political
importance, the article presents two rather different kinds of
material: firstly aspects of the ideology of everyday life of the
population of a particular Tuscan village, and secondly the analysis
of the national propaganda material itself. The relationship between
these two levels is one of the themes of the article and will be
dealt with in the conclusion.

In more detail, the first part of the article will deal with the
social composition of a particular village, Montelaterone, and then
with selected aspects of the religious practice of villagers, indi-
cating in each case the various ways in which participation in
Catholic ritual signifies a political identity in terms of the
major parties. Included in this account is some indication of the
working of the anathema. It should be stressed that the themes
chosen for illustration (the importance of the family and of territorial loyalties) are only part of local religious belief and
practice and are chosen for their relevance to the wider political
context. The second part of the article analyses the posters and
political slogans of the D.C. during the cold-war period, concen-
trating on the way in which the political divisions were represented
as a choice between Christian good and evil. Attention is paid to
the symbols which are employed to express this choice and to the
continuity between these and earlier theological and iconographic
traditions. The conclusion will attempt to draw together the threads
from these two sources and make some general comments on the relationship between religion and politics in Italian society, as well
as pointing out some of the methodological difficulties of this kind
of analysis.

GENERAL HISTORICAL BACKGROUND

The Catholic Church has always opposed political movements derived
from marxism, and anti-clericalism has long been part of the marxist
political tradition. However, in Italy the two did not become direct
rivals in the context of mass political movements until after the
last war. In the years of restricted suffrage from 1870 to 1919
there was no officially approved Catholic Party, while from 1922 to
1945 the left-wing parties were banned under fascism, leaving the
Catholic Church in a privileged position of relative freedom after
the 1929 Concordat. The only exceptions to this are the three
tumultuous years between 1919 and 1922 when the newly formed
Catholic Popular Party and the Socialists not only took off dramatically in electoral terms, but became strong rivals for the rural
vote. It is possible that many of the ideological themes discussed
here were played out in the propaganda of the earlier period.

For the first two years after the Second World War Italy was governed by a tripartite coalition of Christian-Democrats, Socialists and Communists, for whom the gaining of power through the ballot box was already firmly part of their strategy. The left was excluded from government in 1947, and the elections that followed in 1948 were fought out in a period of growing international tension. This and the following years were the period of Marshall Aid, the formation of Nato and the widening division of Europe into Communist and Capitalist blocs. The result of parliamentary elections in Italy was of crucial international importance. Within Italy control of central government determined not only control of outside aid but also a huge range of other resources, including a large public sector control of industry, a fascist legacy. State control of industry and agriculture (through the particular land reform programme), the growth of those employed in the public sector and their recruitment through clientelism, have all increased dramatically in the thirty years of D.C. government which began in 1948.

The Christian-Democrat Party as it emerged in this post-war period was a coalition of economic interests, within which the rural sector was the most important numerically. It should be remembered that at the end of the war nearly half of all Italians were still employed in agriculture, and that outside the red-belt of Central Italy a very large proportion of the landless labourers and small peasant proprietors were aligned with the D.C. party. The high level of illiteracy of this sector should also be noted in considering the form taken by the propaganda material presented below. The D.C. party also had the support of some sections of the industrial working class, and a large proportion of state employees, professional classes, shopkeepers and small businessmen. It did not, on the whole, have support from the large agrarian landlords or of industrial capitalists, who tended to support the minor parties of the right (Liberals and Monarchists) though they often gave their support to the D.C. in coalition governments. It should also be noted that the D.C. has always received more votes from women than from men[2].

This coalition of economic interests has been held together at the ideological level by two major themes. The D.C. defines itself negatively as anti-Communist, and maintains that a strong D.C. party is essential to prevent the Communist rise to power. On the positive side the D.C. defines itself as the party of the Church and of Christian values, and has always maintained that those who consider themselves to be Catholics should support the D.C. ('vote for the cross'). These two themes are central to the argument, which will attempt to show how they reinforce each other through the D.C. claim that to be anti-Communist is to be Catholic (because of the particular definition given of Communism) and that to be Catholic is to be anti-Communist (because of the importance given to certain aspects of 'being Catholic').

If these are the general themes, the D.C. clearly also represented, or claimed to represent, the interest of particular economic sectors, both at the level of government action and ideologically. To return to the rural sector: the D.C. in the cold-war period expropriated many of the large estates in South and Central Italy and distributed the land to landless labourers, creating a great mass of small peasant proprietors, who, however, continued to be dependent economically on the reform agencies and marketing agencies (*consorzi*) controlled by central government and hence by the Christian-Democrat Party. At the ideological level, the small peasant proprietor, the family working their own private property, is stressed as a model of economic organisation, a theme in Catholic social theory which dates back at least to the encyclical Rerum Novarum of 1891, but which receives special emphasis in this period (cf. the privileged position given by the Papacy to the D.C. peasant organisation Coldiretti). This aspect of Christian-Democrat ideology is dealt with in more detail in a recent article by Guizzardi (1976)[3].

Although this article does not attempt to deal with those parts of D.C. ideology addressed to particular economic groups, the parenthesis has been necessary to indicate two further aspects of the material analysed below. Firstly, that the overwhelming importance given to the family in the propaganda is connected also with a particular model of economic organisation, the 'independent' peasant proprietor. Secondly, that for those who would expect to find capitalist relations of production reflected in the ideology, in however a covert or inverted form, the material presents particular difficulties. It is the peasant proprietor not the wage labourer who emerges most clearly as the model Catholic. The Christian worker crushing Capitalism (and Communism) under foot, who appears in one of the 1948 posters may not have stayed long on the stage, but he is by no means an aberration. He is part of a tradition of Catholic social thought and action since the period of Rerum Novarum, through the white leagues of 1919-1923, until the post war years, even if his importance has declined rapidly since the period with which we are dealing.

After this necessarily abbreviated introduction, we can deal with the events of the period, first the Catholic beliefs and practise of a particular peasant village, then the propaganda material itself.

MONTELATERONE

Montelaterone stands at about 2,500 ft on top of a side spur of Monte Amiata in southern Tuscany. The population has declined through emigration from a pre-war peak of about 1,500 to the present

day 800, and is entirely concentrated in the village. Villagers own
land, about 800 hectares in all, in the steep valleys on either side
of the hill, but as until recently the only form of transport was
the donkey, land held was concentrated within a two hour walk of the
village, not very far in this rugged terrain. Landholding is extremely
complicated, there being at least four recognised kinds of right to
land, a great fragmentation of holding (more than 4,000 *particelle*)
and changes in the degree of concentration of land-holding over the
last hundred years. The essential point is that each family owns
some land, but despite the great intensity of cultivation, overall
the land has not been sufficient to keep the population in the village at even subsistence level. Thus although some families held
sufficient land to be full-time peasant proprietors, and a few had
considerable holdings which they let out to other villagers on a
share-cropping basis, many others worked as migrant labour on the
big estates in the coastal plain, the Maremma. These migrants were
often away from home for as much as three months of the year, returning at the end of the summer to cut and harvest their own small
fields which ripened later on the mountain than in the plain. Of
course it was a common ambition to own or share-crop sufficient land
in the village to make this yearly migration unnecessary. They were
also closely involved in the land agitation on the share-cropping
farms where they worked in the summer, participating in strikes and
the occasional symbolic occupation of the land. With the land-reform
in the Maremma in the early 1950s, and the subsequent mechanisation
of agriculture, this possibility of work closed for the mountain
villagers. Only two families in the whole village were given land
in the plain, no redistribution of land would solve the economic
problems of Montelaterone, and massive emigration followed in the
1950s and 1960s.

Those who stayed in Montelaterone have tended to contract marriages with those born in the same village. Until ten years ago,
when a large number of marriages with Calabrian women started to be
contracted, out of more than a thousand village inhabitants, only
half a dozen men and about a dozen women were not born there, and
these exceptions all came from neighbouring villages. In this society
both men and women inherit land, and clearly it was a disadvantage
to marry someone whose land was too distant to be worked. To this
economic motive, people also added some elements of local pride
(*campanilismo*), maintaining that it was impossible to have a harmonious marriage with someone from another place and with other customs.
Conversely the people of Montelaterone have a reputation amongst
their neighbours on the mountain, in their case it is for being
closed, incomprehensible of speech, backward, ignorant, quarrelsome
and violent. Some of this reputation has a political content, to
which I now turn.

Politically, the village shows a greater degree of fluctuations
in party allegiance than is normal in this part of Italy, and a
right wing vote that is higher than the Central Italian norm. In
1946 the Communist Party (P.C.I.) gained 29% of the vote, the
Socialist Party (P.S.I.) 9%, the Republican Party (P.R.I.) 24% and
the Christian-Democrats (D.C.) 34%. Two years later in 1948, with
the formation of the Popular Front (P.C.I. + P.S.I.) and the propaganda battle to be discussed below, the percentages were: Popular
Front 39%, Republicans 7%, D.C. 47% (in both cases other minor
parties were present). In the succeeding years up to 1960 there were
many fluctuations in the voting returns for Montelaterone, but the
D.C. consistently got more than 50% of the vote, with a peak of 62%.
Since 1960 the D.C. has declined steadily.

It is difficult to generalise about the basis of the party
allegiance in a place which is relatively unstable in its voting
habits and very difficult to divide into clear cut social classes.
Although it is possible to obtain fairly accurate information for
the present day, the comments on the previous period are inevitably
rather impressionistic. Nevertheless, it seems that there has been
a tendency for those who since the war have had sufficient land to
be full-time peasant proprietors to support the D.C. This sector,
once the wealthiest portion of the village, now includes many of the
poorest. To this source of D.C. votes can be added all those who
engage in commerce. Those who owned or rented a little land, and
were forced to work as day-labourers in the Maremma, have tended to
support the parties of the left. This group, though no longer working as migrant labour to any extent, continues to be employees for
a large part of the year, in the building trade, the catering trade
and the forestry commission. From the poorest section of the community they are now among the wealthiest, having learnt the advantages of combining sources of income, *combinare*.

Both the left-wing parties have had party sections in the villages
since the war, with meetings held about once a month. The D.C. have
a similar organisation on paper, with about 20 members, but meetings
are in fact never held, and there is only a flurry of informal
contacts at election time.

In a sense the D.C. party does not need a local organisation
because it has a parish priest. Don Raimondo Pellegrini, born in
the village, has been its priest since 1950, and like his predecessor
has never hidden his support for the D.C. or his strong opposition
to the Communists. During the early years of his ministry it is said
that the local much venerated statue of the Madonna was carted around
so many D.C. election meetings that she was nicknamed the Madonna
Pellegrina, the Madonna in pilgrimage, but also a pun on the incumbent's surname[4]. Nowadays he is more discreet but he is conspicuously
present at the D.C. election meetings and no others. As is well known

a parish priest is involved in a number of activities though only a
few can be mentioned here. In the cold-war period he distributed
American aid, particularly badly needed foodstuffs, to young children
in the nursery school he ran. He taught catechism classes (*la dottrina*)
with the help of two local members of Catholic Action (a D.C. flanking
organisation) in which the fundamentals of Catholic doctrine were
mixed with a vigorous dose of anti-Communism which is still clearly
remembered. He was also a supplier of patronage, finding work for
the unemployed and helping to place young girls as servants with
rich families in Rome and Siena. He was also consulted by the larger
landlords in finding new tenants to share-crop land, but his most
powerful position in the economic sphere he held through being
president of the *Ente Morale Parocchiale*. This was a rural relief
agency, later known as the *Cantine Fanfaniane*, set up and controlled
by the D.C. government. These were work gangs, established where
there was heavy unemployment, and paid fairly low wages, in this
case for road-building on the mountain. Don Raimondo retired from
this activity in 1958, the reason given by him being that these gangs,
in that they brought together a large number of village men to work
together, had been very favourable ground for the Communist Party.
   The last aspect of the priest's activity to be mentioned concerns
the relationship between men and women. Don Raimondo not only conducts marriages, he is also involved in marriage negotiations.
Although most of the families in the village know each other, the
man's family frequently consult the priest before a betrothal on
the grounds that he knows more about the moral character of a proposed bride than is generally available. For that reason too,
mothers traditionally told their daughters to go to church regularly
so as to be well seen by the priest, as otherwise they might jeopardise their marriage chances. Although this kind of pressure seems
to have declined it is reported regularly by those who grew up in
the early post-war years.
   The account of Catholicism starts with the importance of the
family in Catholic thought, dealing first with a recent theological
pronouncement and then with Catholic practice in Montelaterone.
Although theological statements are in no way decisive in determining
local practice, an example of the particular importance given to the
family by the hierarchy in teaching and sermons is of value in this
context. The privileged position of the family as an institution is
clear in the Catholic social doctrine of Rerum Novarum (The Worker's
Charter) of 1891, while family metaphors for human-divine relations
are ancient in Catholic thought[5]. The example given here, though
not contemporary with the cold-war propaganda has been chosen for
its clarity. It is a pastoral letter of Lent 1971, written by the
bishops of Siena province to the faithful of the diocese (which
includes the parish of Montelaterone). The occasion was the passing

of the Divorce Bill through Parliament, and as this threat to the
Catholic institution of marriage is also one of the themes of the
earlier propaganda, I shall quote the following extracts.

Dearest children, it is necessary to return to God, but by which
road? By the best road which God has travelled in giving life to
us, and manifesting himself to us, the road of the family. 'God
is love', and he wants to make himself known and to give himself.
But this is a difficult problem which He found and had to resolve:
how to make men understand this mysterious and infinite reality
of God-love. God has resolved the problem by creating the family.
Just as the light of the sun cannot be known by someone who presumes to contemplate it directly, and reveals itself instead to
someone who observes it broken up in the vivid colours of the
rainbow, so the love of God becomes comprehensible in the separate
relationships of love which interlace within the family: the love
of bride and groom, of mother and father towards their children,
of children for their parents, and of brothers and sisters towards
each other.
Thanks to their insertion in the family, men and women can
realize themselves in that giving of self which is as great as it
is shared. It is in the family that one discovers for whom one
works, for whom one suffers, with whom one rejoices, with whom
one confides, by whom one can be pardoned. It is in the family
that the baby becomes capable of life and community, and through
the sweet experience of an unmerited and personal love. The figure of the father and the mother, which are impressed so early
on his soul, remain in him a precious experience of security and
joy. And tomorrow this will be easily transported into his
personal representation of God. Thus the creator, using the
experience of the family, has written in the heart and life of
man the revealing words of a call to Infinite Love.

The bishops continue, by giving us, through biblical quotations, the
sense in which God is like a father, tender as a mother, ardent and
jealous like a husband, and then after a vigorous condemnation of
recent trends, as evident in divorce, ends, "The family is the
mirror of God, and if the mirror is broken or dirtied we will no
longer understand the love of God".
This recent document, with its very tight use of analogy and
homology, gives the clear message that the human family, with the
Sacred Family as model, and the Holy Trinity as inspiration, is an
essential condition for a moral life, and the road to God. It would
take a closer textual analysis than is possible here to show how
for the bishops (and some at least of their flock), all social
relationships are to be conceived of in terms of kinship and the
Divine. However, the indications already given should make clear

that the primary moral relationships are family relationships, and the primary experiences and obligations of life (for whom one works etc.) are family centred.

We can now move on from the theology of the contemporary hierarchy to an examination of Catholic practice as it relates to the family, dealing very briefly with the degree of participation in a series of Catholic rituals. The material is presented in the present tense, because it relates to contemporary accounts collected during fieldwork. Where the practice in an earlier period was significantly different this is indicated.

BAPTISM

All children born in the parish are baptised and usually given the name of a saint, called in Italian their *onomastico*, which they then celebrate every year according to the liturgy. Some are given names derived from an attribute of God or the Madonna: Assunta, Immacolata, Purifica. One child, born on Good Friday, was given the name *Senze Dio*, Without God, which he carried for the rest of his life, presumably celebrating his *onomastico* along with his birthday. Children are frequently named after their grandparents, but passing fancy also plays its part. In Montelaterone names are mostly drawn from the Catholic calendar, but in other villages political motives are more commonly found. The parents first register a name with the officials in the town-hall and then present the priest with a *fait accompli*. Thus there are a number of Ivans and Olgas to be found, from the days when Russia was popularly believed to be the model for Italian Communism, and even one Carlo Marxi in the commune of Arcidosso of which Montelaterone is part. A surprising number of Josephs, Giuseppe, owe their name to Stalin, but at least the parents hedged their bets.

FIRST COMMUNION

Like baptism, this always takes place in the parish of residence, usually when the child is 7-8 years old. It normally involves all one age-set, who receive doctrine classes together and receive their first communion at Pentecost or Corpus Christi. It is one of the most family centred festivals, as many mothers expressed it to me, more joyous even than the marriage of a child, which involves the breaking up of an existing family and the creation of a new. For a girl especially it is a prefiguration of her marriage, expressed in the garment worn only on that occasion, which is a miniature wedding dress. The parallel is continued in the gifts given to the communicant, often of a religious nature, rosaries, gold-chains with a religious icon, little statues of children praying, all of which are displayed in the house of the parents. It is also along with marriage, the only occasion when all friends and relatives are invited into the house to see the gifts and eat and drink together. It has also become a very expensive occasion for the family concerned, but one which it is very hard to back out of, because of the patterns of reciprocity established.

It is during the doctrine classes, taught by the priest, preceding first communion that the child receives the rudiments of Catholic doctrine, and at Montelaterone much of this is presented in terms of a family drama in which the child is encouraged to participate emotionally. First communion begins a period of years during which the child attends church regularly (children and old women are virtually the only people to commune more than once a year), and in which the priest plays an important part in the life of the child.

Expense is not the only objection to first communion, and amongst Communists and Socialists there is often an attempt to prevent the child attending the catechism classes and at least delay first communion. The child's own reaction to exclusion from a whole range of activities in which age mates participate, and in which they are at the centre of family attention, is nearly always sufficient to make the family change its mind. If this fails, the priest or nun involved in religious instruction will intervene with the mother, rarely as involved in left-wing politics as the father, and encourage her to allow the child to attend. In this conflict the church always wins, but it is a conflict which in some households may last several years, with the priest and the mother urging the child to ally against the father. Children may be told to pray for their father's soul, and that their father will go to hell unless he goes to confess. I have mentioned how often families are divided politically, but it would take another article to show in any detail how political choices are presented as moral choices in the socialisation of children. The kind of church pressure described above was particularly strong in the early post-war years, though confined to the households of party activists.

MARRIAGE

Since the creation of the Italian Republic, the possibility of a civic marriage, at which the mayor officiates, has existed as a legal alternative to the religious ceremony. In some northern towns the level of civic marriages has reached 20% of all those celebrated. In the commune of Arcidosso of which Montelaterone is part, there were no civic marriages between 1946 and 1970. Since that year,

which coincides with the introduction of the divorce law, there have
been a dozen, all except two involving divorcees, whom the Church
obviously refuses to remarry. Unlike baptism and first communion,
neither the bride nor the groom are obliged to marry in their parish
of residence, and it is noticeable that many young Communists prefer
to marry in another parish rather than come to terms with their own
priest, but that is about the only acknowledgement of any conflict
in the area. Incidentally in 1974 Montelaterone was one of the few
villages in the locality, or in Tuscany, where the divorce referendum produced an overall majority to repeal the law permitting
divorce.

FUNERALS

On the death of a person, the bells of the church are rung, the
funeral notices are posted round the village, and the body is
prepared for the wake, which lasts a day or two, and during which
most of those who knew the person pay their last respects. Normally
the body is then taken to the church for the funeral mass, and then
in a procession led by the black-cloaked members of the Misericordia,
the burial society to the *campo santo*, the burial ground outside
the village. There are exceptions to the above pattern, when the
body is taken directly from the house to the graveyard, which is
not holy ground in the normal sense, but the property of the commune.
Non-Catholic funerals, unlike marriages, are not registered by the
commune, so there is no sure way of knowing how frequent they have
been over the years, my estimate would be only about two a year in
the whole commune of 5,000 inhabitants, and I have notice of only
one since the war in Montelaterone.

These non-Catholic funerals always involve those who have been
militants in the Socialist or Communist Party, who have never paid
their dues to the Misericordia, and have expressed a wish for a
civic funeral. So instead of a priest and the black cloaks of the
Misericordia, the body is accompanied to the graveyard by the
officials of the party and the red flags of the party section. The
party also puts up its own funeral notices alongside those of the
family. These funerals would be more common, except that the wishes
of a dying person are not always respected, and the family may go
ahead with a Catholic service.

There are a number of contrasts with the situation at marriage.
Marriage is at the heart of all those family based values expressed
by the Church, and at least in this part of Italy, only those whom
the Church refuses to marry, the divorced, will have a civic marriage. This civic ceremony does not take place under the auspices
of any political party, that is there can be marriages between

Communists but not Communist marriages. At death the personal wishes
of the deceased can more easily override those of the family group
(even if they are not always respected), and he can express his non-
belief in the dogma of the Church and his desire to be buried under
the auspices of the party with which he is identified. Note that in
this society some precise non-involvement in the life of the Church,
or agnostic attitude is not sufficient motive for a civic funeral.

Before moving on it should be pointed out that this brief account
of four rituals has been discussing the participation of the main
actors involved. Whatever decisions a person takes, or are taken for
them in their own lives, different degrees of opposition or involve-
ment in the Church can be expressed when it comes to the rituals of
friends and relatives. At the most uncompromising end, one Communist
councillor in Arcidosso recently accompanied his father's coffin as
far as the door of the church, but refused to put a foot inside for
the funeral service. The councillor is not a great believer in
compromise, historical or otherwise. A whole series of less extreme
statements are possible.

PROCESSIONS

We can now move on from a consideration of collective representations
concerned with individual salvation to those concerned with the
spiritual well-being of the collectivity, here the parish. Elements
of this are to be found in the prayers of the daily mass, but it
receives its clearest affirmation in the processions. In Montelaterone
there are still four processions held annually, on Good Friday,
Corpus Christi, the Assumption and All Saints' Day. Two others, one
on the day of the Holy Cross, when all village lands were blessed,
and another on the feast day of the village's patron saint, have
been abolished, and the priest is busy devaluing the remaining four.
It is not possible here to deal with the various significances of
these processions, and only two aspects will be mentioned.

Firstly they are based on the unity of the parish. In the past,
all and only those resident in the parish, and hence the village,
took part, and the procession route, a large figure of eight, encom-
passed all the inhabited area of the hill. Attendance is impressive.
Even in 1975 two-thirds of the adult village population were present
for the midnight procession at Easter, and considering that a third
of the parish consists of those over 65, this is a high figure. In
that year the committee of the local Communist Party had gathered
rather conspicuously in a bar and were sitting it out. They admitted,
however, that in previous years they had all participated, that
there had been no general tendency for the left to abstain from
these processions. The priest, in his homily before the Corpus

Christi procession, told his congregation that it was a form of
collective prayer, that he preferred fifty who went in faith to pray
to five hundred who went to chatter, and it may well be that in a
few years this kind of collective parish based religious practice
will disappear in favour of the community of the faithful.

The second aspect of the processions is the sexual division of
the village which is expressed there. The separation of men and
women in the church is fairly rigorously observed (except for middle-
class summer visitors), as it is in daily life. Friendship across
the sexes is rare, the social life of men takes place in bars, while
women congregate in courtyards in summer, and sometimes in houses in
winter, though in general house visiting is uncommon, especially for
men. In the processions it is the men who go in front, in twos,
followed by the priest in the centre, and then all the women. It was
mentioned above the extent to which the priest often intervenes in
family affairs, the role he plays in marriage negotiations and that
the only legitimate sexual relations between men and women are those
which the priest sanctifies in marriage. In the ordering of the
processions it is hard not to see some more general statement that
relations between men and women are mediated by the priesthood, and
view the anomalous nature of the priest (dress, celibacy etc.) in
this light.

THE BLESSING OF THE HOUSE

The last example of Catholic practice to be considered is the Easter
Blessing of the house. The event provokes a flurry of spring-cleaning
among all the housewives of the village who like to have the house
at its best before this, the only occasion when the priest regularly
enters every house of the parish. It takes place during Lent, and in
day-time when the men are away in the fields. The priest kneels
before the image of the Madonna which is to be found in every kitchen,
and then makes a rapid blessing in each inhabited room, asperging
with holy water, while the altar boys follow behind to collect the
traditional gift of eggs. It is difficult to talk about the exact
significance of the blessing: the priest explains that he places
each house in the hands of God, while local people sometimes say
that it brings good luck. Further questioning usually reveals some
idea that the house has been sanctified and a blessing imparted to
the family life which occurs there.

The most interesting aspect of the Easter Blessing as far as this
article is concerned is the central role it came to play in the years
of the anathema. In 1949 the Pope announced that all those who
belonged to, or supported marxist political parties, in practice the
Popular Front, were to take no part in the life of the Church. The

operation of the anathema has been very much more muted since the
Papacy of John XXIIIrd, and always depended on the discretion and
inclination of the local hierarchy. There are important tactical
considerations here, and a hard-line priest who refused communion
to a third or a half of his parish might have done more to undermine the position of the Church than his opponents. The operation
of the anathema also depended on the extent to which a priest was
in a position to know the political views of his flock. In Montelaterone Don Raimondo concentrated on half a dozen men prominently
involved in left-wing politics and apart from refusing them absolution unless they publicly announced their break with left-wing
politics, he also refused to bless their houses. Of the two measures,
it was the latter which caused the most tension. As one old militant
put it, nobody knew if you had been to confess or not, but everyone
knew if your house had not been blessed. It was a *disgrazia* (disgrace), and caused innumerable rows within the family, between
husband, wife and children.

A further local practice which reveals the same theme was the
circulation, from house to house within the village, of a series of
miniature portable shrines, each containing a reproduction of the
local statue of the Madonna. Each family would tend and light a
candle in this shrine for a night, before passing it on to another
family in the neighbourhood circle. The priest insisted that those
families where the head was prominently identified with the Popular
Front should be excluded from the circle.

Clearly a great deal more could be said about local religious
practice, but from the points made above certain themes should have
emerged. Firstly that Church teaching puts a heavy emphasis on the
family as a precondition for a moral life, and as the focus for
activity in the world. We can add as a corollary to this, one that
should by now be obvious, that the Church condemns all sexual relationships which it has not sanctified, and in its teaching on sin
concentrates heavily on sexual sins. These precepts are followed
very closely by the villagers of Montelaterone regardless of their
political affiliations. Participation in the Catholic *rites de
passage* (which are major occasions of family celebration and the
gathering of wider kin) is also common to all villagers. These
rituals and the processions are the only active forms of participation in the life of the Church for many men in the village, and
there is a special emphasis given to the family, the home and the
domestic domain (i.e., the women's world) in local teaching and
practice. The spiritual excommunication of left-wing leaders was
most strongly felt where it was applied to the domestic domain,
having the effect of excluding the leaders' families from the moral
community[6]. The final theme was the use of a territorial organisation
and the emphasis on local unities in Catholic practice. This theme

is closely linked to the emphasis on *campanilismo* in D.C. ideology, an aspect which will be touched on again below, but cannot be dealt with adequately in this article[7].

PROPAGANDA

We now come to the examination of the electoral propaganda, dating from the height of the cold-war, the years 1948-1953, when a victory for the Communists would have led to "the cossacks watering their horses in the fountains of Rome". The material comes from the D.C. central office and from the *comitati civici*, which were a centrally coordinated group of local action committees, headed by the Catholic hierarchy and various Catholic organisations. Because of the position of the Vatican in Italy, the *comitati civici* could not recommend voting for any particular party, but made their position clear negatively. They were in a sense a political branch of Catholic Action. Allum's detailed study of the Neapolitan politics (Allum 1973) shows how Catholic Action is the major way the Church controls who gets elected in the Christian-Democrat Party, at all levels, using the system of preference voting. In Tuscany, too, the approval of the local hierarchy was and is a pre-condition for success in the D.C.

   Although these are national sources, their diffusion, including some local variations, was very widespread[8]. In the town of Montepulciano (Siena province) I was able to track down propaganda material in the archives of a parish newspaper which duplicates in slogans all the major themes of the posters, while many of the posters themselves are well remembered by the inhabitants of Montelaterone. They are certainly very powerful images, and range in emotional tone from the eschatological to the folksy and coy. (Obviously it has not been possible to reproduce all of them here.) For example, one reason given for voting D.C. was that it preserved femininity, and we are presented with a contrast between a lady portraying 1940s chic, and a dumpy peasant woman giving the clenched fist salute, embodying perhaps, the view of the peasantry as a sack of potatoes. I shall concentrate on the more dramatic themes. Several analyses of this material have already been made in Italy. One stresses the continuity with the Fascist iconography and points to the totalitarian ambitions of the D.C. party of the period. Certainly the propaganda implies little room for dissent, but if political opponents are characterised as not merely wrong, or unpatriotic, but evil, then it is on the latter aspect that I wish to concentrate. Another self-styled structuralist analysis by Quintavalle (in Gaudino & Vittori 1976) emphasises the dynamic aspect of the posters, they tell a story, are fables with a hero, a monster, a menace and a

solution, and the political effectiveness of the propaganda lies in
the recognition of the proponents of the story and the invitation
to participate in the solution, i.e., vote. These are important
considerations, but my own account looks at more specific features
of the propaganda, although I agree with Quintavalle that we need
to look at the posters as a set, a whole, because not all the
elements of the ideology emerge in any of them.

The first aspect of the propaganda to be considered is the presentation of the choice between the Christian-Democrats and the
Popular Front as a choice between Christian good and evil. Apart
from the repeated slogans that characterise the electoral battle as
one between Catholics and Atheists, and the more complex question
of the family (see below), we find in pictorial images, the Christian
worker shown in the manner of the Archangel Michael crushing the
demons of Capitalism and Communism under foot, the Russian soldier
('Vote, or he will be your master') as the angel of death, and
Stalin as the masked devil. The idea of masking in fact runs through
many of these posters: the image of the Popular Front turns out to
be Janus faced, with Garibaldi on one side and Stalin on the other,
the petition for peace by the Popular Front (a reaction to the
formation of NATO) is portrayed as a wolf in sheep's clothing. The
use of masking, the creation of a world where things are not what
they seem, is an important visual form of metaphor, and we shall
return to this aspect of the propaganda in the conclusion.

In the battle between good and evil, the theme of the family
emerges very clearly, and this is the second aspect of the ideology
which can be isolated. Sometimes we just find a child in mortal
danger from Communist tanks, sometimes an exhortation to defend your
children by voting D.C. because in Russia the children belong to the
state. That family ties are severed and parental authority undermined by Communism is underlined by the grim story from Prague of
the man who was hanged after being denounced to the authorities by
his son. This is spelt out verbally in other posters where the so-
called Communist paradise is described as a place where the family
is sacrificed to egoism, divorce and free love. In another, people
are encouraged to heckle Communist meetings by asking how many girls
have emerged safe and unharmed from Communist dances. One pictorial
image sums up this theme with a portrayal of the family unit strong
and unharmed because the Christian vote, represented as a sword, is
about to cut down the serpents of divorce and free love. As with
many of the pictorial images which have a direct biblical reference,
the symbols are taken from the Book of Revelations.

The third aspect is the elaboration of the theme of Christian-
Democracy as a defence, most famously in the emblem of the shield
with a cross (the D.C. campaigning symbol), but also in the image
of the wall and the dam. What is defended is always a feminine

image -- Italy, the motherland, liberty, the family; what threatens
is always a masculine image -- an ape-like brute, barbaric, violent
and violating. Umberto Eco, in an article in the Italian weekly
L'Espresso, suggests that the dominant psychological motif of these
posters is that of cannibalism, but rape might be a more suitable
label. Rape, in this land of metaphor, is not to be understood
always in a literal sense. It is perhaps most explicit in the image
of a Communist fly about to penetrate a fresh rose, itself springing
from an enclosed and defended town, but it is hinted at also in the
smiling countryside secure behind its wall of votes from the attacks
of the clawed Communist demons.

The theme of defence has a number of other dimensions in the
propaganda which can only be outlined here. The simplest of them is
that of patriotism, which opposes the nationalism of the D.C. to the
internationalism of the left, except that the internationalism is
portrayed in a xenophobic and racialist way. The threatening hordes
marching on the town-hall are not just destructive but aliens,
significantly blond-haired. King-Kong is overthrowing the altar of
the motherland on the Capitoline in Rome, while even the fly-swatter
about to eliminate the intrusive Communist fly, has the national
flag on the handle. If the threatening forces are always represented
as coming from outside (aliens), they are also consistently represented as bestial (the ape, the clawed demons, the fly). This
portrayal itself draws on the Christian dichotomy between body and
soul, but instead of being contained within each person, the
attributes are split between opposed sections of mankind, allowing
the Christian-Democrats to arrogate to themselves the spiritual part
of humanity and depict their (atheist) opponents as animals. The
portrayal of this separation also has a time dimension, in that it
draws on the symbolism of the Apocalypse and contains within itself
an apocalyptic message.

The same theme of defence has both a patriotic and local dimension.
The Christian-Democrat Party often chose some symbol of the unity
of the place (a bell-tower, *campanile*, or fortified walls) as a
campaigning symbol in local elections, and in this emphasis on local
unities distinguished itself from the class ideology of its opponents[9].
Not only is this appeal to local loyalties present in the posters,
it is combined again with Christian overtones, in that the turreted
towns and defended gateways, labelled with Christian virtues, refers
also to the City of God (another apocalyptic borrowing from the Book
of Revelations), into which no impure person may enter (hence the
rose springing from the town). Even this is not an entirely new
development. Mediaeval and Renaissance histories of the City-States
often referred to the divine origins of the town and compared them
to the City of God (Weinstein 1968). The same theme is found also

in Tuscan painting. Curiously one picture by Botticelli (The mystic crucifixion of ca. 1500) devoted to the theme of Florence as the City of God, also contains many floating symbols of the shield and the cross, later adopted by the Christian-Democrat Party. Even the smiling countryside secure behind its wall of votes from the demons is not devoid of religious significance, in that there is a long iconographic tradition of portraying paradise as a walled garden, and that the portrayal of rival paradises was a conscious theme on both sides of this propaganda battle.

To summarise: in these posters we find a number of related themes, some of them combined in one image, but never the whole set represented together. The ideology that emerges is structured by a series of interrelated oppositions: order and disorder, inside and outside, female and male, purity and danger, oppositions which not only enable a series of statements to be made about various levels of society (from the family to the town and the nation), but also enable these various levels to be interconnected. The combined force of these statements is to suggest that the conflict between Christian-Democracy and Communism is a religious conflict between good and evil. One of the chief symbols of the good is the family, and thus Communism as the enemy must be made to represent an attack on that most Christian of institutions. Hence there is a Catholic development of the Communist ideology, that the sons belong to the State, divorce, free love, a development which never received much attention from the Communists themselves in Italy. In fact of necessity the Communists presented themselves as defenders of the family, and their leader Togliatti went on record as saying that divorce was not a suitable institution in a country such as Italy, a pronouncement which the D.C. made much use of thirty years later in the divorce referendum. It also follows that at some point an attempt will be made to identify the Communist enemy of the Catholic family with its traditional enemies, egoism and the violent emotions. Hence we find those imputed pillars of Communist doctrine, divorce and free love, represented as serpents, and perhaps at another metaphorical level, the recurring theme of Communism as rape I have already mentioned.

Hopefully it is now possible to understand both the trivial examples of sexual abuse of the 1975 electoral campaign, and the introductory comments on how the two major themes of the D.C. ideology reinforce each other: particularly when political debate is focused on the family, defined as central to Catholicism and denied by Communism. In this reading to be Catholic is to be anti-Communist and vice versa[10].

CONCLUSIONS

a) *Politics and Religion*

In these concluding remarks I shall deal first with the more general points which have emerged for the study of politics and religion in Italy during the cold-war period, and then with the problems connected specifically with the analysis of ideology.

In the first place it is necessary to make a disclaimer. This article has not attempted to expound any kind of monocausal theory that certain categories of people gave their support to the Christian-Democrat Party because of the ideology outlined above. Nor has it given the kind of information which would allow hypotheses about relative motivations -- ideological motives count so much, personal interests or clientelism so much more in the construction of the D.C. block of votes. (This kind of analysis often seems to me mistaken insofar as it treats concepts like 'self-interest' as being unproblematic, transparent, even natural, rather than taking people's conception of their self-interest to be part of the material to be analysed.) Certainly the people themselves are very interested in motivations and have a very articulate set of reasons for why they support given political parties, reasons which vary according to whether they are discussing the matter in public or private, discussing their own motives, those of friends or those of opponents, but this material also falls outside the scope of this article.

What this article has attempted to show is that the Christian-Democrat Party in the cold-war period appealed to the electorate to 'vote for the cross' on the basis of particular presentations of the national and international situation, and on the basis of particular definitions of Catholicism and Communism. One of the themes of these definitions was the family, presented as a pillar of Italian society which the Communists would destroy. The earlier part of the article showed that the Church teaching on the family was accepted virtually without exception by the inhabitants of a peasant village, Montela-terone, and that family values and religious practice that concentrated on the family were essential to 'being a Catholic', the Catholic identity of those villagers. Other ethnographic accounts confirm this emphasis. It seems legitimate to suggest that the account of village Catholicism throws some light on the forms taken by the D.C. propaganda, but it is more problematic to suggest that the propaganda can explain the support given to the D.C. by peasant villagers. That villagers accept the authority of the Church in certain of their social activities does not guarantee that the Church's legitimacy will also be accepted in political decisions, nor does the acceptance of the Church's authority exclude other reasons (including economic advantage) for supporting the Christian-Democrat Party.

To return briefly to the material from Montelaterone, the
Christian-Democrat Party did succeed in increasing its share of the
vote in the first post-war years, as it did at the national level.
This increase, however, came at the expense of the minor parties
(particularly the Republicans who lost much of their *raison d'être*
after the foundation of the Republic), and the left-wing parties on
the whole maintained their support in electoral terms. Those who
were left-wing activists at the time, and subject to the priest's
interpretation of the anathema, did not withdraw from political
life, though they report a sharp drop in membership (as opposed to
votes) of the Popular Front parties from 1948 onwards. Their
accounts would indicate an overall reduction in the extent to which
people were prepared to identify themselves publicly with the left,
and some cases in which the discriminatory tactics practised caused
a change of sides. However, in Montelaterone there remained a core
of left-wing agricultural workers who were employed as day-labourers
for part of the year on the great estates of the Maremma, and were
involved in the class action on those estates. Amongst the rural
sector of the Maremma, scattered on the share-cropping farms, the
Christian-Democrat Party had very much less support and in the purely
rural voting wards the left obtained up to 80% of the vote.

In Montelaterone itself the priest was able to supply some
economic discrimination against left-wing activists, and in the
employment sphere there were one or two patrons who gave jobs in
return for Christian-Democrat votes. But compared with Alan Stern's
account of priests working with local industrialists to exclude left-
wing workers in Veneto, or the control of agricultural credit through
peasant associations and banks found elsewhere, the economic incen-
tives to vote D.C. were minimal in Montelaterone. In fact, the
Christian-Democrat support tended to come from those who were full-
time peasant proprietors rather than those in search of work, from
peasants who sold little and bought less, who at the time were
virtually absent from the market. It came, then as now, from women
more than from men.

These, then, were the people who did 'vote for the cross', for
whom the Church and the Christian-Democrat Party provided a set of
concepts and discriminators which could be applied to the understanding of social conflict at a whole range of levels, and within
which religion and politics were not separable. This cold-war propaganda material now causes considerable amazement to those who once
took it for granted, and provides a measure of one of the changes
which has taken place in Italian society in the last thirty years.
The separation of religion and politics is now much more evident[11],
even if attempts to form political groupings on the basis of
Christian teaching is far from finished at both ends of the political
spectrum. This separation involves, of course, a new conception of

religion, one which is based increasingly on faith, as the cursory remarks on Catholic practice in Montelaterone will have indicated. The responsibility for this development lies not only with the challenge from the left to the Church's hegemony, but has its roots also in the Church's response to this challenge, in its identifi- cation with a particular political party, and in the anathema of the years we have been considering.

b) *Ideology*

It is not possible to deal at any length here with the general problem of the relationship between ideologies elaborated nationally and local beliefs and practice. The configuration in any case varies from one ideology to another: the relationship between Catholic dogma and local practice is not the same as that between Marxism and 'village Communism'[12]. In addition, the material discussed in this article is not the easiest starting point for a general consider- ation of this problem, firstly in that it is electoral propaganda aimed at obtaining consent at the local level (i.e., the two levels, if they are indeed separable, are in this instance confused), and secondly because I do not have detailed information on the circum- stances of its elaboration. In place of the general discussion we can only point to particular themes and problems.

One framework for discussing the relationship between 'great' and 'little' traditions is the use of hierarchical levels of explanation. For example, De Martino (1959), very elegantly relates the particular explanations of misfortune found in South Italian magical practices to the great tradition of the Catholic Church, showing that there is a continuity in the principles underlying both, though different levels of application. Some aspects of the ideology considered here present a similar pattern. Local religious belief and folklore stresses that human beings are *'cristiani'* and that is what dis- tinguishes them from animals, separates the domestic domain, the family and kinship from the profane world of friendship and public affairs dominated by men, separates in a number of ways insiders, those resident in a particular town or village, from strangers. These same themes and oppositions are found in the propaganda material, and in one sense are applied at higher levels, so that strangers are contrasted with patriots, or the free world opposed to the 'enslaved' world of barbarians on the basis of the distinction between humans and animals. But this is only part of the strategy, in that the ideology also incorporates elements from the lower level, precisely because to be successful it must part from that which is familiar, and give universal significance to the institutions of the family or local chauvinism. In this way it is possible to transform the experience of that which is lived daily into the ideological split which divides the nation.

An important aspect of this transformation is the use of visual
images which belong to a very long tradition of Italian and Catholic
iconography. We have mentioned in passing paradise as a walled
garden, and a whole range of other biblical images, most of them
taken from the Book of Revelations and in keeping with the apocalyptic message: the Angel of Death, the serpents, the Archangel Michael
crushing the demons, the City of God. Informants from Montelaterone
when questioned about these posters never volunteered the origin of
these images, though it is safe to assume that those who composed
the posters were conscious of their borrowings, and that some at
least of their public recognised them. The question of for whom, and
in what sense these images are recognised (are symbolic) raises the
general problem of the meaning of symbolism, and here we can only
make a limited observation. If the creators of this propaganda acted
like 'bricoleurs', re-using bits and pieces from earlier traditions,
the elements incorporated in the new structure must also continue to
be considered in their relations with other elements in the structure
which gives them meaning. Thus, for example, if the City of God in
Revelations has to be considered in relation to Babylon, and in
relation to the final separation of Good and Evil, and has been
borrowed for these reasons, the symbol itself gains a new dimension
from the incorporation in an anti-Communist ideology. Thus the
'walled city' continues to be a symbol because of its use in a
present-day political context (as an election symbol for those
political groupings which stress local unities as against class
divisions), but may lose its previous symbolic dimensions, at least
for those not familiar with Revelations or Renaissance iconography.
Other symbols disappear altogether from Christian-Democrat propaganda.

Secondly it should be noted that the elements cannot be borrowed
in a haphazard way, but must be consonant with other elements already
present. The walled city is appropriate to other themes in the ideology, such as *campanilismo* and patriotism, but there are constraints
which make certain transformations impossible (or 'nonsensical') in
a given culture. For example, even after the Catholic party had
obtained a majority and forced the left into a minority position,
the iconography continued to show Catholic 'values' besieged in the
city by outsiders. It would not make sense to reverse the positions
and show the forces of God besieging a town which was an isolated
red stronghold, though possibly (and this is pure speculation), in
other circumstances of political polarisation, such as a pueblo in
the Spanish Civil War, this transformation would be possible.

Finally it is worth re-emphasising the purpose of this propaganda
material. The idea that Italian society was at a turning point in
these years is a constant theme, and given graphic expression in one
poster which shows a cross-roads, where the left-hand path leads to
social disorder and the right-hand path straight to the land of

prosperity. It is continued in the attempt to polarise Italian society at this particular historical moment, one that is mirrored in the apocalyptic references and in the recurring use of symbols of division -- the Christian-Democrat Party is a wall, a dam, a shield[13]. The pronouncement of the anathema in 1949, guided by international considerations, brought this attempt to separate, exclude and excommunicate down to the level of the village and the household, and left an experience which continues to influence attitudes towards the clergy and the Christian-Democrat Party even in the age of the *compromesso storico*.

NOTES

1. The publication of the book by Savelli was itself a political act, aimed at discrediting the present policy of the *'compromesso storico'* of the P.C.I. by revealing the past nature of their hoped for allies in the Christian-Democrat Party.
2. Statistical analyses of party allegiance are to be found in Galli and Prandi (1970) and Maria Weber (1977).
3. Guizzardi's article provides a very good summary of this aspect of Catholic ideology, one which in many ways fills out the picture presented here and provides stimulating points of departure for other analyses. It is therefore even more regrettable that the English version has such an opaque and ungrammatical style, one which occasionally makes nonsense of the argument.
4. Further south, not just statues but the Madonna herself was claimed to have made an appearance in this politically tense period. Fellini dealt with these claimed apparitions in a sequence of 'La Dolce Vita'.
5. W.A. Christian (1972) gives a more detailed account of the subtle shifts in the models of human-divine relations to be found in Church teaching.
6. A similar picture of the working of the anathema and the isolation of the left emerges from Alan Stern's account of political legitimacy in an industrial and a rural setting in the Veneto (Stern 1975).
7. Obviously here we are talking about the basic forms of Catholicism for the laity, because in the Holy Orders the Church has a very important structure not based on territorial organisation.
8. Although I have concentrated on a few of the hundreds of different election posters of the period, it should be made clear that the messages contained in them were also propagated by the other channels of communication used by the Church and the Christian-Democrat Party: mass rallies, pastoral letters, parish newspapers, the pulpit, Papal messages and audiences, Vatican radio and the

State broadcasting system, channels certainly as important as the massive poster campaign. All the themes analysed here can be found in the documentary evidence cited by Falconi (1956), Prandi (1968).

9. A fuller discussion of this point can be found in Pratt (1973 and 1980).

10. It should be added that the left responded to this portrayal of Communism as the enemy of family life with a number of posters showing a united family reading *L'Unità* (the party daily) at the breakfast table, appealing to women to save their children from war by signing the peace petition, and many others employing the classic image of the mother and child. However, in general it was the contention of the left in Italy that this attention to the family and the domestic domain was an attempt to deflect interest away from basic political issues (which concern class relations) and 'depoliticise' large sections of the electorate, especially women.

11. The reader is again referred to Guizzardi's article for a discussion of the problems faced by the Church in privileging a model of economic organisation (that of the 'peasant proprietor') which has become increasingly marginal to Italian society.

12. 'Village Communism' can only be defined by reference to elements which are not Marxist in origin. The same is not true of Catholicism. In other words, membership of a group defined by residence is not a significant or stressed element in a class understanding of society, even if in Italian Communist practice this aspect is of considerable importance. Place of residence is immediately stressed in Catholicism by the fact that the grace of God is mediated through sacraments (including baptism) administered by a parish priest, patron saints and so on.

13. The polarisation of Italian society but on a class basis is evident from the Communist Party posters of the same period (reproduced in Gaudino and Vittori 1976), where there is a division between the workers and the so-called 'big-eaters', who consume more than they produce. The latter, who also have clear foreign connections (with America) are to be expelled from society.

REFERENCES

Allum, P.A.
    1973   *Politics and Society in Post-War Naples*. Cambridge: University Press.
Christian, W.A. Jr.
    1972   *Person and God in a Spanish Valley*. London: Seminar Press.

De Martino, E.
    1959   *Sud e Magia*. Milan: Feltrinelli.
Falconi, C.
    1956   *La chiesa e le organizzazione Cattoliche in Italia 1945–
            1955*. Turin: Einaudi.
Galli, G. & A. Prandi
    1970   *Patterns of Political Participation in Italy*. London:
            Yale University Press.
Gaudino, D. & G. Vittori
    1976   *Via il regime della forchetta*. Rome: Savelli.
Guizzardi, G.
    1976   The Rural Civilization, Structure of an Ideology for
            Consent. *Social Compass* 22:197-220.
Leo XIII
    1891   Rerum Novarum. Published in English as *The Worker's
            Charter*. London: Catholic Truth Society.
Prandi, A.
    1968   *Chiesa e politica. La gerarchia e l'impegno politico dei
            Cattolici in Italia*. Bologna: Il mulino.
Pratt, J.C.
    1973   *Friends, Brothers and Comrades*. Unpublished Ph.D. thesis,
            University of Sussex.
    1980   A Sense of Place. In: R. Grillo (ed.), *Nation and State
            in Europe*. London: Academic Press.
Romano, L. & P. Scabello
    1975   *C'era una volta la D.C.* Rome: Savelli.
Stern, A.
    1975   Political Legitimacy in Local Politics: The Communist
            Party in North East Italy. In: Blackmer and Tarrow (eds.),
            Communism in France and Italy. Princeton: Princeton
            University Press.
Weber, M.
    1977   *Il voto delle donne*. Milan: Fratelli Fabbri Editori.
Weinstein, D.
    1968   The Myth of Florence. In: N. Rubinstein (ed.), *Florentine
            Studies*. London: Faber & Faber.

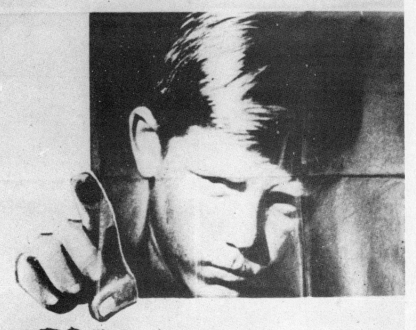

ACCUSO
MIO PADRE E MIA MADRE !

Il 24 novembre 1952 durante il processo di Praga contro Slansky e compagni, il giovane comunista Tomas Frejka chiese la condanna a morte del padre che fu quindi impiccato.

POTREBBE ESSERE TUO FIGLIO
SE VINCESSERO I COMUNISTI

VOTA O SARA IL TUO PADRONE

STATALI
ALTRO CHE AUMENTI
SE VIENE BAFFONE !
LA RIVOLUZIONE PROLETARIA NON DEVE TRASFERIRE DA UNA MANO ALL'ALTRA LA MACCHINA BUROCRATICA, COME E' AVVENUTO FINORA, MA DEVE DEMOLIRLA. LA CONDIZIONE PREVIA DI OGNI RIVOLUZIONE VERAMENTE POPOLARE E' LA DEMOLIZIONE, LA DISTRUZIONE DELLE MACCHINE STATALI ESISTENTI
DEMOCRAZIA CRISTIANA - Spes

Religious Apparitions and the Cold War in Southern Europe

William Christian, Jr., Hamden, Conn.

ALLEGED APPARITION OF THE VIRGIN TO A GIRL IN CACERES

With natural reservations we transmit the following
information. For the last few days Caceres and its
outskirts have been overflowing with thousands and
thousands of persons going to the hamlet of Moret,
where in a certain spot it is said the Virgin appears
to a girl. After a few days it is impossible to cal-
culate how many thousands of persons go daily to the
mining barrio of Moret to be present when the girl
says she is talking with Our Lady. The girl is named
Mercedes Trejo Medina, seven years old. She does not
go to church much; she is the daughter of a widowed
washerwoman; she has three brothers, but they have
not influenced her, for religion is not encouraged in
her house. The girl is strong, well-developed, and
shows no signs of mental disorders. This very humble
child since all this has happened has shown a strange
serenity.
One day recently, the girl was going to get some heads
of wheat from the fields when she stopped suddenly by
the walls of an abandoned building. She said she had
seen a lady with a child. They showed her photographs,
and apparently it was the Virgen del Pilar. Since that
day her mother has tried to keep her at home. But the
child would not be still. The news spread. And since
then the girl goes twice a day to the site of the
supposed apparition. She is taken there at certain
hours. She goes over a certain course on her knees,
and she speaks with the Virgin as if Our Lady were
really present. The girl makes requests and appears
to fall down. While this goes on the multitude is
weeping and praying. The girl has asked the Virgin to
work a miracle. She says that Our Lady promised to do

> it at the end of nine days. External signs? Until now,
> none. The girl walks on her knees, prays, petitions,
> but the people can only see an infant of seven years
> who in the face of enormous crowds neither is fright-
> ened, or perturbed, or loses her normal composure.
> The Church has not intervened yet in this supposed
> apparition, and the ecclesiastical authorities have
> said nothing. CIFRA (*El Alcazar*, Madrid, 6 May 1947,
> 7).

Public visions of Saints, especially Mary, by lay people, some of
them lasting only a few minutes, others intermittant over a period
of days, weeks, or even years, have occurred, particularly in rural
areas, throughout Catholic Europe from at least the fourteenth
century to the present. They have been effective ways to consecrate
a place as holy -- to set up a shrine; they are efficient ways for
towns or regions to obtain the latest word from heaven on how to
avoid collective disasters, especially the plague, and manage the
collective disgrace of military subjection; and occasionally, as
with Jeanne d'Arc and Savonarola, they have influenced the course
of what is conventionally known as history.

I am convinced from talking to friends and casual acquaintances
that very significant numbers of persons have visions. My dental
hygenist in South Boston remembers very clearly a vision of the
Sacred Heart of Jesus out over the water of Boston harbor she saw
from her window as a young child. But until I raised the subject
she had told no one. A student came up after a seminar and told how
she, her sister, and her grandmother saw from the porch of their house
in rural Puerto Rico the three kings ride out of the sky on camels in
1962. They went inside to tell her parents, who just laughed. A
Greek friend tells me that in October, 1942, her father in a
Macedonian village saw two fairies come into the room where his
first-born was lying, and whisper to one another the child's future.
In addition to these one-time, private visions, there are those of
religious virtuosi, whether members of orders or laypeople, who
have frequent revelations, also private.

The kind of vision I have been studying is not intrinsically
different, but it has a different effect -- it is the kind
people find out about and pay attention to. The frequency of such
publicly known visions is an indication of the times and places
that people take visions seriously, of a social need for or
alertness to messages from heaven. Whether one regards the messages and symbolism of these visions as sent from God, or as a kind
of reflection of the collective unconscious, they provide a fascinating counterpoint to political and social history.

According to the best statistics available, visions with a substantial public resonance -- such that they attracted crowds of

spectators -- were most frequent in twentieth-century Europe in the years 1947-1954, especially in 1947, 1948, and 1954. Other times when there were more than the usual number of popular visions were in Spain in 1931, at the time of anticlerical incidents concomitant with the proclamation of the Republic; in Belgium in 1932-1933, and in the years 1937-1940 in Germany, France, and Northern Italy, presumably as tensions built up toward World War II (see Table 1). But the frequency of visions and the popular response to them in the 1947-1954 period were exceptional. On an average there were about four times as many visions per year in the 1947-1954 period as in the rest of the years from 1930 to 1975:

        1931-1946   65 cases in 16 years, about 4 per year;
        1947-1954 112 cases in 8 years, about 14 per year; and
        1955-1975   59 cases in 21 years, about 3 per year.

And this frequency increased not just in one area, but Europe-wide. One is naturally led to inquire to the connections between these visions and the Cold War. What linked 7-year old Mercedes Trejo in the drab company town of Aldeamoret to the struggle that was div-iding Europe and the world into two opposing camps?

The Catholic Church has its representatives in every nook of every country in southwestern Europe -- a stable set of regular clergy and conventual religious, and a cross-cutting network of more mobile religious with headquarters in Rome. And the Catholic Church had been waging the Cold War against Communism since 1917. Before World War II, however, its attention was divided among many enemies. The French Revolution, Freemasons, Republicans, the Mexican Revolution, Marxists and Anarchists in Spain, all fought the Church for people's souls. Secularization in its many forms had by the nineteenth century converted the somewhat somnolent institution of one hundred years before, secure of its base in the countries of the northwest Mediterranean, into a militant organization with well-developed procedures for political mobilization.

But such mobilizations, because of the varying nature of the threats, were by necessity of a national, even regional nature. Separate struggles at different times were waged in France (a con-centrated campaign for the rechristianization of the country from the 1830s through the end of the century), in Spain (the Carlist Wars, the liberal-conservative struggles of the 1890s, and the full-blown Crusade of the Civil War) and Italy (the vain resistance to the loss of temporal power).

By the early 1940s the situation was quite different. The enemy, atheistic Communism, was relatively identifiable and consolidated. It was an international enemy, the same for all the countries, one which posed a threat to the Faith unequaled since the challenge of

TABLE 1: Publicly known apparitions including Mary, Europe 1931-1975[1]

Year of Inception	Total	Italy	Spain	France	Germany	Benelux	Europe East	Europe Other
1931	4		17					
1932	3			1	1	1		
1933	14	1		2		11		
1934	3				1			2
1935	1	1						
1936	3		1	1		1		
1937	5	2		2	1			
1938	6			2	3		1	
1939	2							2
1940	3			2	1			
1941	0							
1942	1							1
1943	1			1				
1944	1	1						
1945	2		1			1		
1946	3			1			1	1
1947	23	9	3	3	3	2	2	1
1948	25	17	1	4			2	1
1949	10	3			4	1	2	1
1950	9	4	2	1	1			1
1951	6	4		1				1
1952	5	2			2	1		
1953	9	8		1				
1954	22	13	3	1	1	2	1	1
1955	2	1						1
1956	3	2		1				
1957	2	1						1
1958	6	4	1				1	
1959	6	3	1				1	1
1960	3	2		1				
1961	5	2	2	1				
1962	1						1	
1963	2	2						
1964	1	1						
1965	1							1
1966	4	3				1		
1967	4	3						1
1968	4	1	2	1				
1969	1	1						
1970	3	1				1		1
1971	3	2		1				
1972	5	3	2					

TABLE 1 (continued)

Year of Inception	Total	Italy	Spain	France	Germany	Benelux	Europe East	Other
1973	0							
1974	1		1					
1975	2		1	1				

the Protestants in the 1540s or the invasion of the Turks.

In Spain in particular the lines between the Church and Communism were clearly drawn. Toward the end of the Civil War, the Communists, supplied by Russia, were a dominant force on the Republican side, and in Republican areas hundreds of priests and religious had been martyred (if often by other groups). The atrocities of Spain were amply circulated throughout the Catholic world, an implicit message as to the fate of Catholics should Communists reach power in other Western countries.

Hence in the thick of war with Germany, the hierarchy and the faithful were preoccupied with the configuration of post-war Europe. Two May Day visions of Jeanne-Louise Ramonet (born 1910), a Breton seer who began her visions in 1938, put the problem succinctly. On May 1, 1941, the Virgin told her:

> Soon Russia will help in the war. It will be a hard blow to your enemies. From then on pray, pray a lot, o Christian souls, for this great country that is an enemy of the Church. Otherwise after the war the Communists will settle in everywhere and the Church will gravely suffer from them. Ask Jesus, through my Immaculate Heart, for the return of sinners and the conversion of Russia (Auclair 1968:100).

On May 1, 1944, Jeanne-Louise saw two tableaux vivants, each as a wing of a double picture.

> On the left half men brandish flags with the intention of putting them up everywhere. Priests try to oppose them, but are insulted and threatened. A hideous character, full of evil joy, who seems to me to be the devil, hidden in the lower left corner of the painting, eggs on the men carrying the flags. In the right hand corner, dressed as she normally appears to me, is Mary. She weeps. Under this picture is an inscription: Image of Communism. In the other half young girls dressed in blue and white recite the Rosary. Beneath them this other inscription: Salvation of Communism (Auclair 1968:103).

Jeanne's vision of 1941 posed the problem; that of 1944 depicted more specifically its social dimensions and offered a solution. In

the picture on the left the flags are carried by men; on the right
prayers are said by girls, dressed as Daughters of Mary. In fact,
in most of Europe the vision was in conformance with reality (and
indeed, still is) in the sense that the left has been an essentially
masculine phenomenon, and the Catholic right overwhelmingly feminine.
France's 'Salvation from Communism' after the war came above all
from the newly awarded suffrage to women.

Consider the figures of Italian membership in Catholic Action,
the Church's activist lay organization. It was rapidly expanded in
the postwar period as part of the mobilization of laity, but throughout the period its membership reflected the sexual composition of
the militant faithful (see Table 2).

TABLE 2: Membership in Catholic Action in Italy [2]

	Men	Boys	Women	Girls
1946	151,000	367,000	369,000	885,000
1954	285,000	557,000	597,000	1,216,000

Membership in the Communist Party and Young Communists would
probably show the exact opposite. To a certain extent the division
within nations between militants of left and right was also a
division within families, along the classic lines of men on the
left, while women were still performing the religious obligations
for the family group.

Here we are already close to the visions, for the composition
of the visionaries reflects a similar gradient (see Table 3).

TABLE 3: Visionary or Vision group, 1947-1954

	Men	Boys	Women	Girls	Mixed (don't know)	Total
Spain	1	1	1	6	0	9
Italy	9	7	12	16	18	62

One of the dynamics leading to the personal epiphanies of some of
the seers was the crystallization of the Cold War not only within
a community, but even within a family.

Part of the Church's strategy, then, in the postwar period, was
not only Jeanne-Louise Ramonet's more metaphysical goal of the
conversion of Russia, but more immediately the conversion of Western
Europe's men. For by the end of the war, especially given the Left's
leadership in the partisan movements, very substantial sectors of
France and Italy were ready to vote for it. As the Blessed Virgin
told Ida Peerdeman, a seer of Amsterdam who had a series of private

revelations, amply diffused, from 1945 to 1959, "This is the era of political Christian warfare" (15 August 1950).[3]

Besides expanding Catholic Action, the Church drew on the immense resources represented by its shrines and venerated images, the friends and sources of spiritual and physical health of devotees whether or not they were active Catholics. One traditional way it did this was through missions -- old-fashioned preaching sessions over a given number of days that made careful use of local traditions and devotions.

According to the Spanish sociologist Aurelio Orensanz, the popular mission summed up Church devotional strategy of the 1940s. It was a carefully calculated effort to revive the religion of whole communities.

> At the reception of the missionaries the total community is present: the local clergy, civil authorities, religious organizations, the teachers, and the people. As the mission develops there is a concentrated program of attention to individual sectors of the population, but not for their own sake, but so they will join in the final apotheosis of conversion and community. ... The preaching aims for the town. Collective symbolism is repeatedly invoked. The Virgin is the main missionary; the patron saint of the town is invoked.

The missions had a double culmination. One was the confession and communion of the largest proportion possible of the population, especially the men. A Jesuit mission manual reads, "On the confessions of the men many times the success of the mission depends, and by the same token the saving of many souls, sometimes of an entire town". The other culmination was an explosive, joyful apotheosis of farewell (Orensanz 1974:10).

Orensanz's description is borne out by newspaper accounts of missions both in cities and in villages in the 1940s and 1950s, and by the memories of older Spaniards. For there are few parish churches in Spain that do not have on their walls commemorative crosses of the missions of this period. The missions of this time were total, emotional events. While the procedures had been perfected over several centuries, there were some new twists. Electricity made possible luminous crosses on the churches and the non-stop broadcasting of prayers and hymns by powerful speakers.

The *Correo de Zamora* reported in April 1953 a Jesuit mission in Gema de Vino, where "loudspeakers on the church tower brought the clear and grave voice of Father Patricio to the pillow of the sick and the laggard and obliged them to follow the rosary of dawn about to begin in streets saturated with Marian fervor". At 11 o'clock in the morning the voice of Father Miguel supplied a "pleasant surprise" for farmers and shepherds working within a radius of three kilometers as he led the prayers of schoolchildren before the microphone. At the end of the mission, all persons who had reached the age of reason accepted communion, according to the newspaper.

A mission in November 1947, in the Mediterranean coastal city of Castellón de la Plana was similar, if on a much larger scale. There the newspaper (*Mediterraneo*, 14 November 1947, 18) reported that in the penitential procession all were participants, none spectators, and this without coercion. Special emphasis was given to the participation of men. 'The number of men spoke loud and clear that the religiosity and piety of Castellón are not solely feminine'. A special communion mass with the Bishop of Tortosa and the Civil Governor present was held for men only in a warehouse, and 3,500 received communion.

Such inclusive community events were only possible in countries like Spain and Portugal where Church and State were close, or in regions of other countries where religious sentiment was strong and united. But another form of mission found favor throughout Western Europe.

The Immaculate Heart of Mary had appeared at Fatima in 1917 and asked for prayers for the conversion of Russia. On 23 March 1943, the day after the consecration of France to the Immaculate Heart of Mary, the *Grand Retour* began at Lourdes. This consisted of the carrying of the venerable statue of Our Lady of Boulogne, one of France's most venerated shrine images, throughout the country from town to town. The image was accompanied by missionaries, and the slow trip was a kind of itinerant mission. According to its organizers, 'The immediate goal of this innovative mission is to support and spread everywhere the consecration of the faithful to the Immaculate Heart of Mary as a means of returning this Catholic country to the law of God'. By November 1946, the image had visited more than 12,000 parishes in 81 dioceses, travelling 45,000 kilometers. The Bishop of Versailles wrote with respect to his diocese, 'The number and quality of conversions obtained are far superior to those of ordinary missions'. The image was carried on a side trip to Rome in 1945, where it was blessed by Pius XII (*Iris de Paz*, 1 June 1947).

The example of the *Grand Retour* and its approval by the Holy Father stimulated other similar ways to bring home the association of Mary with the conversion of sinners and Russia. The apparitions of Fatima were little known outside of Portugal until the early 1940s. But while the war was in progress, not coincidentally, the Fatima story began to circulate throughout Western Europe. In July 1938 was the first national pilgrimage of Portugal to fulfill the Anticommunist Vow. In his 1940 encyclical *Saeculo exeunte*, Pius XII recognized the 'Providential Mission' of Our Lady of Fatima. Luis

Gonzaga de Fonseca's *Las Maravillas de Fatima* went through many editions in the early 1940s. By 1944 there were even children's books, like *Tre Fanculli Guardano in Cielo* by Paolo Liggeri, with illustrations of the Fatima visions for children to see. And in May 1946 the image was canonically crowned, Pius XII speaking by radio.

So when the first 'Voyage-Mission' of the Virgin of Fatima to Lisbon in November 1946 was an overwhelming success, it was a short step to imagining an international version of the *Grand Retour*. The first was a trip to Holland to a Congress of Marian Congregations at Maastricht. The Fatima image slowly made its way through Spain and France, leaving in May 1947, and returning in March 1948, and causing a wave of conversions, miracles, and revivals wherever it went. The *Bulletin of the Diocese of Salamanca* reported in May 1947, "people have been seen weeping on their knees who have not entered a church for a long time; and people have confessed and received communion who had not done so for years, returning to their lost faith".

More international missions followed, both of the original image and of reproductions. In Spain a wealthy devotee, Pascual Arias, dedicated himself to supplying cities and dioceses with copies (2800 by 1950), and many of these copies were sent off on their own missions. In 1948 and 1959 such missions had been held in the majority of Spanish dioceses. One aspect of the missions that people found most persuasive was that doves accompanied the statues, roosting at their feet.[4]

The Bishop of Madrid, whose 25th anniversary as Bishop was one of the motives for the visit of the Fatima image to Madrid in May 1948, wrote, "It was nine days of heaven. There was such religious fervor, so many conversions, such delirious manifestations of love for Our Lady, that I believe that she came to begin in Madrid the Crusade for purification of Christian customs that she wants from Spain in order to convert Russia".[5]

The image paused overnight in Toledo on its return. Priests who were there remember the time the Fatima image came as the zenith of post-Civil War religious fervor in the city; they worked in the confessional nonstop for 24 hours; masses were said all night in the cathedral. Villages went *en masse* to the city and spent the night in its squares or churches. Again, conversion, return to the Church, especially of men, was a constant, the Diocesan Bulletin (1948:187) reported, "The hearts of the faithful were moved by an inner impulse; thousands asked for confessions, and about 10,000 communions were distributed". The next morning an open-air mass and healing session was held for the sick of the diocese in the city's largest square, and thousands wept as the image passed them.

The active and massive participation of children in missions was

a time-honored practice, and before missions in collective penitential processions. In the Fatima missions that had a special
significance, for it had been small children who had seen the Virgin
in 1917. Typically some of them were dressed to represent the seers
of Fatima, as can be seen from photographs in *Iris de Paz*, the organ
of the Missionaries of the Immaculate Heart of Mary, the order
founded by Antonio María Claret whose members often accompanied the
Fatima statues. The children of Málaga in 1950

> were meticulously prepared in school, under the orders of the
> teachers, always our enthusiastic collaborators. They made little
> flags, blue for the boys, white for the girls. Some were dressed
> in regional costumes, others from past eras, some representing
> the scene of the apparition of the Virgin, others representing
> little shepherds[6].

In Spain the Fatima missions received governmental cooperation.
When the Virgin of Fatima arrived in Madrid on 24 March 1948, the
image was given flowers by Franco's wife and daughter, and on 27
March the image was taken for a private visit to the Prado Palace,
where the Caudillo was photographed in the act of veneration. A
year later he repaid the visit in Portugal, and decorated the
Bishop of Leira[7].

Since in post-war Spain there was little or no possibility of a
Communist takeover, the missions rather served to consolidate the
position of the Church and win back some lost sheep. But in Italy,
the missions inevitably became part of electoral campaigns. As the
fragile post-war coalition broke up, the movement for a Christian
Left was dissolved, and Communists and Catholics faced off, mass
preachers like Padre Lombardi held a series of campaigns and
crusades. In 1949 the excommunication of Communists was decreed,
and the Pope called for Italy's own *Grande Ritorno* for the Holy
Year of 1950.

In Italy, too, images of the Virgin of Fatima were circulated.
In February 1947, the Pope blessed a Madonna Pellegrina for the
Diocese of Udine, and on 12 May a grandiose Marian pilgrimage in
Milan stimulated similar missions throughout the nation. Leonardo
Sciascia described the arrival of an image of Fatima in his town in
Sicily:

> In 1948 before the elections, the Dominicans carried the images
> of Fatima from one town to another, a wind of miracles blew over
> Sicily, promises and offerings rained on the new image of the
> Madonna, and it was said that at the feet of the Madonna deaf-
> mutes mumbled words and the paralyzed had been able to drag
> themselves a few steps through the crowds.
> The Madonna came to us at Regalpetra from the neighboring
> town of Castro. The people of Castro carried it seven kilometers

in procession, and at the gates of Regalpetra, where they were supposed to hand over the Madonna, they found the priests, the municipal band, and the townspeople. But the people of Castro wanted to carry it on their shoulders inside the town and leave it in the main church, as those of another village had done in their town. The Regalpetrese held that the instructions were to hand it over at the gates of the town, an argument started, it was poisoned by old grudges, derogatory sentiments were shouted back and forth. The fight sharpened, rockets of blasphemy exploded around the celestial image, the Fathers raised their hands to placate the tempest. Never as on that day had the Madonna been so blasphemed by the citizens of Castro and Regalpetra. The Communists were the first in the fray; if the election had been held in the days that the Madonna of Fatima was in Regalpetra, the Communist Party would not have had a single vote. It was held a month later, and the Communist Party had a thousand (Sciascia 1956:94-95).

The special value of the messages of apparitions, once authenticated, is that they provide information on what the Divine Will is at a given historical moment. It is much simpler, if the visionaries can be believed, to hear what God has to say through his messengers about such-and-such a place right now, than to try to extrapolate correct conduct from what Christ said 2,000 years ago and the accumulated wisdom of the Church. The visions of Rue de Bac, 1830, La Salette, 1847, Lourdes, 1858, and Pontmain, 1870, had tremendous impact in France, when duly diffused, in the recuperation and reinvigoration of French Catholicism after the Revolution. In the early twentieth century the Lourdes story was known to rural and urban Europeans far beyond France's borders. The French experience had not been lost on the ecclesiastical authorities of Portugal, and in that country the apparitions of Fatima during the nation's first lay government, inevitably had a political significance. During World War II the Fatima story was particularly relevant for the nations at war, because of the explicit connection of the Fatima visions with World War I.

But the new emphasis on Fatima throughout Europe had a side effect of producing a new wave of visions. That it stimulated visions, especially by children, is not surprising. The imagery and message of Fatima entered the subconscious of Catholics.

Consider the case of a valley in Northern Italy. In 1942 the Archbishop of Milan wrote in a pastoral letter on the 25th anniversary of the apparitions of Fatima,

History teaches us that in the most tragic moments of the history of the Church, in the situations of greatest anguish, in the gravest of dangers, the Most Holy Madonna has always intervened to help Christians. We are therefore certain ... that she will

have the final victory over the devil, impiety, and heresy
(Ballini 1947:42-43).

Subsequently, in May of 1943 the parish priest of Bonate (Bergamo)
preached a sermon on the Fatima story. And around December 1943 the
sisters who ran a nursery school in the Bonate valley put on an
'operina' or skit, in which children played the Virgin, Saint
Joseph, and the three seers of Fatima. The moment of apparition
was represented by bringing in the Saints when the lights were out
and suddenly turning them on. Just so in medieval mystery plays
the same effect was gained by drawing a curtain to reveal a candle-
lit image.

   With this kind of exposure it is not surprising that eight-year
old Adelaide Roncalli of Bonate often prayed, posing like the children
of Fatima, that the Madonna would also appear to her. On 13 May,
1944, the anniversary of the first of the Fatima visions, Adelaide
had her first vision. The visions continued, thirteen in all, to a
crescendo of popular attention. It was estimated that on 21 May,
150,000 persons were present, and at the final vision on 31 May,
200 - 300,000. As at Fatima, so at Bonate the seer brought word
that the war would end soon -- in two months, she said at first.
Her visions had enormous resonance throughout northern Italy, even
though, as with almost all of the postwar visions, the Church did
not accept their supernatural character.[8]

   The next year in Spain there was a Fatima-like vision series --
in La Codosera (Badajoz), a town on the Portuguese border. There a
girl of ten first, then eventually hundreds of other people, saw
Our Lady of the Sorrows on or near a chestnut tree, near what was
known as a haunted house, the *Casa de Miedo*. Two other seers, a
girl of 17 and a married woman of 31, subsequently became major
visionaries; thousands came to the site from surrounding towns
in Spain and Portugal; the visions were publicized by a series of
articles in the Madrid newspaper *Informaciones*; and eventually,
with the permission of the bishop, a chapel was built, partly with
funds from the Spanish Ministry of Education. By June 1946, La
Codosera was referred to in *Informaciones* as the 'Spanish Fatima'.
Its precocious connection with the Cold War series of Fatima-like
visions can be explained by the town's proximity to Portugal
(Marcelina, the first seer, was on her way back from an errand at
the border when she had her vision). In 1945 the people of La
Codosera knew the Fatima story far better than most Spaniards.[9]

   The circumstances of both the Bonate and the Codosera apparitions
illustrate why the main question for historians is not whether
visions occurred, but rather why attention was paid to them. A week
or two before Adelaide had her visions in Bonate, some boys had a
vision in Verdello nearby, a fact known in the Roncalli household.
But the boys' visions did not make the big time. Similarly, there

had been visions at the Codosera site around 1870, provoking little more than an outdoor mass at the chestnut tree; and some years previously a shepherd had seen Christ in the sky there, but had not even told his wife, knowing, he said later, that he would not be believed.[10] In 1945 it was a girl who was believable, and in 1945 a vision was read by the people to mean something it did not mean in 1870.

There were many other subsequent visions in which, as with that of Bonate, the influence of the Fatima story, or the subsequent Fatima missions, was patent. A man in the Toledo village of Yunclillos saw the Virgin on 7 June 1948, eight days after the Virgin of Fatima had passed by on the way from Madrid to Toledo, and many townspeople had gone out on the road to salute her.

The influence of the Fatima story can also be seen in the content and dramaturgy of the visions. As at Fatima, many of the postwar seers received secrets which they could reveal only to the Pope, or only after a certain number of years.[11] The importance of the unrevealed third secret of Fatima was very much in the news, as the Patriarch of Lisbon had revealed in September 1946 that it was fair to infer that the secret would place 'the salvation of the world in this extraordinary hour ... on the Immaculate Heart of Mary' (*Iris de Paz*, 1 December 1948). Because Jacinta and Francesco, two of the Fatima seers, had died not long afterwards, it was feared by both seers and spectators that visionaries would die soon, and such predictions were sometimes part of the postwar vision messages.[12]

Like the visions of Fatima, many postwar visions were supposed to end with a great miracle, a kind of visionary equivalent to the apotheosic final day of a mission. At Fatima people saw the sun spin in the sky. The postwar visions were ordered throughout like missions, lay missions in which the Virgin was the missionary, speaking through the seer, and in which the daily or weekly visions built up to the great climax. The visions of Mercedes Trejo at Aldeamoret, the mining suburb of Cáceres, built up toward a miracle on the ninth day, when many people saw the sun spin in the sky and give off streamers of light. One witness I talked to had a partially detached retina to remind her of the event. Similar solar phenomena were seen by at least some of those present at Ibdes (Zaragoza) in 1954, in some Italian visions, and I have been present for similar alleged solar 'miracles' during contemporary visions.

Other episodes did not have such satisfying outcomes. While a mission was in progress in Castellón de la Plana in November 1947, ten year old Raquel Roca was embarked on a perilous mission of her own in the village of Cuevas de Vinromá, some 60 kilometers away. She supposedly began to have her visions in March, but they became known only in mid-November, when she began to have visions daily at 11.30 in the morning and foretold a great miracle for 1 December at

which the sick would be healed. The word spread in the coastal cities
by mimeographed leaflets; caravans of cars came from Valencia,
Tarragona and Castellón. By 24 November thousands of people were
arriving every day. On 30 November 40,000 were present. Raquel was
admonished by her parents and the priest of the dire consequences
of deception, but she stuck to her prediction. On 1 December the
hillsides of a great natural amphitheatre were packed with people,
a crowd estimated at between 200 and 300 thousand. All the blind of
Lérida and Castellón came to have their sight restored. Some of
the visionaries from apparitions in the 1930s turned up from
Zaragoza. The police had to open all the houses of the village to
put up the sick. But there was no miracle; no cures worth men-
tioning, and the girl left the village in disgrace. Similar predicted miracles failed to occur at Casaseca de los Chanes (Zamora,
1950) and Villaesteva (Lugo) in 1961.[13]

Many Italian visions followed the Fatima pattern to culminate
in solar phenomena. At Gimigliano (Ascoli-Piceno), for instance,
on 18 May 1948, 80,000 persons from Le Marche, Abruzzo, Sabina,
and Romagna stayed awake all night praying to see the miracle of
the sun at sunrise. And at Acquaviva (Caltanissetta) thousands
were present from larger towns, and as the sun was spinning they
sang the hymn of the Virgin of Fatima, 'The Thirteenth of May'.[14]

The visions of the 1940s and 1950s were undoubtedly informed by the
Fatima story. It remains to be seen why they were paid attention
to, what it was in them that spoke to the historical moment of
the Cold War. All of them performed the age-old role of providing
a sacred place and sacred relics for curing. Those of Spain pointed
out sacred trees (as, indeed, had that of Fatima), variously chestnut, ash, olive, pear, almond, and pine trees, whose leaves were
used by the public for talismans and cures. In Italy pilgrims
especially removed the dirt from the ground above which the Virgin
had hovered. At four Spanish sites caves were sacralized as holy
places, echoing the visions at Lourdes, and as at Lourdes and many
older Spanish shrines, the Virgin pointed out holy springs whose
water had curative powers. But in these aspects the postwar visions
were indistinguishable from village apparitions in the preceding
500 years.

What does seem to key them in to the Fatima missions, the crusades
of Father Lombardi, and the ethos of each nation's particular
'Christian political warfare', is their emphasis on conversion. The
conversion theme is most explicit in the countries where the enemy
was most salient. It is dramatically evident in the descriptions
of East European visions that circulated in Western Europe, quite
clear in Italy, and more implicit in Spain.

According to the Spanish magazine *Iris de Paz* (1 March 1948,101),

there had been four sets of visions in Yugoslavia in recent years.
Whether or not these visions really took place, especially under
the circumstances described, I do not know. But the credence they
were given in Spain points to the more general connection of
visions and anti-communism. The four visions were said to have
taken place at Josujici (Slavonia) on the site of the alleged
execution of 500 Croatian members of Catholic Action; at Marburg,
where the Virgin cried, 'Penance, Penance; Convert before the
terrible chastisement comes'; at the Isle of Zrec in Croatia, where
Christ Crucified surrounded by mocking enemies appeared to two
Communist women and converted them; and on an island in Dalmatia
(11 May 1946) in which in the climatic vision, with 10,000 persons
present, Mary was seen surrounded by priests and laymen killed by
the Communists.[15]

On the whole, the Western European visions were more subdued, in
keeping with a more subdued level of conflict. The Italian vision
that received the most publicity, the only one of more than eighty
between 1947 and 1953 that was explicitly encouraged by the Church,
was that of the Virgin of Tre Fontane to a Seventh-Day Adventist,
Bruno Cornacchiola, in Rome on 12 April 1947, in which he was converted after first his children, then he, saw Mary. Cornacchiola,
who subsequently presented a Protestant Bible to the Pope, was a
perfect example of the redemption of the wayward. The Virgin said
to him, 'You persecuted me. Ora Basta! Enter the heavenly fold, the
heavenly court on earth, the nine Fridays of the Sacred Heart have
saved you'.

Enrico Contardi, whose pamphlet on the visions was distributed
throughout the Catholic world in 1948 by various religious orders,
commented on the meaning of the visions of Cornacchiola as follows,
"It is all too clear that God, angered and offended by the way-
wardness of men, who forget to render homage to their creator, and
who fight among themselves like savage wolves, wishes to punish
humanity with individual and collective chastisements. But then
the sublime Lady whom he chose for Immaculate Mother and Virgin,
and whom he left at the foot of the Cross to be our Mother, intervenes in our favor, interposes herself between the wayward sons on
earth and the Divine Son in Heaven" (Contardi 1947:5).[16]

The other Italian and French visions for which I have detailed
information share this moral and theme. The messages of the Virgin
to Angela Volpini (born 1940) in a village of Pavia from 1947 to
1956 constantly refer to the conversion of sinners. Similarly at
Île Bouchard (Touraine) in France, in December 1947, Mary asked
girls, 7-12, to pray for France.[17] In these countries the enemy
was present and overt. At Acquaviva in Sicily Mary asked the 12-year
old seer to come back on the same afternoon with her nieces and
nephews, at a time when the Communist children's league, Associazione

dei Pionieri Italiani (A.P.I.), was going to have a meeting in the town. The author of a booklet about the vision, Giuselli, provides us with a gloss of what must have been running through the Virgin's mind,

> On this very day the godless ones are holding a perfidious campaign against children: to destroy the concept of God in the hearts of innocents (1950:38).

By contrast in Spain irreligion was not organized or open, did not distribute comic books about the class struggle like those of the A.P.I. In Spain irreligion was merely an unspoken presence in the scepticism and silent hostility of many of those who had fought on the Republican side.

Hence the individuation by the Virgin of certain teenagers in Aldeamoret whose parents were Republicans and who had never received communion was the exception, and general recommendations like that to the seers of Ibdes in 1954 to 'pray for the conversion of sinners and the world' were more the rule. But there was a message buried in the choice of seers, as with Bruno Cornacchiola, and also in the effect of the visions in converting casual observers, which show that the Spanish visions, as much as the Italian ones, were addressed to a society in deep conflict.

Marcelina Barroso of La Codosera was the grand-daughter of the socialist mayor of the town, and both her grandfather and her father were killed by the Nationalists, along with about 30 other townspeople for political reasons. The seer Mercedes Trejo of Aldeamoret was not from a religious household. Her father had been a Socialist, and Aldeamoret itself was a workers' enclave in an area dominated by caciques. The Castellón village of Cuevas de Vinromá had voted and still votes socialist, and according to a newspaper article 'had always been very irreligious'. The seer's father too had been on the losing side of the war, had lost his job as a telegraphist and had been banished from Extremadura. Adult male visionaries at Yunclillos (1948) and Ibdes (1954) were known as blasphemers and infrequent church-goers before their visions. The seer of Ibdes explained obliquely in 1977, 'Some of us think we are better than others. But it can happen that to someone who speaks badly the Virgin appears. And to someone else who speaks well she does not appear'. I include in Appendix 1 an excerpt from an interview with a Civil Guard telling how he was present when four men were converted by an apparition of Mary in rural Galicia in 1961.[18]

So to the spectators, who knew the background of the seers, the very apparitions were sacred dramas of conversions that concerned seers, their families, or their towns. And in a context of divided communities and regions, still riven by the bitter hatreds of the Civil War, some of the visions seem to have served as a kind of collective catharsis. Aldeamoret was a workers' town, but Aldeamoret believed Mercedes Trejo in 1947. Nearby Falangist Cáceres, a diocesan seat, did not believe the daughter of a Socialist. During the final apparition a young woman from a leading family of the city, a member in the *Sección Feminina* of the Falange, addressed the multitude, denouncing the child's visions as a ploy to get alms. To the horror of those present, the woman was struck with a heart attack, and died later on the same day, a grim point in favor of the authenticity of the visions.

The reaction of Cáceres against Aldeamoret paralleled that of ecclesiastical authorities throughout Spain, with rare exceptions, to the postwar visions. The local press was silenced; circulars and leaflets without Church approval were condemned, and printing presses were destroyed (the case of a hapless printer in Madrid who published in 1951 the miracles worked by Mary in Yunclillos). Local authorities, civil and religious, distrusted these seers of dubious backgrounds and were probably a little afraid of their power. None of the postwar seers were forcibly interned in mental hospitals, although this happened in 1932 in Guipúzcoa and in 1938 in Heede (Germany). But every effort was made to keep the visions local, controllable phenomena.

The position of the church hierarchy, one of extreme prudence born of extreme scepticism, was not shared by all of the clergy. Parish priests and religious were sometimes convinced by the undeniable sincerity and inspiredness of the seers, and were often responsible for permitting the first efflorescence of an apparition sequence. The Vatican itself was somewhat divided over the matter. Throughout the period, Vatican radio reported the existence of supposed visions. And Pius XII in a 1948 address printed in the *Osservatore Romano* (of 11 March) seemed to appreciate the visions.[19]

> Do you not see how the force of attraction of earthly goods is not able to prevent people from feeling lifted, as by instinct, toward spiritual and religious things? The most consoling aspect of these times is the ever-growing manifestation -- even at times flowering in visions of marvelous grandeur -- of the confidence and filial love that leads souls to the most pure and Immaculate Mary.

But by 1951 this flowering of visions was too much, and Alfredo Ottaviani, advisor to the Santo Officio, published an article, 'Proceed, Christians, with more Prudence', that was reprinted in many Diocesan Bulletins, decrying the visions as an outbreak of 'natural religion'. 'The period we are traversing lies between the excesses of open and shameless irreligion, and a religiosity that is blind and out of control'. Ottaviani recognized that a revival of great proportions was taking place, and that the visions were

playing a part in this. But he wanted to ensure that the Catholicism
produced by the revival was orthodox and clerical. 'In the undeniable
return to God that we are witnessing, the faithful should overcome
all their reservations and come back to live in community of feelings,
thoughts, and faith with the priest'.[20]

Indeed, in this period the visions, the byproduct of the Church's
mobilization of the faithful, had become a kind of parallel mobilization. While in August 1947, the hierarchy of Almería organized a
youth pilgrimage to the shrine of Saint Indalecio, the man who
supposedly first brought Christianity to the area, as a symbol of
'the great task of rechristianization that the youth of Spain has
undertaken', another, more effective rechristianization was underway
nearby. Ginesa Simón Casanova, age 14, was having a series of visions
in a mountain village that attracted thousands of praying spectators
who said all fifteen mysteries of the Rosary. While in the presence
of the Bishop of Tortosa 3,500 men were receiving communion in Castellón, 10,000 persons were flocking daily to an erstwhile Socialist
village in the hills, to watch the daughter of a Republican talk
with Mary, in spite of the opposition of the bishops of all the
neighboring dioceses.

The vision-missions were more effective, I think, even than the
Fatima missions. At ordinary missions the symbolic missionary was
the local shrine image; at those of Fatima it was a famous and
miraculous international image; but at the vision-missions the
missionary was the Virgin herself, or Jesus Christ, or the Holy
Family. The effect was deep and lasting. For days, weeks, even years
a sacred climate prevailed in some of the vision towns. I have
spoken to priests and religious who received their vocations at
visions, either as visionaries or as spectators. And the level of
emotion -- collective weeping, petitions, and prayers -- seems to
have been very high at the vast majority of these events.

In part their attractiveness for a Spanish population that was
deeply religious yet in some regions justifiably resentful of the
alliance of the Church with the powerful lay precisely in their
unofficial character, precisely because they were rejected by the
bishops. The vision events provided a way that religious persons
of all political backgrounds could come together from divided
regions, towns, or families, in intense communion with the divine
presence. I suspect that visions in France, Germany, and Italy to
some extent also served as emotional counterweights to the deep
divisions in the postwar period.

But however uncontrolled or aclerical the visions, the movement
of piety they represented fed into the Mission campaigns of the
Church and contributed to the genuineness of the revival of West
European Catholicism after the war. So although Ottaviani could
deplore their excesses, he could not treat them as a major threat

to the Faith. In fact in some dioceses bishops adopted an attitude
of cautious cooptation. While the visions (and much less the
visionaries) were not certified as partaking of the supernatural,
the piety they engendered was channeled into new shrines and devotions. One way chosen to redirect the new piety in old channels
was to counter the vision-mission with a regular mission.

In 1953 a Sicilian bishop certified the supernatural character
of a kind of vision that presented far fewer problems than the
reception of messages through seers. An image of Mary wept in
Siracusa -- the Immaculate Heart of Mary. Here there were no
special seers; when the image wept it could be seen by everyone.
The message was clear and simple: Mary was sad, presumably at the
state of affairs of mankind.[21] This kind of epiphany was part of a
very old tradition in Southern Europe, known also in the pagan churches,
that images wept in times of crisis. In Spain weeping or bleeding
images came into vogue in the seventeenth century during periods
of national or regional disaster (Christian 1981:195-200). In
central and eastern Italy the eyes of a number of images were seen
to move during the Napoleonic invasion (Marchetti 1799)[22] and also
when Rome was threatened in the 1850s. In 1853 a Tuscan shepherdess
was told by a vision of Mary weeping in the rain, 'Help me to weep.
I cry for so many sinners! Do you see how much it is raining? There
are more sins than the drops of water that fall'. A commentator wrote,
"Most Holy Mary, to alert Catholic Italy to be on guard against
the terrible aggression of pagan Italy, had already in 1850 worked
prodigious movements of the eyes in her images in Rimini, Fossom-
brone, and Sanginesio".[23] With this kind of tradition well kept up
locally, the meaning of the tears of the Immaculate Heart of Mary
in 1953 was no great mystery.

The bishop's swift approval of the supernatural character of the
tears inevitably provoked, during the Marian year of 1954, more
cases. Of the 22 apparitions of Mary we know about from November
1953 to 31 December 1954, thirteen were lacrimations of pictures
reproducing the image of Siracusa, and the phenomenon has continued
intermittently ever since, the latest an image of Lourdes at Niscima,
near Caltanissetta, in August 1980. Similarly, stimulated by the
case of Siracusa, propagated through the magazine of religious
orders, people in two towns in Galicia also had images that 'wept'
what chemists determined to be real tears. A similar case occurred
in a village of Cuenca in 1959, and in Granada in 1982. In all of
these instances the weeping of images provoked the weeping and in
some instances the conversions of those who watched.[24]

After 1954 the number of visions dropped back to the rate
characteristic of the pre-war period, and this rate has continued
to the present. But the Church is no more in control of visions
than it was when Ottaviani wrote his article, and since that time

many visions have run counter to Church policy and strategy. For although to all intents and purposes the Church ended its Cold War at the Second Vatican Council, contemporary visions continue with the conversionary, apocalyptic tone of the late 1940s. In particular those of Garabandal in Northern Spain and San Damiano (Piacenza) in Italy, which both began in 1961, have found worldwide audiences among those distressed by changes in Church policy, a slackening of Church discipline, and a softened attitude towards Communism.

As in the times of the Flagellants, the Cathars, the beguines, and the Protestants, the Catholic Church in the twentieth century continues to engender movements of piety that escape its control. The Church's acceptance of certain visions and revelations, and their very widespread deployment, has shown lay people how to have direct, public converse with the Saints, which is especially problematic now that the Church has far fewer ways to enforce discipline.

To the question, what made people take visions seriously in large enough numbers for them to find their way into newspapers, radio, or newsreels, we answer the Cold War -- its electoral and local conflicts in Italy and France, its social and personal trauma in divided nations, and the oppression of one faith by another in Spain, Portugal, and Eastern Europe. The recourse to the solutions proposed by past apparitions led to new apparitions. But to the trauma of division and oppression we should add the fear of a devastating international atomic war. For even in the United States a phenomenon not unlike that of visions was going on at the same time -- the sighting of UFO's, interpreted as aliens, whether those of Russia or those from outer space. The months of June and July 1947, when the European wave of visions began, were also the beginning of the great American saucer scare. A tireless researcher, who read through 140 daily newspapers from 90 North American cities for the year of 1947, found over 850 separate sightings of flying saucers in the months of June and July (cf. Bloecher).

Writing in 1950, Lewis Mumford argued, "It is plain that we are now facing something even worse than war : we are threatened with an outbreak of compulsive irrationality. By reason of the fears and suspicions and hatreds that have been introduced into the affairs of nations during the last four decades, no small part of mankind lives in a state of self-enclosed delusion..." (Mumford 1950). The explosion of atom bombs on Hiroshima and Nagasaki, the V-2 rockets of Peenemünde, the possibility of germ warfare, signalled a new era in the technology of destruction in which all were vulnerable, and in which death would come from the sky. Hear Ida Peerdeman tell of her vision of 26 December 1947 (untitled booklet, p. 28)[25]:

The vision fades and now I see a sort of cigar or something
shaped like a torpedo flying past me at such great speed that
I can hardly discern it. It seemed to be of the same color as
aluminium. I see it spring open suddenly. I feel with my hand
and experience different frightening sensations. The first is
a total loss of feeling. I live and yet I do not live. Then I
see faces before me (broad faces) disfigured with repulsive
ulcers like leprosy. Then I feel terrible diseases (cholera
etc.). Then I see little black things whirling about me. I
cannot perceive them with my eyes and it is as if I am expected
to look through something. And then I see beautiful white
fields with those little things enlarged in them. I do not know
how I must explain this. (Bacilli? I ask.) Then the Lady says,
'It is hellish'. I feel my face swelling as it were and it
feels swollen to the touch. It is bloated and quite stiff. I
cannot move. Then I hear the Lady saying again: 'And that is
what they are inventing', and then very softly: 'Russia, but
the others too'. After that the Lady says, 'Nations be warned'.
And then the Lady disappears.

In this context the old apocalyptic warnings of a divine chastisement of world-wide proportions has a referent in the techniques of
mass annihilation that is unmatched in history, with the possible
exception of the Black Death. And the division of nations in the
Cold War made the use of the weapons a real possibility. At Heede,
near the Dutch border in a divided Germany, Jesus Christ told seers
late in 1945, after the bombings of Hamburg, Dresden, and Hiroshima,
"Humanity has not listened to My Holy Mother who appeared at
Fatima to ask for penance ... I am very close. The earth will
tremble and contract; it will be terrible, like a smaller version
of the Last Judgment" (*Iris de Paz*, 1 December 1948, 326). Small
wonder, under the circumstances, that people wanted direct word
from their saints as to what course of action they could take and
what prayers would avoid God's wrath.

In conclusion a more general observation. A village-based, or even
nation-based analysis of an unusual event like an apparition would
miss much about it. As earthquakes, seemingly spontaneous and
unconnected, are in fact systematic manifestations of shifts in
the earth's surface, so apparition episodes may arise from movements very deep in the individual consciousness with a collective,
often systemic etiology. This kind of trans-national pattern of
visions is by no means a novelty of the Cold War. In the period
from 1450 to 1515 remarkably similar visions were occurring throug-
out southwest Europe.[26] Perhaps in the seventeenth to nineteenth
centuries nation-states with national churches somewhat compart-
mentalized European religion, but in many respects the nation-state

is no longer the real arena of culture. In 1947 a circuit of
mutual influence could probably have been detected that linked
the visions of Mercedes Trejo in Aldeamoret to the *fanshen* of a
Chinese commune.

APPENDIX 1. Conversions in Galicia.

In December 1961, Manuel Moreira, a sergeant in the Civil Guard,
went with some friends to a place on a hillside near Villaesteva
(Lugo) where lights were supposed to be seen, lights supposedly
connected with visions of the Virgin Mary seen by four children a
couple of months previously. In 1977 he recounted what he had seen
sixteen years before.

> We came to the edge of the village in order to take the path
> that goes up the hill, and I saw a car from Sarria parked
> there. This was about 11 at night. We didn't think anything
> about the car and went up the path on foot, when we heard, 'Ay
> Virgen Santísima! Ay Virgen Santísima!'
> And I said to myself somebody has been hurt, or someone was
> killed or something awful has happened -- because of the wailing.
> Because for a man to cry ---- And I left the others behind and
> ran ahead to see what I could do to help.
> I came upon four men kneeling soaked in the rain, weeping in
> the mud, saying, 'Ay Virgen Santísima!'
> I said, 'What happened to you? What's wrong?', looking around
> with the flashlight for a dead body, but I saw nothing.
> 'Ay, we just saw the Virgen Santísima'. The four crying like
> children.
> When I heard that I stepped back and said, 'Listen, you some
> kind of clowns? Do you really think the Virgin is going to come
> down here like this?'
> And one said, 'Ay, if it is not the Virgen Santísima, when I get
> to Sarria let me find my parents dead'. Just like that. This
> was a boy in his thirties, who worked in the government unions
> in Sarria -- he has since died. He was a man they kicked out of
> Spanish Sahara, Venezuela; he never entered a church, and was
> a semi-savage, because he was a blasphemer and -- he was the
> one who said, 'When I get to Sarria let me find my parents
> dead if it wasn't the Virgin'.
> Then a man in his sixties with white hair got up and came
> over to me and said, 'Listen. Until today they were just four
> children and nobody paid any attention to them. Today we are
> four men, and disgracefully four unbelievers, but what we have
> seen is the authentic Virgen Santísima, and neither you nor
> Franco can stop me from saying it'.

Then since he was a man who expressed himself well, I said, 'All right then, what did you see?'

He said, 'Listen. I was in the store around 10 in the evening. These friends came in and said, "Do you want to come and see the Virgins of Villaesteva?" As if to go and make fun of it. As we were coming up the path from the car we were looking and saying, "What are we here for? With this weather you can't see anything". Then we saw light from behind the hill that kept getting closer and brighter. And someone said, "That's just a car on the road -- the reflection of its lights". But then the light itself appeared. It was an oval shape, just over a meter long, that was giving off the light. And in the middle of this light was the Virgin. She was wearing a white mantle and a crown, and we could not see her face as it was covered with a blue veil. But the crown was giving off stars, and the stars followed behind her in procession. She came here above us. The others just dropped to their knees and began to weep. I had the presence of mind to say to her, "Virgen Santísima, come close to us". And she came so close that she almost touched us with her hand. Now we are going to Sarria, and the first thing we are going to do when we get there is go to a priest to regenerate our lives'.

APPENDIX 2. Spanish visions referred to in the text.

Place	Seers/Date	Saints seen
La Codosera (Badajoz)	Girl, age 10, then others, many visions. 27 May onwards.	Above all: La Dolorosa
Aldeamoret (Cáceres)	Girl, age 7, nine visions. 29 April - 6 May 1947	Virgin of Pilar
Los Cerricos (Almería)	Girl, age 14, five visions 31 July - 10 August 1947	Virgin Mary, for Rosary
Cuevas de Vinromá (Castellón)	Girl, age 10. ? March - 1 December 1947	Mary in various forms
Yunclillos (Toledo)	Man, middle-aged family head, one vision, 7 June 1948	Virgin, vocation to preach
Usagre (Badajoz)	Two teenage girls, then many others, many visions. 3 May 1950 onwards	'Inmaculada del Calvario'

APPENDIX 2 (continued)

Place	Seers/Date	Saints seen
Casaseca de los Chanes (Zamora)	Girl, age about 12, then other, older girl from Benavente. Circa 1950, over several months until 15 November 1950	Virgin Mary
Entrecruces (La Coruña)	11 February - 21 April 1954	Image of La Milagrosa weeps eleven times
Foz (Lugo)	1954 - 1955	Image of Immaculate Heart of Mary weeps
Ibdes (Zaragoza)	Two girls, ages 11, 12; then man, age 51; many times. 6 June 1954 onwards	La Dolorosa, Pascual Bailón, Santiago, Sacred Heart
Jorcas (Teruel)	Eight boys, two girls, ages 7 - 11. 6 - 24 June 1958 onwards	Virgin, baby in cave
Villalba de la Sierra (Cuenca)	18 September - ? November 1959	Print of Our Lady of Mount Carmel weeps
Villaesteva (Lugo)	Four children, ages 7,7,11, 11; then others; several times. 17? September, October, November, December 1961	Mary as in church
Garabandal (Santander)	Four girls, ages 10,12,12,12; very many times. 18 June 1961 - 1965	Our Lady of Mount Carmel, other Maries, St. Michael

NOTES

* Research for this paper was conducted with a grant from the Tinker Foundation, and revisions were made while I held a Fellowship from the American Council of Learned Societies. I thank Father Theodore Koehler and Bro. William Fackovec of the Marian Library, Dayton, Ohio, and Father Giuseppe Besutti of the Marianum of Rome for access to their libraries and Lynn Eden and Alexander Popovic for their suggestions.
1. This table is based on the revised listing of Bernard Billet in the latest edition of *Vraies et fausses apparitions dans l'Eglise*. I have separated out the European visions, substituted my own list of the Spanish ones, and augmented the

Italian ones with others given in Falconi (1956:96-120, "La sete del prodigioso e le suggestioni del sopranaturale"). Since Billet's sources probably used different criteria for what was or was not a vision, and whether or not to include private revelations, one should not take this table with undue seriousness. It probably includes the most well-known visions of Western Europe, and those visions elsewhere that became known in Europe.

2. Falconi (1956:399, from *Annuario dell'Azione cattolica italiana*, 1954).

3. Untitled booklet in English, without author (Louis Knuvelder?), publisher, or date (but between 1959 and 1968) about the visions of Our Lady of All the Peoples of Amsterdam, p. 42. See also R. Auclair 1977.

4. Jiménez (1960) and the same author's additions to his translation of *Las Maravillas de Fátima* are prime sources for the Fatima trips in Spain.

5. On Fatima in Madrid, *Iris de Paz*, 16 June 1948, 180-186, and *Las Maravillas*, 324.

6. Photos of children dressed as seers in *Iris de Paz*, 16 November 1947, 341, and 1 October 1947, 289. Málaga quote, *Iris de Paz*, 1 March 1950, 95.

7. Franco photo, *Iris de Paz*, 16 June 1948:183.

8. See Fatima preparation at Bonate, Cazzamalli (1951:47, 71, 105).

9. The best sources on La Codosera are the articles of José de la Cueva printed in *Informaciones* (Madrid) June-September 1945, and subsequently as a pamphlet. See also two articles in the same paper, 27 June 1946 and 8 July 1946 by Hilarión Sanchéz; a collection of early reports edited by Fr. García (1973) and *La Codosera*, a booklet with photographs published by Arias in Madrid (1953). As with all of the Spanish visions discussed, I have also drawn on interviews with witnesses to the vision and visits to the vision sites.

10. The Verdello visions are mentioned by Cazzamalli (1951:70). The Codosera pre-visions are noted by De la Cueva, pp. 18 and 47 of the pamphlet edition (see note 9).

11. True for Aldeamoret (1947) and Casaseca (1950) and in Italy Bonate (1944), Tre Fontane (1947), Gimigliano (1948), Tor Pignattara (1948) and in France Île Bouchard (1947) and doubtless many others.

12. Predictions of early death were made in the vision messages of the seer in Yunclillos in 1947, in Palermo in 1954 (Falconi 1956:109) and assumed by spectators at Villaesteva (Lugo) in 1961.

13. For Cuevas de Vinromá the only printed sources I have found are newspaper articles between 18 November and 7 December in the

press of Castellón, Valencia, Murcia, Almería, and Tarragona.
I talked to townspeople in 1977 and 1980.

14. *La Pastorella di Gimigliano; I Miracoli delle 25 visioni celesti,* etc. (1948); Giuselli (1950).

15. A recent work on a postwar Polish vision series is that of Kudera (1975).

16. See on spread of story Carloya (1955:3-7).

17. *Messaggi della Madonna ad Angela Volpini* (1959); *Les faits mystérieux de l'Île Bouchard* (1951).

18. Much was made at the time, and this was also true in Italy, of the conversion of sceptical observers. Several spectators at La Codosera were divinely chastized for sacriligious remarks, in particular a 24-year old Portuguese woman who said to a female companion when the latter's boyfriend was approaching, "We haven't seen the Virgin, but here comes Jesus Christ". She was immediately struck blind, and converted, only later regaining her sight. At La Codosera, Usagre (Badajoz 1950), and Ibdes (1954) as at earlier visions of Ezquioga and Guadamur in 1931, the visions were contagious and seen by as many as a hundred people, and that was the surest way to be converted.

19. Cited in *Iris de Paz*, 1948:324.

20. The Ottaviani article was cited in the most comprehensive analysis of visions by Staehlin (1954). This sceptical book had a great impact on Spain's already sceptical clergy, but it was considered to have gone too far, particularly in its criticism of Fatima, and new editions and foreign translations were never published.

21. The best work on Siracusa, which cites whole portions of the official investigation verbatim, is the unpublished thesis of Carlo M. Ramondetta, "La Madonnina delle Lacrime di Siracusa", 129 pp., in the Marianum Library, Rome. The work that most spread the story was that of Ottavio Musumeci (1954).

22. Also *Raccolta di Varie Lettere che descrivono e attestano i prodigiosi segni veduti costantemente in vari luoghi della Marca, in alcune sante religie ed immagini* (1796).

23. *Relazione storica sulla recente apparizione di Maria Santissima Addolorata alla Pastorella Veronica Nucci avvenuta nel territorio di Sorano diocesi di Pitigliano il 19 di maggio 1853* (1860:19).

24. For Niscima, Domenico del Rio, "Sigillate quella madonna versa lacrime dispettose", *Repubblica* (Roma), 26 August 1980. For Entrecruces (La Coruña), where the Milagrosa wept, there have been only brief articles, like that of Daniel Vega, "La Milagrosa de Entrecruces", *La Milagrosa*, November 1957. The image was seen to weep eleven times from 11 February to 21 April 1954; a similar case occurred in the township of Foz (Lugo), in the church of San Martín de Mondoñedo a few months later. In the village of

Villalba de la Sierra (Cuenca), a lithograph of Our Lady of Mt.
Carmel wept intermittently in October and November 1959. The
event was well chronicled in *Diario de Cuenca* by Bort Carbó,
and excellent photographs appeared in *Blanco y Negro* of 24
October. In all three Spanish cases the weeping stopped when
the images were put behind glass.
25. See note 4 above.
26. Cf. Christian (1981) and Niccoli (1979:500-539).

BIBLIOGRAPHY

Arias, P.
  1953   *La Codosera*. Madrid: Gráficas Matasanz.
Auclair, R.
  1968   *Kerizinen. Apparitions en Bretagne*. Paris: Nouvelles
          Editions Latines.
  1977   *La Dame de tous les peuples*. Paris: Nouvelles Editions
          Latines.
Ballini, A.
  1947   *E apparsa la Madonna alle Ghiaie?* Bergamo: Ed. Tavecchi.
Billet, B.
  1976   *Vraies et fausses apparitions dans l'Eglise*. Paris:
          Letheilleux.
Bloecher, T.
  --   *Report on the UFO Wave of 1947*. Washington D.C.
Carloya, M.
  1955   *La vera storia delle apparizioni alle Tre Fontane*. Roma:
          Diffusione del Libro.
Cazzamalli, F.
  1951   *La Madonna di Bonate*. Milano: Fratelli Bocca.
Christian, W.A. Jr.
  1981   *Local Religion in Sixteenth Century Spain*. Princeton, N.J.:
          Princeton University Press.
  1981   *Religious Apparitions in Late Medieval and Renaissance
          Spain*. Princeton, N.J.: Princeton University Press.
Contardi, E.
  1947   *Le 'apparizioni' alla grotta delle Tre Fontane. Primo
          documentario sulla 'Vergine della Rivelazione'*. Roma: Ed.
          Cosmos.
Falconi, C.
  1956   *La Chiesa e le organizzazioni cattoliche in Italia, 1945-
          1955*. Torino: Einaudi.
García, A.C. (ed.)
  1973   *El Santuario de Chandavila*. Cáceres: Ed. Cruzada Mariana.

Giuselli, S.
  1950   *I fenomeni di Acquaviva (Caltanissetta)*. Catania: Scuola del Libro.
Jiménez, F.
  1960   *La Virgen Peregrina y sus palomas*. Bilbao: El Mensajero del Corazón de Jesús.
Kudera, E.
  1975   *Arme Seelen erscheinen in Oberschlesien 1945/6: Ein Tatsachenbericht*. München: S. Hacker.
Marchetti, G.
  1799   *Mémoires concernant les prodiges arrivés à Rome dans plusieurs images*. Hildesheim: Imprimerie de Christ. (A translation of the 1797 Italian edition published in Rome by Zempel.)
Mumford, L.
  1950   In the Name of Sanity. *Common Cause*, January.
Musumeci, O.
  1954   *Ha pianto la Madonna di Siracusa*. Siracusa: Marchese.
Niccoli, O.
  1979   Profezie in piazza. *Quaderni Storici* 41 (May-August):500-539.
Orensanz, A.L.
  1974   *Religiosidad Popular Española, 1940-1965*. Madrid: Editora Nacional.
Sciascia, L.
  1956   *Le parrochie di Regalpetra*. Bari: Ed. Laterza.
Staehlin, C.M.
  1954   *Apariciones*. Madrid: Razón y Fe.

OTHER SOURCES AND DOCUMENTS

  1796   *Raccolta di Varie Lettere che descrivono e attestano i prodigiosi segni veduti costantemente in vari luoghi della Marca, in alcune sante reliquie ed immagini*. Roma: Zempel.
  1860   *Relazione storica sulla recente apparizione di Maria Santissima Addolorate alla Pastorella Veronica Nucci avvenuta nel territorio di Sorano diocesi di Pitigliano il 19 di maggio 1853*. Roma: Tip. Cesaretti.
  1948   *La Pastorella di Gimigliano: I Miracoli delle 25 visioni celesti, etc*. Roma: G. DM.
  ca.1951 *Les faits mystérieux de l'Ile Bouchard*. Tours: Gibert-Clarey.
  1959   *Messaggi della Madonna ad Angela Volpini*.
  --   *Las Maravillas de Fátima*. Barcelona: Gráficas Claret (7th Spanish edition, expanded).

Index of Personal Names

Index of Geographical Names

Names which are marked with an asterisk (*) are pseudonyms for places (villages) studied by social anthropologists.